T0333998

Delaying Doomsday

BRIDGING THE GAP

Series Editors:
Goldgeier James
Jentleson Bruce
Steven Weber

Delaying Doomsday

The Politics of Nuclear Reversal

RUPAL N. MEHTA

OXFORD
UNIVERSITY PRESS

OXFORD
UNIVERSITY PRESS

Oxford University Press is a department of the University of Oxford. It furthers
the University's objective of excellence in research, scholarship, and education
by publishing worldwide. Oxford is a registered trade mark of Oxford University
Press in the UK and certain other countries.

Published in the United States of America by Oxford University Press
198 Madison Avenue, New York, NY 10016, United States of America.

Library of Congress Control Number: 2019035266
ISBN 978–0–19–007797–6

1 3 5 7 9 8 6 4 2

Printed by Integrated Books International, United States of America

For my parents, Vasanti and Naresh Mehta

CONTENTS

LIST OF FIGURES

LIST OF TABLES

ACKNOWLEDGMENTS

I remember my first serious introduction to the study of nuclear weapons in Ron Hassner's WAR! course at the University of California, Berkeley in 2002. The course surveyed the causes and consequences of conflict over time and ended with seminal readings from Kenneth Waltz and Scott Sagan. This course, and Ron as an early mentor, friend, and role model, made the decision to pursue a PhD in Political Science easy. My path to graduate school was fortuitously sidetracked by a year working at the Center for International Security and Cooperation (CISAC) at Stanford University, where I had the opportunity to work with two of the pillars of the nuclear security discipline—Scott Sagan and Sig Hecker—and reaffirm my passion to pursue this field for my career. My progress over the next twelve years, including the evolution and completion of this book, originated by being immersed in the intellectual environment at Stanford.

My mentors at the University of California, San Diego were instrumental in guiding me along this path and provided me encouragement and support to grow and thrive in graduate school. I am especially grateful to David Lake and Erik Gartzke who agreed to co-chair my committee and guided me every step of the way. I have immensely benefited from the mentorship of Branislav Slantchev, Susan Shirk, Barbara Walter, Christina Schneider, Miles Kahler, Emilie Hafner Burton, Samuel Popkin, and Steph Haggard. I am so appreciative of your support, guidance, feedback, encouragement—all of which has made me a better scholar, teacher, and person.

In addition to my graduate school mentors, I have been fortunate to have colleagues (many of whom participated in a book workshop at UCSD in January 2017) who have provided well-reasoned and thoughtful comments and feedback on my work, and support for my professional growth. I thank Matthew Fuhrmann, Todd Sechser, Matthew Kroenig, and Neil Narang for their extensive comments on my book manuscript and their unparalleled support of me as a junior scholar.

After graduating from UCSD, I had the opportunity to spend a year as a Stanton Nuclear Security Postdoctoral Fellow at the Belfer Center at Harvard University's Kennedy School of Government. I thank my mentors—Matthew Bunn, Lynn Eden, Marty Malin, and Steven E. Miller—for their guidance and feedback in helping me revise and improve this manuscript. Belfer was also one of the most professionally and personally rewarding experiences of my academic career. I was fortunate to be in the company of some of the smartest and most engaging young scholars who constantly encouraged me to think critically and work hard. Special thanks to Rachel Whitlark, Gene Gerzhoy, Evan Perkoski, Gaëlle Rivard-Piché, Christopher Clary, and Mark Bell.

During my time at the University of Nebraska-Lincoln over the past four years, I have been surrounded by thoughtful and supportive colleagues and friends who have made the start of my career at UNL rewarding and fun. I am grateful to Kevin Smith, Patrice McMahon, Courtney Hillebrecht, Alice Kang, Ingrid Johnsen Haas, Tyler White, Ursula Kreitmair, and Robert Schub for their mentorship, guidance, and the opportunity to turn my dissertation into this book.

Many other friends and colleagues have contributed their time to help my research and this book in a variety of ways. I thank Molly Berkemeier-Harvey, Målfrid Braut-Hegghammer, Paige Cone, Fiona Cunningham, Michael Horowitz, Joshua Kertzer, Sarah Kreps, Alexander Lanoszka, Austin Long, Julia MacDonald, Aila Matanock, Eleonora Mattiacci, Nicholas L. Miller, Vipin Narang, Jaime Settle, Joshua Shrifinson, William Spaniel, Caitlin Talmadge, Jane Vaynman, and Jessica Weeks for their support. I apologize in advance to any colleagues that I have forgotten to thank.

For generous financial support along the way, I thank the Belfer Center at Harvard University, the Stanton Foundation, the Naval Postgraduate School's Project on Advanced Systems and Concepts for Countering WMD (PASCC) Grant, and the Department of Political Science, the College of Arts and Sciences, and the Senning Foundation at the University of Nebraska-Lincoln.

I am especially grateful for the support from my editor at Oxford University Press, Angela Chnapko, as well as the Bridging the Gap Series Editors, Jim Goldgeier, Bruce Jentleson, and Steven Weber, for their faith in me and this project. I also thank three anonymous reviewers who provided helpful and constructive feedback to significantly improve this book.

I received moral support and endless words of encouragement from close friends who have become family—Nicole Bonoff, Karen Boyd, Maya Duru, Naushin Hussain, Donya Ahourai Ladunga, Brad LeVeck, Dusty Lowry, Claire McConnell, Anjali Mohlajee, Lindsay Nielson, Parisa Azizad-Pinto, Sheena Reddy, Chelsea Reeds, Christina Reginaldo, Ashley Richter, Brigitte Seim, Sjuli Senn, Mona Vakilifathi, Camille Yabut, and Luhua Zhang. I thank them all.

Most importantly, I am eternally grateful for my family, without whom none of this would have been even remotely possible. My sister, Sonal, has always been my best friend and role model. She instilled in me the true meaning of passion, hard work, and perseverance. She often reminds me that the most important relationships in life are those with family and friends. And despite her unbelievably busy life, she has never missed the big or small moments in my life—that has meant more to me then I can ever say.

My parents, Vasanti and Naresh, have set a phenomenally high standard for me throughout my entire life. In addition to teaching me the basics of life and challenging me to work harder every day, they provide the greatest model for unconditional love and support. My father, Naresh, has read every word of this manuscript numerous times and has uniquely provided the best feedback on this book—this could not have been completed without his help. My mother, Vasanti, has provided the unwavering love and support that singularly gives me the strength I need to pursue my dreams. I owe my accomplishments and future successes entirely to my family.

The Puzzle of Counterproliferation

> There are indications because of new inventions that 10, 15, or 20 na-
> tions will have a nuclear capacity, including Red China . . . This is ex-
> tremely serious . . . I think the fate not only of our own civilization, but
> I think the fate of world and the future of the human race, is involved in
> preventing a nuclear war.
>
> —John F. Kennedy
> Third Nixon-Kennedy Presidential Debate, October 13, 1960

Introduction

The twentieth century was to see an expanded club of nuclear actors. States across the world were projected to develop nuclear arsenals to address security threats from proximate and distant adversaries, to provide stature and esteem, and to change the nature of interstate relations. President Kennedy bleakly envisioned a new world: the emergence of a nuclear Red China to rival American and Soviet primacy; a nuclear South Asian subcontinent with nuclear-armed missiles spread along the borders; and nascent nuclear weapons states in Latin America eager to shed their second-world status and enter the fray as regional powers. President Kennedy feared that, by the close of the twentieth century, the international community would be faced with managing the horizontal and vertical proliferation of nuclear weapons to the far corners of the world, "a world in which there are large quantities of nuclear weapons is an impossible world to handle."[1]

Yet, despite President Kennedy's fateful prediction in 1960 that the world would see nearly twenty countries with a nuclear capability, this is not the world we see today. For more than seventy years, the international community has managed to stem the tide of nuclear weapons. Since the inception of nuclear weapons during World War II, more states have opted to give up their nuclear pursuit or relinquish existing weapons than have maintained their arsenals.

Delaying Doomsday, Rupal N. Mehta. Oxford University Press (2020). © Oxford University Press.
DOI: 10.1093/oso/9780190077976.001.0001

Many more, in fact roughly three times as many countries, have reversed the direction of their nuclear weapons programs than stand today as nuclear weapons states.

While some scholars and policymakers have argued that "in the past half-century, no country had been able to prevent other countries from going nuclear if they were determined to do so,"[2] the majority of Cold War and post–Cold War governments have stubbornly focused on how best to disincentivize nuclear proliferation. In recent decades, in the United States for example, nonproliferation policy has oscillated between calls for preemptive action against "rogue proliferators" (following in the footsteps of the Israeli destruction of the Osirak facilities in Iraq in 1981 and of the Al Kibar nuclear reactor in Syria in 2007) and demands for continued diplomacy (mirroring U.S. reactions to previous instances of proliferation in Europe or Latin America).

However, as the nuclear club threatens to expand, especially with the introduction of new state and non-state actors that engage in increasingly bellicose behavior, questions remain regarding the most effective ways of curbing nuclear proliferation and ensuring international stability. Despite an overall decline in actors seeking nuclear weapons, these are not irrelevant or baseless concerns. The clandestine acquisition of nuclear weapons materials and technology in Iraq, Syria, and North Korea, among others, has reinforced the fear of nuclear weapons in the wrong hands, especially rogue states, and reaffirmed the U.S. commitment to pursuing aggressive nonproliferation/counterproliferation strategies over the past seven decades. Faced with Saddam Hussein's belief that nuclear weapons would allow Iraq to "guarantee the long war that is destructive to our enemy, and take at our leisure each meter of land and drown the enemy with rivers of blood,"[3] and Muammar Qaddafi's declaration that "soon the atom will have no secrets for anybody [. . .] Tomorrow we will be able to buy an atom bomb and all its parts . . . the nuclear monopoly is about to be broken,"[4] it remains imperative that the U.S. formulate an effective and fruitful counterproliferation policy that prevents the spread of nuclear weapons.

Evaluating the decisions of states that start down the nuclear path—such as Libya, South Africa, Brazil, and Sweden—and their motivations for stopping further development may help us to better address these questions. While there is little evidence to suggest that all nuclear proliferators are made equal, understanding the causes of nuclear reversal and establishing general patterns of behavior provide invaluable insight into the challenges of forming a successful counterproliferation policy. This book thus focuses on the experiences of the often forgotten: countries that ventured down the path of nuclear weapons but were stopped short. In doing so, I concentrate on two critical questions. First, given the benefits that nuclear weapons bestow their possessors, why would states opt to end their nuclear weapons pursuit? Second, if the international community can exert pressure on proliferators to abandon their nuclear programs, which set of policy levers is most likely to succeed?

Argument in Brief

Nuclear decision-making, including the decision to end a nuclear program, is significantly impacted by external factors. This observation incorporates two elements. First, states are willing to end their nuclear weapons programs when extended positive and negative inducements by the international community. Because the United States is often at the forefront of nuclear negotiations, the success of these policy levers in exerting pressure on states to reverse nuclear weapons programs depends on the proliferator's relationship with the U.S. Second, the shadow of military force influences the bargaining process. The possibility of military intervention incentivizes proliferators to accept an agreement and end their nuclear pursuit.

Inducements Given the Proliferator's Relationship with the United States

My theory argues for the necessary inclusion of positive inducements while imposing negative incentives, even when faced with difficult proliferation challenges. By employing them in tandem as mutually reinforcing instruments, these external inducements have a powerful impact on domestic-level nuclear decision-making, especially during periods of leadership change. And, perhaps more importantly, from a policy perspective, rewards and sanctions can work on both allies and adversaries that have divergent relationships with the U.S.

In assessing the influence of external factors on nuclear reversal, I examine the strategic interaction between a state that has begun nuclear weapons activity (the proliferator) and the United States (as a representative of the international community). In doing so, I follow the literature's emphasis on "the interaction between two or more states as the object to be analyzed . . . the strategic interdependence of the actors."[5] While proliferators seek to acquire nuclear weapons to reap the benefits they may confer upon their possessors,[6] the United States aims to counter the diffusion of nuclear technology and curb the expansion of the nuclear club. Each interaction is shaped by the relationship between the two actors: their beliefs about what these programs can be used for, how resolved the U.S. is to use any means necessary to stop a proliferator, and the similarity of their policy preferences, that is, how opposed or agnostic the international community may be to that proliferation attempt given the proliferator's status in the system. For states that share preferences with the United States, the latter can simply offer rewards to make the proliferator indifferent to the program and be satisfied to end it. This logic accounts for many of the instances of nuclear reversal observed among friends, and often allies, of the United States. For these states that may have embarked upon the nuclear path, perhaps as a result of security concerns or simply because they had the technical capacity to do so, the U.S. can provide an adequate package of rewards to compensate for reversing their nuclear course. Increases in military or economic assistance, civilian nuclear assistance, or even security guarantees may satisfy these proliferators. Agreements that offer "carrots" should effectively motivate nuclear reversal among states that share preferences with the United States.

On the other hand, for states whose policy preferences diverge from those of the international system, the United States is more likely to be opposed to the program and to resort to a combination of rewards and sanctions to encourage nuclear reversal. The U.S. may employ economic sanctions to identify states that are amenable to negotiations and those that may remain resistant to bargaining. In these interactions, sanctions play a critical role in revealing the preferences of states engaged in nuclear weapons activity. However, while sanctions can serve to differentiate differently motivated proliferators and serve as an impetus to negotiate, by themselves, they are unlikely to delay or stop nuclear development. Instead, sanctions must be employed in tandem with rewards to motivate leaders to reverse their nuclear course and agree to accept a deal to forego a nuclear deterrent in exchange for compensation for the lost capability. To encourage nuclear reversal, the United States and other states in the international community must provide the necessary face-saving incentives for leaders to claim domestic victories after forgoing nuclear weapons.

Background Threat of Military Force

Underlying these interactions is the resolve of the United States to resort to the use of military force to counter a state's nuclear weapons activity. While not an option against all proliferators, especially states allied with the United States, the shadow of military force plays a critical role in influencing how proliferators view offers of rewards and sanctions. This revelation of resolve by the United States impacts the willingness of the proliferator to accept an agreement to avoid an escalation in punishment, even conflict. The U.S. can credibly threaten the use of force against states that continue down the nuclear path, while simultaneously offering inducements in exchange for nuclear reversal that may satiate domestic constituencies and provide the necessary political cover for a foregone program. In tandem, positive and negative inducements may incentivize all types of proliferators (even those with divergent or revisionist policy preferences) to reconsider and ultimately abandon their nuclear efforts to prevent war.

Implications for Analysis:
Success and Failure in Counterproliferation

What then are the conditions for successful nuclear reversal? Negotiated settlements that privilege positive inducements (over negative inducements) are most likely to be effective with states friendly to the United States. Positive and negative inducements together are effective even for states with divergent preferences to the U.S., especially when the U.S. can credibly threaten the use of military force if the proliferator were to continue. The extension of inducements is most likely to fail when imposed against revisionist proliferators, with divergent preferences to the U.S., and for whom threat/use of military attack cannot credibly be employed. Under this condition, proliferation has the highest likelihood of success. However, using my theoretical framework, the United States should be able to exert pressure to end most proliferation instances.

Nuclear Proliferation and Reversal

Given its importance in international relations, nuclear abandonment is surprisingly understudied by scholars and policymakers. There are two key reasons for this lacuna. First, while the question of nuclear reversal lies at the crux of an expansive literature on nuclear weapons proliferation, thus far, the majority of this scholarship has focused on two alternative, albeit important, questions: why do states pursue nuclear weapons and what is their impact on the international system? This literature has been largely successful in understanding and identifying, both theoretically and empirically, the primary motivations behind nuclear weapons exploration and acquisition: threats in the security environment, available technological capabilities, and domestic-level bureaucratic and organizational factors.[7] Similarly, this scholarship has made significant strides in analyzing the substantial impact that nuclear weapons have had on various issue areas—regime change/transitions to or from democracy, inter-state conflict, economic growth, and civil strife, suggesting that nuclear weapons have differential effects for their holders in conventional versus nuclear crises or broader bargaining interactions.[8] Only recently have scholars begun to systematically address the corollary question of why states may reverse their nuclear course.[9]

For the most part (with the exceptions noted previously), prior scholarly and policy focus on nuclear reversal has been ad hoc and situational. As

administrations and policymakers sought (and continue to desire) detailed understanding and data on the crisis du jour, academics have similarly centered
their research and analysis on addressing those pressing cases. The literature
to date has identified some conventional wisdoms for how best to counter
the spread of nuclear weapons. First, one prevailing notion—in both the academic and policy communities—is that states are more likely to give up nuclear
weapons as a result of changes in domestic political factors, that is, a resolution
of a threat to national security, endogenous changes in regime leader or type, or
institutional changes in the domestic political structure. But is this the case for
all states that have given up their nuclear weapons programs? There is some evidence to suggest that changes at the domestic political level can contribute to
reversal decisions.[10] Indeed, a fairly common explanation for cases such as South
Africa, Brazil, and Argentina, among others, is that leaders or governments
seeking to maintain their own political survival acquiesced to abandon their nuclear weapons programs.[11]

For example, one branch of scholarship on nuclear proliferation, and in part,
the foundation of this study, seeks to examine why states proliferate, the variance
in doing so, and to forecast which states are the most likely new proliferators.[12]
These scholars argue that states pursue nuclear weapons for various reasons including security concerns, organizational or bureaucratic interests, or to gain
enhanced prestige in the international community.[13] Further, the scholarship
assumes that these factors similarly influence decisions to abandon nuclear
weapons programs. While the current state of the literature on proliferation has
thus far been able to account for many cases, it has had limited predictive power
for some key aberrations found in the empirical record.

To the extent that we seek to identify cross-national patterns to more effectively disincentivize future instances of proliferation, I deviate from the extant
literature, and these assumptions, for two reasons. First, the literature seeks
primarily to explain why states renounce nuclear weapons proliferation as a
mirroring process to the initial pursuit of nuclear weapons. But this may or may
not be the case. While many states (Germany, South Korea, Taiwan, Iraq, and
Libya) may have chosen to pursue nuclear weapons as a result of domestic political pressures, these states may in turn choose to voluntarily dismantle their
weapons programs because they receive strategic incentives from the international community that ameliorate their pursuit (e.g., to revise the status quo, increase their share of the distribution of resources, or both). This may have an
indirect effect on mitigating internal pressures, but it may not necessarily be the
precipitating cause of nuclear reversal. Indeed, these are not necessarily opposite processes, whereby the presence and subsequent absence of organizational
biases explain state proliferation behavior; to the contrary, states may choose to
proliferate for specific reasons and reverse for varied and unrelated reasons. In

the event that one external threat is alleviated, or a dispute is settled, states may still opt to maintain their nuclear weapons programs, keeping the capability to restart the program if another threat arises.

Further, these demand-driven models of proliferation often fail to take into account supply-side or "opportunity" factors that are necessary for successful acquisition of nuclear weapons. States may desire acquisition of nuclear weapons but may lack the capabilities necessary for successful weaponization. An external security threat may persist, but a proliferating state may ultimately decide to dismantle its program because the costs of continued development are outweighed by the benefits of counterproliferation. This is especially true if the international community is able to provide an inducement, such as a security guarantee, or establish a military alliance that helps to alleviate an external threat that may have contributed to the initial decision to acquire nuclear weapons. Indeed, some have argued that while Japan and South Korea have both the opportunity (a high latent nuclear capacity) and willingness (an increasingly aggressive regional adversary, North Korea), they both remain non-nuclear states because of the promise of an extended nuclear deterrent by the United States. Both determinants are crucial for explaining the process of proliferation, but neither is sufficient for understanding why states may voluntarily reverse their weapons programs. Perhaps more crucially, this type of analysis may not yield implications about future instances of proliferation.

Second, the scholarship on nuclear proliferation has highlighted the efficacy of the Nonproliferation Treaty and international institutions in effectively curbing the spread of nuclear weapons and technology beyond the original nuclear club.[14] This explanation suggests that the normative constraints by these institutions limit the desire of states to pursue nuclear programs in contravention of the international law and nonproliferation norms. And perhaps more importantly, they are effective in regulating the spread of fuel-cycle technology to ensure that states that do go down the nuclear weapons path are prevented from fully developing an operational nuclear weapons arsenal. Under this logic, international institutions can incentivize changes in nuclear behavior.

Yet, a careful examination of the universe of nuclear activity presents a challenge to this argument. First, many instances of nuclear pursuit occurred after the creation and ratification of the Nonproliferation Treaty, suggesting that the NPT was not always a significant barrier to nuclear weapons interest and pursuit. Second, the existing scholarship on the NPT, and the nonproliferation regime in general, reveals the mixed effects of export control and regulation of nuclear materials. More often than not, international treaties contributed to the spread of nuclear technology and capacity that underpinned the eventual proliferation of nuclear weapons.[15] Further, some states like Iran and North Korea openly scoffed at the efficacy of the nonproliferation regime and the NPT by pursuing nuclear weapons while NPT signatories. These empirical deviations from conventional wisdom suggests that there may be alternative logic than NPT restraint that is a better fit for the historical record.

Finally, the policy community's recent approach to challenges to the non-proliferation regime has focused on a trigger punishment strategy—threatening to respond with the "worst" possible punishment. In the case of a recent proliferation attempt (Iran), hawks within the government, and policy and academic communities have supported the prospect of a preemptive military strike against Iranian nuclear facilities. A response of this kind, primarily as a substitute to other non-military approaches to curb the Iranian nuclear program, would aim to permanently dismantle, and erect a prohibitive obstacle to restarting, a nuclear program. Matthew Kroenig states:

> A preventive operation would need to target the uranium-conversion plant at Isfahan, the heavy-water reactor at Arak, and various centrifuge-manufacturing sites near Natanz and Tehran, all of which are located aboveground and are highly vulnerable to air strikes. It would also have to hit the Natanz facility, which, although buried under reinforced concrete and ringed by air defenses, would not survive an attack from the U.S. military's new bunker-busting bomb, the 30,000-pound Massive Ordnance Penetrator, capable of penetrating up to 200 feet of reinforced concrete.[16]

Yet, as critics of this policy approach have pointed out, this strategy presents its own challenges and threats to broader security goals.[17] First and foremost, a military strike against Iranian nuclear facilities may ignite a full-scale war, a global economic crisis, or both that would further destabilize the region and the international community at large. Second, given the already tense relationship between the United States and Iran, a military attack (in lieu of more diplomatic approaches) may yield limited international support for U.S. policy. Lessons from the 2003 U.S. war in Iraq yield important implications for how allies, friends, and other states in the international community may respond to this strategy. Lastly, this stark punishment mechanism may set a dangerous precedent for how states, beyond just the United States, respond to future proliferation challenges from latent nuclear states and true nuclear weapons aspirants alike. Indeed, the Obama Administration's Iran policy consisted of a "dual track" of pressure and engagement. The strategy exerted pressure in order to force Iran to the bargaining table for a period of engagement and negotiations which ultimately led to the signing of the Joint Comprehensive Plan of Action in 2015.

A survey of the historical record and the contemporaneous cases suggests that rationales for case-specific responses to nuclear proliferation are neither sufficient nor entirely satisfying. To fully understand why *any* state may choose to reverse its nuclear weapons program, we must zoom out from individual countries and examine behavior at the global level, specifically how other countries can influence states to stop their nuclear pursuit. My book contributes to extant scholarship by building on literature that focuses on this dynamic, specifically by examining how external incentives (both positive *and* negative) offered by the United States can impact domestic nuclear decision-making.

Despite the prominence of these issues in present-day politics, multinational summits, and international relations writ large, the aim of this book is not to rehash the conventional wisdom (often demarcated along party or ideological lines) to justify particular political decisions or fret about the remaining nonproliferation challenges (such as North Korea). Rather, the overarching goal of this book is to use the entirety of the historical record (including both wins and losses for the nonproliferation regime) to enhance our understanding of these dynamics and to articulate a better strategy and range of solutions for the future. I take a necessary step toward addressing these gaps by conducting a systematic, mixed-method analysis of the impact of foreign influence on nuclear reversal since the end of World War II through the recent conclusion and aftermath of the Joint Comprehensive Plan of Action (JCPOA) with Iran in 2015. My book will also contribute in defining and guiding approaches to the difficult case of North Korean nuclear proliferation. In doing so, these analyses reveal the steady, slow improvement and evolution of U.S. nonproliferation/counterproliferation policy over time that support the core arguments of this book.

Defining Nuclear Weapons Activity

I begin by discussing state choices regarding the acquisition and subsequent abandonment of nuclear weapons programs. Over the past seventy years (essentially since the earliest nuclear weapons pursuit), nuclear reversal has taken on many forms. Norway, for example, is not widely remembered as one of the world's foremost nuclear entrepreneurs but it was one of the first states to acquire a nuclear reactor.[18] After years of experimental research at the start of the first wave of global nuclear proliferation in the 1950s—including the difficult-to-attain capability to manufacture the fissile material necessary for a bomb (the separation of plutonium)—Norway ultimately opted to end its nuclear weapons program in the late 1960s. In contrast, South Africa quietly pursued nuclear proliferation into the 1980s, even successfully completing the production of six operational weapons and acquiring suitable delivery vehicles, before ultimately agreeing to dismantle its weapons in 1993 in adherence with regulations from the International Atomic Energy Agency (IAEA).

Before explaining why states that begin nuclear weapons programs choose to renounce their nuclear ambitions, it is important to first consider the proliferation process. The definition of the start of a nuclear weapons program has been subject to a wide variation in interpretation but has resulted in two key points in the nuclear weapons development process: (1) opportunity/capability, and (2) willingness/intent.[19] The difficulty arises when using one point or the other as the defining characteristic of starting a nuclear weapons program. By placing either capability or intent as senior to the other, one can introduce biases that result in overestimation or underestimation of nuclear weapons activity. To mitigate this potential bias, I mirror the current standard in the literature and incorporate both simultaneously as necessary conditions. Thus, I define a state's nuclear weapons program as a motivated effort to acquire a nuclear explosive device and access to the necessary technical capabilities for building such a device.

Not surprisingly, the question of what constitutes nuclear reversal is similarly complex. To parallel initial proliferation decisions, a definition of nuclear reversal must also incorporate elements of deliberate action (e.g., dismantlement of existing facilities) and intention (i.e., adherence and compliance with the international nonproliferation regime). For the purposes of congruence with other analyses in the field, I adopt, but slightly modify, a definition for nuclear reversal suggested by Ariel Levite:

> "The phenomenon in which states embark on a path leading to nuclear weapons acquisition but subsequently reverse course, though not necessarily abandoning altogether their nuclear ambitions. . . . including a governmental decision to slow or stop altogether an officially sanctioned nuclear weapons program" as a basis for selection into my population of interest.[20]

This definition allows for the possibility that despite the intentions of the international community and the proliferator, and the institutional mechanisms in place to ensure a non-nuclear status, a proliferator may at some point in the future restart its program. I allow for this flexibility because it reflects reality. As interstate relations evolve over time, states (such as South Korea or Saudi Arabia) that seem unlikely to want to pursue nuclear weapons may opt to do so even after receiving incentives from the international community that discourage proliferation behavior.[21]

To be classified as engaging in nuclear weapons activity, there must be evidence of some form of technological behavior (such as indigenous production or receipt of nuclear technology or materials) and political conduct (discussions leading to a decision to pursue a nuclear weapons program). To that end, nuclear reversal is the observable process of reversing a state's decision to pursue nuclear weapons and a commitment to refrain from continued development, construction, or possession of nuclear weapons. Reversal can then take on any of the following forms: suspension or freezing of an ongoing nuclear weapons program; permanent abandonment of active weapons development; returning full weapons systems to another state or non-governmental organization; or the voluntary dismantlement of an operational nuclear arsenal.

By incorporating all of the states that have ever pursued nuclear weapons activity since 1945 in the scope of my analysis, a rather different picture emerges: the phenomenon of nuclear reversal overwhelms that of nuclear weapons acquisition. Table A1.1 in Appendix 1.1 presents detailed coding for nuclear weapons activity for each case included in the analysis. Figure 1.1 below summarizes cumulative counts of nuclear proliferation and reversal occurrences over time between 1945 and 2015. I also show the number of states that have proceeded to successfully acquire nuclear weapons during the same period. Thirty-two states have embarked upon the path of nuclear proliferation, out of which twenty-three have opted to reverse their nuclear programs. In other words, almost 72% of states that initiated nuclear activity chose to abandon weapons pursuit.

This figure yields some interesting take-aways. First, nuclear reversal is not as rare as is often presumed in policy circles or some extant scholarship. In fact, nuclear abandonment reflects the behavior of the strong majority of states who have undertaken some form of nuclear weapons activity. Second, the graph also reveals interesting variations over time. After a steady growth during the period 1945–1970, the introduction of new states with nuclear weapons activity stagnated in the mid-1970s, and essentially ended in the early 1990s when Belarus, Kazakhstan, and Ukraine, who had inherited their programs after the fall of the Soviet Union, returned their arsenals to the Russian Federation.[22] The late 1990s also saw the conversion of long-time proliferators, India and Pakistan,

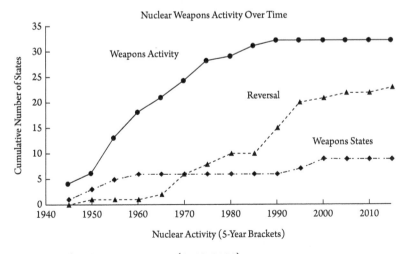

Figure 1.1 Nuclear Weapons Activity (1945–2015)

to de facto nuclear states. On the other hand, nuclear reversal was negligible until 1960, grew steadily in the 1960s, stagnating between 1970 and 1985, ultimately skyrocketing after the mid-1980s. Temporal variations lend themselves to thorough theoretical and empirical investigations to help answer key questions about the evolution of nuclear reversal in the international system. And understanding the diversity of these countries—representing different motivations for proliferation, progress on the weapons activity spectrum, and types of nuclear reversal—provides novel insights into the best inducements for encouraging nuclear abandonment.

Bargaining with Rewards and Punishments

Figure 1.1 further illuminates that understanding the variation in nuclear reversal is especially important because it sheds light on which policy instruments the international community has, and in the future, should choose in countering proliferation. So, what are the best policy levers for the U.S. or other weapons states to use in addressing counterproliferation?[23] As with most other issues of compellence and deterrence in the modern era, policymakers traditionally have used a variety of policy levers for bargaining. The Cold War's ushering in of a bipolar nuclear world revealed the necessity for the superpowers and other major actors to establish a set of instruments with which to modify or prevent certain state behaviors, especially those in opposition to the aims of the nonproliferation regime.

Scholars and practitioners traditionally categorize "influence" into two broad classes: (1) political or economic assurances; and (2) the use of force or economic coercion, most commonly, economic sanctions.[24] The origin of both branches of literature on inducements can be traced back to the work of Thomas Schelling. In contrast to leading work at the time that emphasized the role of military power as central to the success of a state and a predictor of state behavior, Schelling argued for a critical examination of the strategic interaction between states, specifically how states choose to act in response to another state's behavior.[25] He further drew the distinction between the blunt use of force and a limited, coercive threat of force that could be used to compel or deter action of an adversary. This type of coercion, according to Schelling, was essentially structured bargaining that depended on both a state's strengths and preferences. To some extent, there is a reasonable differentiation between blunt and soft coercion in the use of military force and the threat of economic sanctions; while costly to both actors, they tend to operate in different ways.

Using work by Schelling and others as foundation, scholarship and foreign policy eventually diverged into two separate strands of debate about the use of military and economic inducements in bargaining. The literature on coercion and bargaining yielded powerful implications for a more general understanding of positive and negative inducements: (1) a state's preferences matter almost as much as the valuation it places on the issue in question; (2) successful bargaining entails both coercion and cooperation, where a set of demands and promised rewards adapt as a result of changes in the environment; (3) the use of costly sanctions or military coercion may backfire, potentially resulting in the escalation of the use of force to inefficient levels; (4) positive inducements may encourage longer, cooperative relationships; and (5) information asymmetries create significant problems for effective, credible bargaining and the ultimate establishment of credible commitments.[26]

Yet, some of the existing scholarship and conventional wisdom on nuclear reversal suggests that actors can and should only be targeted with one form of inducement to change behavior. Thus far, this scholarship and policy have emphasized the efficacy of negative inducements or punishments to alter behavior. As I demonstrate later, the disproportionate political emphasis on the punishment side of the spectrum is often followed by counterproliferation failures. Further, this seems surprising given the positive externalities of bargaining with rewards. According to some scholars like Baldwin, the form of inducement can have long-lasting psychological effects on how states bargain. Positive inducements, in contrast to damaging sanctions, may produce virtuous cycles of success or spillover that work to build trust within the international system in the future.[27] Indeed, I find that for successful nuclear reversal, states cannot solely rely on the use of rewards or coercion to alter behavior, but must employ threats of coercion and the promise of rewards simultaneously in the same offer. These tools are mutually reinforcing in providing a set of incentives to modify nuclear decision-making.

Even within this simplified single framework, there remains a significant theoretical gap in our understanding of how inducements operate. If, for example, rewards and punishments are used in tandem, which is actually doing the heavy lifting in providing incentives for leaders to shift their behavior? How can we be certain that it is the promise of sanctions relief (a "future" reward) that is not bringing countries to the negotiating table when they were hit with U.S.- or UN-imposed economic sanctions? To answer these questions and gain clarity on causal mechanisms at play, I employ the intuition that initially guides analyses of deterrence and coercion. The success of nuclear reversal is incumbent upon the willingness of a state, the United States or some other member of the international community, to negotiate with a variety of (even positive) policy instruments. Rewards can serve as face-saving political cover that allows leaders of adversarial states to stop their nuclear weapons programs and survive potential challenges to their political survival. Sanctions (and the prospect of their ultimate lifting) can also help persuade domestic populaces that accepting a settlement to end their nuclear programs is better than continuing to suffer political and economic costs—or face an escalation in punishment.

Critically, these dynamics are underpinned by the United States' willingness to credibly threaten military force—that the United States or another member of the international community will choose to terminate a nuclear weapons program rather than risk its continuation and eventual success. This game-ending move, which restructures and shapes the entirety of the negotiation process for some proliferators, is unique in the context of nuclear counterproliferation. While it is generally non-credible to threaten military strikes in most other arenas of international relations, the ultimate option to use military force to end a nuclear weapons program reinforces the utility of a combined strategy of rewards and sanctions as effective policy tools to change nuclear decision-making.[28] And though we should take comfort that inducements under these conditions are effective, it is also important to determine which types of policy tools have the greatest likelihood of success across a variety of proliferation cases. Further, extensions of this logic help isolate the causal forces behind decision-making under different conditions, such as during periods of domestic political changes (including changes in leadership) as well as among various types of proliferators—friends and foes.

Road Map of the Book

Less studied by both scholars and policymakers focused on particular cases mired in controversy are the more quotidian cases of nuclear reversal that result in the belief and practice that only some friendly countries could be compelled with incentives. The variation among proliferators is important as it highlights the notion that all states can be incentivized to reverse their nuclear programs and an effective counterproliferation strategy relies on a variety of policy levers. Accordingly, in Chapter 2, I develop a theory of nuclear reversal that examines the strategic interaction between the international community and the proliferator when the latter opts to begin a nuclear weapons program. Building on traditional bargaining models in international relations, I argue that the negotiation process itself provides critical information about the preferences and aims of the proliferator. By differentiating among different types of proliferators (those that are truly committed to acquiring nuclear weapons and those that may be more pliable), the international community, primarily the United States, is better able to tailor a strategy toward a particular state. Through these negotiations, the United States is trying to send messages about its own willingness to stop the program with inducements, or military force, and to determine the resolve of the proliferator. My theory of nuclear reversal develops a framework that can retroactively help guide our understanding of historical instances of nuclear counterproliferation *and* provide a lens through which to better examine current and future proliferation attempts.

Neither carrots nor sticks work all the time. Thus, existing studies in both political science and economics find mixed evidence of their effectiveness. However, my theory provides a more complete framework for why states reverse their nuclear weapons programs, outlining testable and falsifiable hypotheses for the efficacy of some policy instruments over others, and identifying the conditions under which states negotiate away their nuclear weapons endeavors. It is important to note that while this theory can predict which end of the policy spectrum will result in nuclear reversal, it cannot predict what tools the United States or other members of the international community will choose to employ and implement. That is a distinct question requiring a different theory and a subject for future study. It is similarly important to consider the potential selection bias in these cases: the international community may levy sanctions and threats of attack at the most intransigent and belligerent of proliferators, while it may prefer to reward friendly states or allies. By properly specifying how the international community can act to encourage states to stop their weapons programs in different situations, I can minimize the impact of this potential bias and provide evidence that even adversarial proliferators can effectively be targeted with rewards and sanctions to abandon their programs.

Prior to Chapter 3, I present an overview of the empirical evidence presented in this book. Specifically, I highlight the necessity of a mixed-method research design that includes both quantitative and qualitative analyses (including original archival and interview data). Then, Chapter 3 conducts a series of large-*n* analyses to examine the effects of these policy tools in inducing nuclear reversal. Taking into account important distinctions in the international system—allies or adversaries; states with high or low levels of industrial, economic, and latent nuclear capacity; states that experience transitions in leadership—these findings lend support to my theory of nuclear reversal and thus provide a cause for optimism as to the role of the United States and the broader international system in more effectively and permanently encouraging nuclear reversal. These analyses illuminate the general impact of available policy tools and provide an estimate of how rewards, when employed in tandem with economic sanctions, can successfully result in nuclear reversal over time. The evidence from these empirical tests reveal strong support for my theory.

In a set of qualitative analyses, Chapters 4 through 7 examine examples of counterproliferation successes and failures. Derived from the theoretical framework and probabilistic conditions, I identify exemplar cases that exhibit the variation described in the theory and assess what types of inducements are most effective. These chapters also examine how the U.S. and the international community can present inducements to leaders of the proliferating states to influence nuclear decision-making. For example, Chapter 4 introduces the Libyan (a success story in counterproliferation) and Chinese (a counterproliferation failure) nuclear programs to trace these dynamics.

In the three chapters that follow, I further investigate the mechanisms of nuclear reversal through comparative in-depth case study analyses. It is often difficult to establish causal identification or relationships through observational data; these chapters seek to use qualitative data to test whether the empirical implications of my theory approximate reality. Chapters 5, 6, and 7 focus, in detail, on three instances of nuclear pursuit: the Indian nuclear weapons program (1974 to present); the Iranian nuclear weapons program (1974 to 2015); and North Korean nuclear weapons program (1959 to present). For each, I describe the origin and evolution of its nuclear weapons activity over time. India and Iran, for example, provide interesting examples of two relatively similar states that embarked on nuclear weapons programs early on, with only one ultimately acquiring a nuclear weapon. Both states were (and are) considered to be regional powers that often play leading roles in international politics. At the time of their initial exploration of nuclear weapons, both were considered to be viable candidates for proliferation: they had a latent nuclear capability, economic and political resources, and serious external security concerns that paved the way for political decision-makers to pursue nuclear weapons. Interestingly, they lie in contrast to the North Korean nuclear program which developed in contravention of policymaker and analyst expectations. According to most theories of nuclear proliferation, North Korea was an unlikely candidate for being able to successfully acquire nuclear weapons.[29] Supply-side theories, for example, argue that states are not able to develop nuclear weapons unless they have the financial capacity and the technical knowledge base required to do so. Despite these obstacles, North Korea has emerged as a de facto nuclear power and has posed a formidable challenge for both U.S. leaders as well as the broader nonproliferation regime.

Further, I examine India as a within-case comparison. A series of sanctions and offers of sensitive nuclear assistance after the 1974 peaceful nuclear explosion temporarily froze further nuclear development. However, India accelerated its nuclear program in the mid-1990s and was ultimately deemed a nuclear weapons state in 1998, after multiple successful detonations. Yet, during this nearly twenty five-year period, the international community had successfully induced nuclear reversal, that is, the suspension of India's nuclear program in response to economic sanctions and the United States' offers of other forms of military assistance. Given this long hiatus from nuclear development, India's sudden shift to de facto nuclear status in 1998 surprised many in the international community and raised concerns about the spread of nuclear weapons beyond the original nuclear club. Indeed, in short order after the Indian nuclear tests, its neighbor Pakistan successfully conducted a series of underground nuclear tests to emerge as another de facto nuclear state.

The sudden proliferation in the South Asian subcontinent raised a host of questions for the international community and the United States to address. How did India, and Pakistan, manage to clandestinely acquire the bomb within the confines of the nonproliferation regime? Would this surprise nuclearization incite other neighboring or regional states to also pursue the bomb? Lastly, and most importantly, were there opportunities lost along the way to influence India's nuclear course? Much of the existing scholarship on India's path to proliferation has centered on the causes and consequences of New Delhi's acquisition of nuclear weapons.[30] Less attention, however, has been paid to opportunities the international community may have had to prevent India from getting the bomb.

Chapter 5 explores India's acquisition of nuclear weapons and its relationship with the international community, primarily the United States, during its rise to nuclear status. My analysis suggests that the global community, especially the United States, missed various opportunities throughout India's nuclear development—from its participation in the Atoms for Peace program to the unofficial announcement of its shifting nuclear intentions with the Peaceful Nuclear Explosion in 1974 to secret nuclear weapon detonations in 1998—to change the course of nuclearization on the subcontinent. In particular, I examine how the United States could have applied pressure on the Indians to help alter their nuclear intentions through the offer of rewards, perhaps in combination with the threat of punishments, at appropriate times along its long nuclear pursuit. These inducements may have altered India's path to proliferation and structured its future interactions with the international community as a de facto nuclear state. This case study analysis also provides an in-depth, nuanced story of the potential mechanisms at play in the international community's application of pressure during India's pursuit of nuclear weapons.

Iran, on the other hand, ended its nuclear weapons program in 2015, after years of negotiations and decades of political isolation and economic punishment. Most analysts saw (and some continue to see) Iran—given its security concerns, desire for national prestige, and early cooperation with other proliferators—as a natural candidate to achieve a nuclear weapons capability. Evidence suggests, however, that Iran's ultimate decision to stop pursuit of nuclear weapons was the result of growing Iranian discontent with its isolation from the international economic system and its pariah status within the international community. Indeed, these two factors were the primary drivers for the election of President Hassan Rouhani, a relative moderate that sought to reverse the nuclear weapons development in exchange for the promise of positive inducements. These included assurances of relief from punishing economic sanctions and the ultimate restoration of political and diplomatic relations with key members of the international community, after decades of isolation.

At times, Iran's proliferation story appears in some ways to be similar to those of other successful proliferators. It seemed unlikely that Iran would ever reverse its nuclear program and equally unlikely that it would give up its nuclear deterrent if it were to successfully acquire one. Yet, as my theory would suggest, the process of negotiating with the international community provided an opportunity for a new leader in Iran to reveal his evolving (and declining) preference for pursuing nuclear weapons *at all costs* in exchange for political and economic benefits. Indeed, Chapter 6 highlights the Iran nuclear agreement (the Joint Comprehensive Plan of Action) to stress this key finding: rewards, used timely and strategically, can persuade even the most persistent of proliferators.

As a nuclear proliferator in the latter half of the twentieth century and as the latest of the twenty-seven instances of successful international involvement in nuclear reversal, Iran provides a useful example of how the international community can apply pressure on a proliferator to abandon a nuclear weapons program. Lastly, as the international community had previously attempted with negative inducements to negotiate an end to Iran's nuclear program, I am able to examine why the joint rewards and sanctions strategy inherent in the JCPOA was eventually successful in incentivizing reversal.

Next, Chapter 7 examines the North Korean nuclear trajectory. North Korea's nuclear program remains the most surprising and significant challenge to the nonproliferation regime. North Korea's nuclear ambitions began in the aftermath of the Korean War and growing tension in the newly divided Korean peninsula. Exacerbated by the U.S.-ROK alliance and fueled, in part, by Soviet and Chinese assistance, Pyongyang has devoted decades to its nuclear pursuit. And this persistence and dedication has significantly shaped, and often damaged, relationships between the North Koreans and the international community, especially the United States and China.

Yet, despite continued efforts by the U.S. and other key members of the international community to negotiate with Pyongyang, North Korea remains committed to its nuclear program. And given the historical failures to negotiate the end to their nuclear program, there remains a significant debate about how the United States needs to manage the threat they pose and whether the U.S. would seriously consider the use of military force against the North Koreans.

How can we explain why the United States has continually been unsuccessful in reversing North Korean nuclear progress? To answer this question, Chapter 7 first describes the evolution of the North Korean program over the past three decades. I then examine how prior American leaders (Clinton, George W. Bush, and Obama), have engaged Pyongyang on this issue. By examining their bargaining strategies in the context of my theoretical framework, I am able to explain historical, political missteps and identify a strategy that may potentially be effective, going forward, in reversing the DPRK's nuclear program. This analysis reveals a difficult realization: despite the valiant efforts of the international community, especially the United States for taking on the lion's share of the burden of engagement, North Korea may ultimately represent a failure for the nonproliferation regime.

Finally, Chapter 8 concludes with a survey of the contemporary nuclear landscape. The questions raised no doubt play a significant role in current U.S. foreign policy debates about how the United States, and the international community more broadly, should deal with North Korea and potential future proliferators. I discuss fruitful levers that the United States and the international community may use to provide incentives for nuclear reversal among current and potential nuclear proliferators, and in dealing with states that are interested in acquiring nuclear latency. Contrary to the conventional wisdom, the acquisition of nuclear weapons may be prevented, even among the toughest of proliferators. This book contributes both to the scholarship on nuclear reversal, and on the utility of rewards and punishments, to highlight how nuclear decision-making can be influenced by international actors. Despite the historic successes of counterproliferation policy that employed external policy instruments to motivate nuclear reversal, the international community is still confronted with significant challenges that require innovative thinking and new approaches. The book concludes with a discussion of recommendations for U.S. counterproliferation policy moving forward.

Concluding Remarks

This book provides a novel examination of the question of nuclear reversal with regard to the role of the international community's menu of policy instruments. Specifically, I argue that nuclear proliferators may be more willing to give up their weapons pursuits if approached with positive and negative inducements that operate as mutually reinforcing policy levers. Contrary to conventional wisdom and decades of non- and counterproliferation policy, the sole use of punishment strategies, such as the use of economic sanctions, may have an unforeseen and unfortunate consequence of actually persuading proliferators to continue their nuclear weapons programs. Successful reversal requires a tailored approach that includes both ends of the inducement spectrum.

I aim to make several contributions to the academic scholarship by providing a new framework with which to understand the set of conditions under which proliferators may be willing to abandon their nuclear programs. First, rather than using either carrots or sticks, I argue that these tools must be used in tandem. My

theory reveals the necessity of inducements as face-saving tools meant to provide political cover to leaders, particularly new leaders, to abandon their nuclear
weapons programs. Second, and relatedly, this book reiterates the necessity of
credible consideration or the use of military force as a bargaining tactic.[31] Third,
I evaluate my theoretical propositions through complimentary approaches: (a) a
large-n quantitative analysis of the determinants of nuclear reversal; (b) shorter
analyses of successes and failures in counterproliferation; and (c) detailed
analyses of the Indian, Iranian, and North Korean nuclear weapons programs,
with original interview data from interlocutors involved in nuclear negotiations
over the past quarter century. This research aims to provide a nuanced picture
of the causal relationship between the United States ascertaining how best to
bargain with proliferators and the proliferator's decision to continue or stop
its nuclear pursuit. By empirically testing the theory of nuclear reversal in such
granular detail, I can better identify the specific conditions under which the
United States can motivate a fundamental change in nuclear decision-making
and provide answers to the central questions put forward in this study.

This book is also aimed, in no small part, toward an engagement with
policymakers and to contribute to broader policy discussions on how the international community, especially the United States, can best incentivize a change
in nuclear policy among early proliferators, and potentially, reduce the likelihood
of nuclear proliferation in the first place. Patterns that emerge from the empirical
analyses provide a useful framework with which to discuss potential next steps
for the U.S. and global nonproliferation policy. I delve into these implications in
greater detail and provide a set of recommendations that stem from the theoretical and empirical analyses for policymakers to consider when bargaining over
nuclear policy with potential proliferators.

The two questions that motivate this book—why states are willing to reverse
their nuclear course and the best means or conditions for yielding successful
outcomes—advance our understanding of nonproliferation by moving beyond
the academic and policy community's focus on "crisis" cases and the predispo-
sition to punishing proliferators. The international community is likely to face
new challenges to the nonproliferation regime in the coming years, both from
current proliferators like North Korea, and new state and non-state actors, like
Saudi Arabia, that are interested in acquiring nuclear weapons or nuclear latency.
One of the most important and difficult questions for the future of U.S. foreign
policy will be to determine the optimal strategy for engaging these players and
ideally, preventing the spread of nuclear weapons beyond the existing nuclear
club. This research takes a step toward answering these questions and yields
provocative suggestions for countering current and future proliferators, and
ensuring stability and security in the international system.

Appendix 1.1

Table A1.1 **Detailed Case Coding**[32]

State (Years of Program)	Proliferation Evidence	Reversal Evidence
Algeria (1983–1991)	Uranium exploration began; intention to launch program was announced (1981)	Acceded to the NPT
Argentina (1968–1990)	Established National Atomic Energy Commission (CNEA); mining and processing uranium core; began production of research reactor	Gaseous diffusion enrichment facility shutdown; ratified Treaty of Ttatelolco; ratified NPT
Australia (1956–1973)	Australian Defense Committee recommended that the government approach UK about purchasing nuclear weapons from them; Prime Minister asked British Air Chief Marshall and Foreign Secretary whether UK could "supply" Australia with atomic weapons	Ratified the NPT
Brazil (1955–1990)	Established National Nuclear Energy Commission (CNEN); began production of first nuclear research reactor (5000 KW)	Ratified Treaty of Ttatelolco and IAEA Safeguards Agreement; spent fuel reprocessing facility decommissioned
Canada (1944–1969)	Participated in Manhattan Project (provided expertise on uranium mining, refining, and conversion on heavy water production); began to develop a pressurized heavy water nuclear reactor (basis for CANDU, Canada Deuterium Uranium reactor system)	Ratified NPT; began removal of U.S. nuclear weapons from Canadian bases

(continued)

State (Years of Program)	Proliferation Evidence	Reversal Evidence
China *(1955–Present)*	Publicly announced decision to pursue nuclear weapons, with assistance from USSR; established Ministry of Nuclear Industry to begin construction of uranium enrichment plant	
Egypt (1955–1980)	Creation of Egyptian Atomic Energy Authority; began development of first research reactor	Ratified NPT and IAEA Safeguards Agreement
France *(1946–Present)*	First research reactor went critical; began to extract small amounts of plutonium	
India *(1945–Present)*	Establishment of Tata Institute for Fundamental Research by Dr. Homi Bhabha; statement by Prime Minister Nehru calling for development of "atomic force for constructive purposes"	
Indonesia (1965–1967)	Established Commission of Radioactivity and Atomic Energy; began construction of first nuclear research facility	Suharto's government formally agreed to international safeguards for sensitive nuclear materials and equipment
Iran (1974–2015)	First research reactor at Tehran Nuclear Research Center (TNRC) went critical—produced small amounts of plutonium	Dismantled centrifuges, poured concrete into reactor core at Arak; Signing of the Joint Comprehensive Plan of Action (July 2015)
Iraq (1976–1995)	Established Iraqi Atomic Energy Commission; began developing first research reactor	UNSC Resolution 687 directed the IAEA to find and dismantle Iraq's nuclear weapons program, require Iraqi compliance with the NPT through comprehensive ongoing monitoring and verification; UNSCOM/IAEA reported dismantlement

State (Years of Program)	Proliferation Evidence	Reversal Evidence
Israel *(1949–Present)*	Secretly established Israeli Atomic Energy Commission under control of Defense Ministry; perfected uranium extraction and developed procedure for making heavy water	
Italy (1955–1958)	Began exploration of possible joint nuclear development activities with France and West Germany; began development of first research reactor	Ratified NPT; ratified comprehensive safeguards agreement with the IAEA
Libya (1970–2003)	Qaddafi publicly announced desire for nuclear weapons; unsuccessfully attempted to purchase a weapon from China	Qaddafi renounced unconventional weapons and surrendered all nuclear-related equipment and long-range ballistic missiles
Japan (1945–1970)	Began development of uranium enrichment technology; began development of first nuclear research reactor	Ratified NPT
North Korea *(1959–Present)*	North Korea and USSR signed nuclear cooperation agreement; began production of Yongbyon Nuclear Scientific Research Center	
Norway (1949–1962)	Created Norwegian Defense Research Establishment and directed to do nuclear research for defensive purposes; began development of experimental heavy water research reactor	Ratified NPT
Pakistan *(1957–Present)*	Established Pakistan Atomic Energy Commission under direct military control; began development of first research reactor	

(continued)

State (Years of Program)	Proliferation Evidence	Reversal Evidence
Romania (1985–1993)	Began uranium mining activities; beginning of covert nuclear weapons program	Ceausescu overthrown and nuclear weapons program abandoned; agreed to full-scale IAEA inspections and command of facilities
South Africa (1969–1993)	Established first uranium mining plant; began large-scale research and development of uranium processing plant and indigenous power reactor production	de Klerk ordered termination of nuclear weapons program; acceded to NPT
South Korea (1959–1978)	Established Office of Atomic Energy; began development of first nuclear research reactor	New democratically elected government came to power, stifled military's involvement in nuclear program
Soviet Union/ Russia (1945–Present)	Stalin launched Soviet program to develop an atomic bomb, headed by Igor Kurchatov	
Spain (1959–1975)	First nuclear research reactor (Coral-1) went critical; suspicions arose that military dictatorship had begun to develop nuclear weapons facilities	Franco's death led to abandonment of nuclear weapons program
Sweden (1954–1969)	Created nuclear authority, Atomenergi, with intent to exploit uranium deposits for civilian and military purposes; Defense Research Establishment (FOA) began research on nuclear weapons	Leaders officially renounced nuclear weapons; ratified NPT
Switzerland (1946–1969)	Atomic Energy Committee given mandate to investigate defensive protective measures for country and determine requirements to develop nuclear weapons	Ratified NPT

State (Years of Program)	Proliferation Evidence	Reversal Evidence
Syria (1976–2007)	Established Syrian Atomic Energy Commission	Destruction of nuclear facility (suspected of containing partially constructed nuclear reactor of North Korean design) in Deir ez-Zor region; full-scope IAEA safeguards in place
Taiwan (1967–1988)	First nuclear research reactor went critical	Agreed to return all spent fuel from research reactor to the U.S.; began to shut down nuclear-related facilities and return remaining heavy water to the U.S. and ban any nuclear weapons–related nuclear research
United Kingdom (1945–Present)	Began Manhattan Project (in conjunction with the U.S.) to develop atomic weapons	
United States (1945–Present)	Began Manhattan Project to develop atomic weapons	
West Germany (1957–1958)	Defense Minister Strauss began diplomatic initiative to acquire nuclear arms in joint project with France and Italy	Ratified NPT; began comprehensive safeguards agreement with the IAEA
Yugoslavia (1954–1998)	Established first research reactor center (Vinca Institute of Nuclear Sciences); Tito decided to develop a capability to produce nuclear weapons	Staggered reversal in newly formed states after breakup of Yugoslavia; Macedonia acceded to NPT in 1995; Serbia approved for ratification of Additional Protocol in 2004

Theory of Nuclear Reversal

Introduction

Given the benefits that nuclear weapons bestow upon their possessors, why
do states stop pursuing them? As briefly noted previously, the existing literature has focused on a set of domestic-level explanations ranging from bureaucratic hurdles to leadership personalities to explain decisions to stop nuclear
weapons programs. Yet, these explanations clearly do not tell the entire story.
Discussions with U.S. policymakers, policymakers in current or former nuclear
aspirants, and officials in international institutions highlight another factor: the
prominent and long-standing role that the international community has played
in altering domestic-level nuclear decision-making. Academic scholarship is
also beginning to focus on the strategic interaction between proliferators and
members of the international community, especially superpower patrons such
as the United States.[1] And while much of this scholarship focuses on threats of
military force or other negative inducements, a careful survey of the historical
record illuminates that the United States, as both a clear leader of the nonproliferation regime and the primary contributor of carrots and sticks in the international community in a variety of security and non-security arenas, plays an
important role in motivating changes in nuclear decision-making.

Argument in Brief

I argue that nuclear decision-making, including the decision to end a nuclear
program (or nuclear reversal),[2] is significantly influenced by external factors.
Specifically, I argue that nuclear reversal is most likely when states are threatened
with sanctions and offered rewards that are tailored to compensate for a lost nuclear weapons deterrent. Because the United States is the leader of the nonproliferation regime, the success of these policy levers depends on the proliferator's
relationship with Washington. Yet, the shadow of military force underscores the

Delaying Doomsday, Rupal N. Mehta. Oxford University Press (2020). © Oxford University Press.
DOI: 10.1093/oso/9780190077976.001.0001

negotiation process. In an effort to reduce the likelihood that the United States would use preventive military force against them, proliferators are willing to accept an agreement to end their nuclear pursuit.

This logic yields two probabilistic conditions for examination. First, I consider a proliferator's type—and its relationship with the United States. States differ in their desire (largely though not exclusively as a function of their external threat environment) and ability to produce nuclear weapons. In turn, the international community and its key actors differ in their reactions to these weapons programs as a function of what these programs can be used for and the similarity of their policy preferences to the proliferators', that is, how opposed or agnostic the international community may be to that proliferation attempt. On the one hand, if the members of the nonproliferation regime charged with inducing nuclear reversal (most often the United States) share policy preferences with the proliferator, they will be less opposed to the program and can offer incentives to make the proliferator indifferent or satisfied to end the program. This logic accounts for many of the instances of nuclear reversal observed among friends, and often allies, of the United States. The United States' offer of rewards, such as security guarantees, is sufficient to persuade these states to abandon their nuclear efforts.

On the other hand, if the United States and the proliferator are more distant in their policy preferences and the latter aims to develop a nuclear deterrent to revise the status quo in its favor, the United States is more likely to be opposed to the program and to resort to a different combination of inducements to encourage nuclear reversal. Specifically, the United States may impose sanctions against these states to help distinguish among differently motivated proliferators that may be seeking to acquire nuclear weapons to revise the status quo against that set by the United States and other major powers. It is important to note that sanctions by themselves are unlikely to delay or stop nuclear development. Rather, they must be employed in tandem with rewards to motivate leaders to reverse nuclear course and agree to accept a deal to forego a nuclear deterrent. Given the domestic costs of nuclear reversal for the proliferator, the United States and other states in the international community must provide the necessary political and economic incentives to do so.

Second, I consider another condition on the impact of pressure campaigns for nuclear reversal—namely, the role of leaders. The extension of inducements plays a critical role in shifting how leaders view their nuclear weapons programs. New leaders may have some preference with which they too may be willing to come to the table and negotiate nuclear reversal. This calculus may evolve upon their entry into office as policy positions change after coming into office. Both instances—new leaders that come into office potentially willing to negotiate and those who do not—serve as a screening effect that affects the likelihood of getting the leader to come to the table in response to offers from the international community. For leaders concerned about political fallout if they were to abandon their nuclear weapons programs, these inducements provide crucial political cover and a "face-saving" mechanism for satisfying their domestic constituencies. To compensate for the political costs of succumbing to external pressures, leaders of nascent nuclear states can highlight the political benefits of positive inducements and demonstrate the potential costs of negative inducements if they were to continue their nuclear efforts. In doing so, leaders can justify reversing nuclear pursuit, especially decades-long unsuccessful programs, without jeopardizing their own political futures.

However, accompanying these inducements for states to reverse their nuclear weapons programs, the United States can issue a credible threat of military force to effectively terminate the nuclear program. This revelation of such resolve by the United States impacts the willingness of the proliferator to accept an agreement, to avoid an escalation in conflict. If the U.S. is able to credibly threaten the use of force against states that continue down the nuclear path, while simultaneously offering inducements in exchange for nuclear reversal, that may satiate domestic constituencies and provide the necessary political cover for a foregone program. The positive and negative inducements may incentivize all types of proliferators (even those with divergent or revisionist policy preferences) to reconsider and ultimately abandon their nuclear efforts to prevent costly conflict.

This critical difference is absent from other arenas of international relations, even discussions of nonproliferation prior to the start of nuclear weapons activity. The ability of the United States or other members of the international community to impose a "game-ending" move enhances the efficacy of rewards and sanctions to influence nuclear decision-making. While it seems implausible that the U.S. would carry out a military strike when states commit human rights violations, renege on trade deals, or violate international institutional commitments, there is significant evidence that the United States or its proxies have contemplated and implemented military strikes to prevent certain states from acquiring nuclear weapons.[3] Indeed, it is the shadow of a military attack that provides the necessary backdrop for the international community to incentivize nuclear reversal.

This chapter begins by briefly highlighting the existing literature that provides the foundational support and primary motivations for my theory of nuclear reversal. Next, I introduce new logic for how the intersection of international influence and domestic political changes can provide a strong impetus for proliferators to abandon their pursuit of nuclear weapons programs. This argument leads to a more exhaustive survey of the historical record and yields a compelling explanation of the motivations behind nuclear reversal by focusing on a different level of analysis. The chapter then introduces a set of hypotheses that examine the core theoretical logic, and its scope conditions, and concludes with a discussion of the broader implications of my theory for policy. These additional hypotheses can tell us about the parameters of my theory beyond average treatment effects. For example, consider a scenario where a proliferator has revisionist preferences, but the U.S. has little resolve to escalate to military force to stop a weapons program, what options are best to incentivize nuclear reversal? Similarly, in the event that a new leader has come to power, as a result of domestic and external pressures, how best can the U.S. leverage this opportunity to incentivize nuclear reversal? By identifying these probabilistic conditions, my theory can speak to the broadest set of cases.

Alternative Explanations

The phenomenon of nuclear reversal—the process by which states stop pursuit of a nuclear weapons program or return or dismantle an existing weapons arsenal—belongs at the center of a well-developed literature on nuclear weapons proliferation that helps inform important policy decisions toward current and future proliferators. To date, this literature has been largely successful in understanding and identifying, both theoretically and empirically, the primary motivations behind nuclear weapons exploration and acquisition. The second strand of scholarship on nuclear proliferation, and in part, the foundation of this study, seeks to examine the variance in proliferation, and to forecast which states are the most likely new proliferators.[4] This branch of proliferation scholarship has also been the foundation of more recent work examining counterproliferation and nuclear reversal, and seeks to understand how the international community, and the United States in particular, can encourage a change in nuclear decision-making.[5] This literature suggests that states may be persuaded to give up nuclear weapons as a result of changes in international dynamics, that is, alliance coercion by superpower patrons, threats of military force, and most recently, the extension of rewards and sanctions as part of national and global nonproliferation policy.[6] Scholars have focused primarily on case-specific rationales that examine changes in domestic or regional environments, including reduced threats to national security, institutional changes in domestic political structures, bureaucratic pressure, and regime and leadership change.[7]

There are, however, three limitations to this scholarship that this book aims to address. First, the literature on counterproliferation to date has centered primarily on realist-based, demand-driven explanations for state behavior that emphasize resolution of security concerns (or other factors that lead to proliferation in the first place) as a key motivation for nuclear reversal. Country-specific accounts for nuclear reversal, from Reiss's 1995 study to more recent analyses by

Levite, describe nuclear renunciation as the result of an absence of external security threats. In this model, states make the decision to acquire nuclear weapons to deter potential aggressors and secure their territories from attack without acquiring more territory or developing substantially larger conventional military capabilities.[8] In the event that this external threat is alleviated, or a dispute is settled, proliferating states, such as South Korea, may decide to reverse their programs and stop further development. These states can thereby retain a level of nuclear latency, that is, the capability to restart the program if another threat arises.

From a theoretical standpoint, the decisions underlying nuclear reversal are likely to be different than those underlying nuclear proliferation for a couple of reasons. Proliferators may decide to reverse their nuclear weapons programs not because a security threat from a foreign aggressor has been resolved or the search for prestige has faded but because the United States may provide a security guarantee or the retention of a civilian nuclear program. On the other hand, the decision to reverse a program may be made by a different actor than the one who started the program. For example, these security-driven models of proliferation fail to take into account other non-security motivations for the acquisition of nuclear weapons (such as national prestige or pressures from the military and civilian bureaucracies to pursue this capability) and supply-side or "opportunity" factors that are necessary for successful acquisition of nuclear weapons. States may desire the acquisition of nuclear weapons but may lack the technical capabilities necessary for successful weaponization.[9] And, a latent external security threat may persist, but a proliferating state may ultimately decide to dismantle its program because the costs of continued development outweigh the benefits of proliferation. This is especially true if the international community is able to provide positive inducements, such as a security guarantee, or establish a military alliance that helps to alleviate an external threat that may have contributed to the initial decision to acquire nuclear weapons. While Japan and South Korea have both the opportunity (a high latent nuclear capacity) and willingness (an increasingly aggressive regional adversary, North Korea), they both remain non-nuclear states because of the promise of an extended nuclear deterrent by the Unites States. Relatedly, democratic proliferators may experience changes in leadership such that the actor that initiated the program is potentially no longer in office. In that case, the motivation for reversal may be orthogonal or no longer related to the reasons a predecessor started a program with (especially if it was the result of bureaucratic pressures or prestige that differentially affected the predecessor).

Second, the most recent scholarship on nuclear reversal has focused primarily on providing state-level explanations (and often, although not exclusively, case-specific rationales) for why states decide to renounce nuclear weapons programs. Both Hymans and Solingen present domestic-level factors for nuclear reversal.[10] Hymans provides a leader-specific theory that argues that certain types of leaders are more likely to voluntarily stop further development of nuclear weapons programs, using the Australian case to illustrate his causal logic.[11] Solingen, on the other hand, looks to regime-specific factors to outline her argument that the political-ideological orientation of the ruling coalition in the country may determine if the state is likely to continue to pursue nuclear weapons (e.g., Argentina) or opt to voluntarily dismantle (e.g., Libya). She argues that domestic coalitions have varying preferences for nuclear policies, depending on how those coalitions view the value of nuclear weapons on regime security. Outward-looking elites that place a premium on economic openness and integration in the international community see nuclear weapons as a source of friction and may choose to reverse course, while inward-looking elites see the nuclear deterrent as a means to attain or retain security, prestige, and independence.[12] By contrast, Liberman's analysis of South Africa stresses the need for incorporating both domestic and system-level explanations into a single case study.[13] He argues that the South African case was unique in that the decisions to arm and disarm were not mirroring. South Africa initiated its nuclear program in response to organizational and leader biases, while the improving security environment of the late 1980s and outward-looking politicians who sought the benefits of economic openness and interdependence drove its decision to give up an operational nuclear arsenal. This study highlights two important assumptions that I rely on in my analysis: there may be a different mix of causal factors at work in proliferation and reversal decisions, and it is necessary to consider different forms of strategic interaction in our examination.

Third, my study builds on, but diverges in critical ways from, more recent scholarship that examines the impact of coercion, specifically by the United States, and the nonproliferation regime writ large, on nuclear decision-making.[14] This recent literature suggests that punishments, namely in the form of economic sanctions, conditional threats of alliance abandonment, and external military intervention, are the most effective policy tools in persuading states, especially those motivated by security concerns, to reverse their nuclear development or prevent it from the outset.

As such, I ground my analysis in recent scholarship on the utility of preventive military force in counterproliferation. For example, Fuhrmann and Kreps, and Whitlark examine the efficacy of preventive attacks in nonproliferation—often finding mixed effects of their impact.[15] Further, Bas and Coe study the mixed success of U.S. intelligence in identifying opportunities in a non-ideal environment, where there are limited opportunities for nonproliferation agreements. Their research shows that while intelligence can decrease the likelihood of proliferation, it may increase the likelihood of preventive attacks.[16] Importantly, their work highlights a critical empirical selection bias in counterproliferation: often, the punishment side of the policy spectrum is employed against proliferators that have revealed their enduring commitment to nuclear weapons acquisition. These are the hardest proliferation cases, and it makes sense that these states fail to reverse their nuclear course.

At the core of their theory on nuclear decision-making, Debs and Monteiro zero in on the importance of underlying strategic considerations of opportunity and willingness—security concerns, relative power, and the reliability of allies.[17] They argue that as critical and informative as these conditions are for understanding why states may want to acquire nuclear weapons, they are also useful in understanding why states may wish to *forego* or *counter* nuclear pursuit in the first place. States may wish to not pursue nuclear weapons for fear of being too vulnerable to external military intervention, that is, out of preventive war concerns. Specifically, Debs and Monteiro argue that "the efficacy of softer counterproliferation and nonproliferation measures depends on the underlying credibility of threats to use military force against or in support of the potential proliferator."[18]

While this analysis is the core foundation on which my study builds, I diverge on four main points. First, Debs and Monteiro identify the security environment in which the proliferator is operating as playing a significant role in its decision-making regarding its willingness to pursue a nuclear program. I am agnostic to the nature of the environment and potential threats faced by proliferators. Indeed, to ensure that the initial motivations for nuclear weapons do not influence reversal decisions, I include theoretical and empirical measures of rivalry and dispute environment, to control for the security context. Second, Debs and Monteiro are mostly focused on understanding the decision-making calculus for protégé states allied with stronger patron states. While I am interested in the underlying relationship between states, my theory seeks to account for all types of proliferators, not just those that are in alliances with strong patrons. I assess the impact of these relationships to ensure that the commitment nature of alliances is not driving the outcome. Third, Debs and Monteiro argue that the effectiveness of the carrots or sticks approach offered by the stronger patron will depend on the proliferator's strength relative to its adversary. My theory focuses on how the U.S., regardless of security conditions or alliance dynamics, can motivate nuclear decision-making among all types of proliferators irrespective of the state's strength vis-à-vis its adversary. Lastly, in my framework, it is not sufficient to threaten states with military force to motivate changes in their nuclear decision-making. States interested in stopping the spread of nuclear weapons must also offer incentives to proliferators that compensate for the benefits of a nuclear weapons program *and* provide political cover for leaders forgoing their nuclear pursuit.

Other studies stress the impact of the United States as a powerful patron in bilateral alliances in motivating changes in nuclear decision-making, by threatening punishment if states decide to pursue nuclear weapons.[19] Relatedly, Coe and Vaynman argue that leaders in the nonproliferation regime, including nuclear patrons, have colluded this way to manage the spread of nuclear technology and weapons.[20] Further, Gerzhoy and Lanoszka each discuss the important role that alliances, more specifically the fear of alliance abandonment, can play in motivating nuclear weapons activity.[21] All these studies stress the importance of alliances and existing political relationships with superpower patrons, in understanding proliferation decisions. I argue this dynamic can also be applied to counterproliferation decisions—where patrons are able to leverage their influence to discourage even non-allies from continuing down the nuclear path.

Lastly, when considering how best to manage potential challenges to nonproliferation regime, scholars often point to the use of punishment, especially economic sanctions, as the best way to change, delay, or stop nuclear weapons development.[22] For example, Miller states, "many scholars of nonproliferation are similarly optimistic about the role of sanctions, arguing they are an important component of the nonproliferation policy toolkit."[23] The use of punishments, or sanctions, has also been a favorite tool of the policy community as it confronts actors who are seeking to challenge the nonproliferation regime by pursuing a nuclear weapons option, in contravention to or outside the guidelines of the nonproliferation regime. This policy emphasis on economic sanctions, often to the exclusion of other policy levers, has become particularly forceful in the United States in the context of recent cases of rogue proliferators that have embarked upon the nuclear path. For example, when asking Iranians, Americans, and other third-party interlocutors about what eventually brought Iran to the negotiating table after years of failed attempts, all parties stress the importance of sanctions, though for different reasons.[24]

Surprisingly, the reliance and emphasis on sanctions or military force, alone, in the nuclear policy realm often run counter to the broader academic literature in international relations that stresses their inefficacy. The majority of scholarship on economic sanctions in international relations, especially with regard to issues of trade, human rights, repression, and other types of strategic interactions, suggests limited utility in achieving outcomes commensurate with their aim given their high costs.[25] In other policy spheres, punishments rarely have their intended effect, and, with some actors, may even encourage prolonged behavior the tools were meant to deter.

This irony is salient and interesting when considering the relative neglect of other policy instruments (such as rewards or positive inducements) in policy discussions *despite* their historical use and success in countering the spread of nuclear weapons and other issues in foreign policy. A survey of the historical record reveals the very real and important role that rewards and punishments play in motivating changes in decision-making both with regard to nuclear proliferation and other policies that run counter to U.S. preferences. This evidence is in contrast to the recent emphasis on choosing from more unsavory policy tools that may not result in the preferred outcome. And while some U.S. policymakers recognize the importance of offering carrots, in addition to or in lieu of sticks, much of contemporary U.S. foreign policy discussed in academic scholarship emphasizes the necessity of punishments, often resulting in the continuation of nuclear weapons programs. While this reaffirms the important role the United States can play in motivating changes in nuclear decision-making beyond factors at the domestic level, it raises significant questions about the manner in or conditions under which states are actually incentivized away from the nuclear weapons path.

My study yields several important contributions to this literature on nuclear reversal by building and improving on existing scholarship. First, taken together, these studies assemble both important theoretical implications and other relevant factors that are necessary not only for case studies but also for a broader, large-*n* analysis. These foundational pieces provide the motivation for my analysis, which uses the universe of nuclear weapons activity in an effort to establish a more generalizable logic that can help explain similar behavior by states that renounce their nuclear weapons programs. Second, my analysis highlights the necessity of examining multiple explanatory factors at all relevant levels, especially how proliferators interact with the United States and other key members of the international system who strive to incentivize nuclear reversal. Third, my theory seeks to address limitations and prior mixed findings, and to resolve existing tensions in scholarship by incorporating a new element for consideration in counterproliferation policy: the use of rewards *in conjunction with* sanctions, in the shadow of military force, to incentivize states to abandon their nuclear efforts in order to avoid military action. Relatedly, it provides a logical basis for why some states (especially those with divergent or revisionist policy preferences) are targeted with sanctions, and why even these states can be motivated to reverse their nuclear course without resorting to the use of military force or other escalatory punishments. Importantly, this study argues that while the specter of preventive military force is a necessary part of the counterproliferation equation,[26] it is not sufficient on its own to incentivize nuclear reversal: it must be threatened *with* an offer of inducements to help politicians save face after abandoning their nuclear efforts. Lastly, this analysis provides an opportunity to forecast the types of positive and negative inducements that are most associated with persuading future proliferating states in curbing their nuclear ambitions and preventing the spread of nuclear weapons in the international system.

The Strategic Logic of Negotiating Nuclear Reversal

The combination of elements articulated in the previous section yields a new theory of nuclear reversal. First, I emphasize the importance of superpower influence in the study of nuclear reversal. Because the United States is the foremost opponent of nuclear proliferation, it is the primary negotiator in most bilateral and multilateral attempts at counterproliferation. As such, the U.S. is also the largest donor and contributor of positive inducement, and often, if not exclusively, the primary and most active imposer of negative inducements.[27] The U.S. differs in its reactions to nuclear weapons programs partly as a function of what those programs could be used for. While aiming to avoid expanding the nuclear weapons club even for allies or friends, the United States and other major powers are far more concerned about and opposed to proliferation in states with divergent policy preferences—namely among revisionist states interested in changing the status quo in their favor by developing active nuclear weapons deterrent capable of threatening regional or distant adversaries.

Second, as with any military capability, there remains an uncertainty about the true motivations for and intentions behind nuclear programs, and what is sufficient to compel a change in behavior. What challenges the interaction is the uncertainty about the true intentions of proliferators as they continue down the nuclear path. Even more importantly, in the context of negotiating nuclear reversal, the circumstances under which they are willing to abandon their efforts are unknown a priori. To deal with these unknowns, it becomes necessary for the U.S. to decipher critical information about a proliferator's intentions and strategy. The extension of policy tools and a proliferator's response to those offers help reveal this information. In these instances, the U.S. can employ policy levers designed to distinguish between proliferators—those for whom attempts to dissuade nuclear proliferation is possible, and those for whom simple attempts at negotiation or diplomacy may not suffice and the threat of escalatory punishments is necessary.

The historical record includes many examples of such interactions between the proliferators and the United States. In some instances, states pursued nuclear weapons overtly, and potentially even with the assistance of states in the international community. This was certainly more likely prior to the ratification of the Nonproliferation Treaty in the early 1970s than it is now.[28] However, during the Cold War, and especially more recently, states have embarked upon the nuclear path with clandestine investments in either civilian or weapons programs—aimed at keeping states such as the United States in the dark about their intentions and progress. Furthermore, some of the first nuclear proliferators were technologically capable, wealthy states that acquired nuclear technology primarily for civilian purposes, as they lacked significant security threats that would necessitate a nuclear deterrent. Many other states opted to pursue nuclear weapons because they faced external security threats that prompted the acquisition of a nuclear deterrent to prevent foreign aggression.[29] More still aimed to reaffirm their status as a regional power or to use nuclear weapons to coerce or compel adversaries to change the status quo in the former's favor. Indeed, some states pursued a nuclear weapons capability (without necessarily being successful) to gain this bargaining advantage.[30]

Finally, underlying this strategic interaction and the conditions under which the international community is ultimately able to change nuclear decision-making, is the presence of a game-ending move, that is, a credible threat to destroy the nuclear program if necessary. This policy tool may seem implausible for other issue areas of foreign policy such as human rights abuses or trade violations because of the high costs of consideration (having to withdraw from redlines) and implementation (increasing the likelihood of actual war). Yet, there is a robust literature that articulates the strong theoretical and empirical rationale behind the threat or actual use of preventive military force as an effective nuclear counterproliferation tool.[31] This growing literature also addresses how nonproliferation regime leaders make decisions regarding the consideration of the use of preventive military force for counterproliferation.[32]

Despite this compelling rationale, there are three conditions under which the use of military force to destroy a nuclear program is not credible.[33] First, despite the expressed political will and current policy rhetoric, it may not be particularly credible that the United States would employ military force against some proliferators (such as North Korea) for fear of retaliation against itself, allies, and other states in the region. For these proliferators, the U.S. (or another state charged with steering counterproliferation policy) can be deterred by the threat of a conventional counter-attack or possible retaliation against an ally, even under an extended nuclear umbrella (e.g., North Korea overrunning South Korea). While the United States may want to stop North Korea from acquiring nuclear weapons, it is not seen as credibly resolved to do so with military force. Second, the United States is unlikely to choose to threaten the use of military force to prevent proliferation against erstwhile friends and allies, such as Norway or Pakistan. In the late 1970s, the U.S. considered attacking Pakistan's uranium enrichment facility at Kahuta, despite its complicated but favorable relationship with Islamabad, but ultimately decided not to.[34] Though the U.S. was seemingly resolved to stop the proliferation of nuclear weapons on the subcontinent, it ultimately gave up serious consideration of the use of military force because it was deemed too challenging and costly (given its friendly relationship with Pakistan). Both cases also reveal that while a proliferator's relationship with the United States may be useful in understanding how the U.S. establishes its counterproliferation policy, there is important variation to explore empirically. Third, and relatedly, the United States may be unwilling to consider and publicly threaten the use of force against proliferators if an operation is deemed technically challenging or impossible (i.e., the U.S. learns about the program after the state has already acquired nuclear weapons; intelligence about the program is limited and constrains a successful military strike). For example, South Africa finally revealed its decades-long nuclear weapons program once it had successfully built a nuclear weapons arsenal and purchased delivery vehicles for nuclear use. It would have been nearly technically impossible and likely undesirable to use military force to destroy the program given the risks of accidental detonation and conflict escalation against a nuclear weapons state.

Thus, while not an option for all states, the shadow of a military attack importantly shapes the bargaining dynamic between the U.S. and proliferators. However, one common objection to threats that the United States may indeed be willing to use force is that this force may be selectively employed. It will be directed mostly at targets that are not considered friends or allies of the United States. This bias may appear to be the case with distinct adversaries of the U.S., such as Iraq or Iran. But, the threat to terminate nuclear weapons programs through military force can actually apply to a broader set of proliferators, *if* the proliferator has signaled that it is more committed than most to the pursuit of nuclear weapons. One may consider the U.S. response to early signs that Beijing was planning to pursue a Chinese nuclear deterrent. Declassified documents from the Kennedy and Eisenhower administrations suggest that both leaders considered the use of force to stop China's nuclear weapons program.[35]

This case illustrates some important considerations, and limitations, about the use of military force. First, the consideration of military force does not necessitate the threat or use of military force. It reveals to both the United States and to proliferators that the U.S. is not sufficiently resolved to terminate the nuclear weapons program at any cost, such as actually implementing military force unilaterally or working with adversaries (such as the USSR) to successfully do so. Second, despite concerns over proliferation, even among adversaries, the consideration of military force may not be deemed credible to either the proliferator or to the United States. This, no doubt, has important implications for the type of agreement ultimately reached. Third, and equally importantly, there may be a somewhat non-linear relationship between affinity with (proximity to) the United States and the likelihood of threatening or using military force to stop a weapons program.

Rewards and Sanctions in Nuclear Reversal

If the international community—particularly the powerful permanent five members, P5, of the U.N. Security Council (and the only de jure nuclear weapons states)—is willing to exert pressure on proliferators to abandon their nuclear programs and potentially escalate it to the threat of military force, which set of policy levers is more likely to work? While there is consensus among policymakers and scholars regarding the necessity for diplomacy and negotiations with proliferators, there is little agreement about the best forms of statecraft for the task.[36]

Advocates of sanctions in the policy community argue that positive inducements may encourage future transgressions and the diffusion of proliferation attempts in the international community, while those who favor rewards highlight the limitations of economic sanctions in their intended effect of curbing nuclear development. On their own, rewards or sanctions may actually encourage proliferation under a "wait and see" approach. First, using sanctions alone may encourage a proliferator to further develop its nuclear weapons program as it seeks to see how the U.S. will respond to its proliferation attempt, that is, how costly it may get while continuing to assess the likelihood of its ultimate success. In addition, while sanctions may peripherally target nuclear programs, they may not actually delay or deter technical nuclear progress (i.e., further development of nuclear capabilities, the establishment of the delivery vehicles, etc.), especially if there is limited broader international support for sanctioning the proliferator.[37] Also, sanctions alone may stall negotiations, or, in the worst case, actually encourage strongly committed states to continue their nuclear progress (barring military destruction of the program). Second, using rewards in isolation may actually counterintuitively encourage some states to wait and see how much they can wrest from the United States.

To resolve this tension about the utility of sanctions versus rewards in the literature, I argue that rewards and sanctions must be used in tandem as mutually reinforcing tools to motivate nuclear reversal. Given the mixed results for the efficacy of sanctions as a counterproliferation tool (i.e., empirically, sanctions do not have a significant impact on nuclear development) and the high costs they impose on allies involved in universal or third-party sanctions, there may in fact be a limit to the scope and extent of sanctions the United States is willing to impose, especially if there is significant resistance from its adversaries in imposing sanctions against the proliferator.[38] Thus, it is still necessary to offer some form of inducement—monetary reward, military aid, sanctions relief in other arenas, or some political benefit—to compel decision-makers to abandon their nuclear pursuit.[39] This requisite stems from domestic political constraints and demands from constituencies within the proliferating states. For leaders of sanctioned states, the offer of rewards as a part of the negotiated agreement provides sufficient domestic political cover for ending a nuclear weapons effort. To avoid being seen as "capitulating to Western political demands" after being sanctioned bilaterally or multilaterally, or foregoing the nuclear option despite potential external security threats, leaders require a "deal" to take home to their constituents.

In tandem, these policy levers offer face-saving incentives for states forgoing continued nuclear weapons development. Sanctions allow leaders to demonstrate that their hands are tied, in a manner of speaking, and that they must go through with nuclear reversal for fear of enduring (further) sanctions. Rewards provide the actual mechanism by which leaders are willing to accept the negotiated settlement and satisfy domestic constituencies that may otherwise be opposed to efforts to denuclearize. By employing both instruments in a mutually reinforcing manner, the United States is better able to buy off potential proliferators without paying an exorbitant cost and simultaneously provide political cover for leaders that may face costs for forgoing their nuclear efforts.

As discussed above, the core distinction in understanding why inducements work in altering political decision-making in nuclear arena, more than most other areas in international relations, is the ability for the United States to ultimately decide to use military force to end the nuclear program. If the United States is resolved enough to use military force to end a nuclear weapons program, states are more inclined to abandon their nuclear pursuits to avoid being attacked. This strategy works for various types of nuclear weapons proliferators: states that were previously offered smaller rewards to end the program *and* states that were previously sanctioned by the United States. When faced with the potential threat of U.S. military force (or the use of force by other allies or proxies in the international system such as Israel), states are more inclined to stop their nuclear weapons attempts, accept whatever rewards are being offered, and prevent future economic punishments. For example, the discussion in Chapter 6 reveals that *both* positive and negative inducements along with more credible threats of military force may have ultimately brought Iran to the bargaining table. These dynamics yield the core hypothesis for empirical testing:

Hypothesis 1: External inducements (rewards and sanctions) increase the likelihood of nuclear reversal, given a credible threat of military force.

In what follows, I expand this core logic to examine how important probabilistic conditions, including how the existing geo-strategic relationships between these actors may impact the counterproliferation equation.

Implications of Probabilistic Conditions
Leadership Change and Pressure Campaigns

From this core theoretical logic, we can consider probabilistic dynamics that may be associated with pressure campaigns and nuclear reversal. First, are there specific moments in the bargaining dynamics between the United States and a proliferator that can be more effective in inducing nuclear reversal? To answer this question, I draw upon scholarship on crisis bargaining that examines whether there are indeed critical moments when the dynamic between actors shifts to alter the likelihood of particular outcomes.[40] In the nuclear realm, leaders (sometimes in conjunction with other domestic political actors) make the final decision about their state's nuclear trajectory. This includes the decision about whether to continue to invest in the infrastructure, technology, and know-how or, to eventually stop their nuclear pursuit in response to external incentives.[41] This logic builds on previous literature to examine how inducements from the United States can more directly impact domestic-level decisions and to better understand or even predict when it may be the best time to pursue negotiations with leaders to encourage reversal.[42] New leaders are often chosen or elected specifically because they have different domestic and foreign policy preferences than the incumbent.[43] Their rise to power may be a rare opportunity to signal their adherence to constituent concerns and preferences to end a nuclear weapons program, especially if a threat of military force or other forms of punishment seem credible and even likely. A new leadership position may allow a leader to reap the domestic benefits of being the key figure in negotiations that yield military and economic assistance, after years of coercive measures and political isolation.[44] New leaders may view the opportunity offered by a nuclear agreement to repair the economy, increase security through military assistance or security guarantees, and reengage the international community, as being critical to their domestic political survival and re-election.

This logic may apply even when leaders are handed long and unsuccessful nuclear weapons programs. While some heads of states are anchored by the weight of sunk costs of a long-running nuclear weapons program, new leaders may be more willing to cut ties to a lengthy and costly program. New leaders may be unencumbered by such concerns over their past decision-making acumen. They may also worry less that their peers will question their present judgment based on past mistakes. It is during this "honeymoon period" that they should have an opportunity to examine inherited policy and, ideally, be more willing to reevaluate whether a nuclear initiative should continue or cease. New leaders who alter their political stance during this timeframe may also side-step criticism and political repercussions for abandoning the policy positions of the previous leader. A change in leader personality and policy preferences is a way to signal a change in course that does not necessarily negate a previous administration's position on nuclear weapons or jeopardize a country's international standing or reputation.[45]

This dynamic helps explain why new leaders may be willing to accept the offer of rewards in exchange for stopping their nuclear programs. Moreover, leaders who continue down the nuclear path despite offers that would either stop existing punishments or yield some positive rewards, face both international and domestic costs for ignoring such incentives. This logic suggests that nuclear reversal could be more likely to occur upon entry into office of a new leader and in turn implies that this effect may be short-lived and will likely attenuate (or potentially reverse) over time, especially if the leader has initially signaled his preference for continuing an inherited nuclear weapons program. Consider here the election of President Hassan Rouhani in Iran in 2013. A relative moderate in Iranian politics, President Rouhani campaigned on both increasing transparency of the nuclear program as well as broader engagement with the United States.[46] Importantly, however, this logic does not imply that *all* new leaders will be amenable to nuclear negotiations. For example, in 2012, Kim Jong-Un assumed his position as the new leader of North Korea with little known about his preferences for maintaining North Korea's illegal status as a nuclear weapons state. His subsequent actions—including nuclear testing, the purported development of a hydrogen bomb, and threats of preemptive nuclear attacks against the United States—provide strong evidence that he was resolved to continue North Korea's nuclear weapons program and has in fact rebuffed attempts to dismantle its nuclear weapons. These two different outcomes highlight the importance of approaching and striving to negotiate nuclear reversal as a screening mechanism when new leaders first enter into office.

Thus, new leaders may be more amenable to nuclear negotiations than their incumbent predecessors. Consistent with this logic, states in the international system, such as the United States, have an incentive to challenge new leaders to assess their resolve or willingness to engage in negotiations to abandon their nuclear weapons programs. Leaders who are truly committed to the pursuit of nuclear weapons have an incentive to signal high resolve to develop a reputation for future bargaining. Others who are open to negotiation and prefer to prevent further punishment or even the use of military force may use this opportunity to achieve the best settlement for their state. For new leaders who inherit nuclear weapons programs from their predecessors, it is politically beneficial to voluntarily abandon nuclear weapons programs *with* the promise of certain military or economic benefits offered by the United States or other members of the international community, especially to avoid additional or escalatory punishments, such as sanctions or even threats of military action. New leaders may use their arrival in office as an impetus to signal a potentially new preference to reverse the country's nuclear weapons course or stay the course. If they choose to reverse course, new leaders may concede their nuclear weapons programs during the first round of negotiations.

> *Hypothesis 2*: External inducements, conditional on a credible threat of military force, increase the likelihood of nuclear reversal during periods of leadership change.

Again, it is necessary for these policy levers to be used in tandem. The offer of rewards alone, without the threat of potential future punishments, may encourage states to continue down the nuclear path to leverage a better offer down the road. Similarly, the threat of sanctions alone may encourage leaders to continue their proliferation attempt as they view these tools as undue punishments, with no face-saving political benefits that satisfy domestic constituencies. This is especially true for new leaders under sanctions held over from previous administrations who may be concerned about negative reaction by the domestic population if they entertain a non-nuclear status. By providing inducements, the U.S. helps to both cement the proliferator's non-nuclear status and stave off domestic problems for the new leader—providing them the opportunity for a domestic political victory.

Friends vs. Foes States with Smaller and Larger Policy Distance to the United States

The historical record reveals rich variation in the types of states that have pursued or contemplated nuclear proliferation, requiring a variety of responses to counter them. The process by which nuclear reversal occurs is varied and complex. Some states began nuclear exploration in the aftermath of World War II and introduced a nuclear weapons option as part of their interest in and access to enrichment and reprocessing technologies, ostensibly for generating electricity. Others focused from the outset on the procurement of nuclear weapons as the result of insecurities in regional or global environments. The story of adversaries like Libya or North Korea is, no doubt, markedly different from that of allies such as Brazil or Sweden. These differences are important to advancing our understanding of how the process of nuclear reversal has evolved over time and how it may look in the future. Perhaps more importantly, however, by examining the full universe of this phenomenon, we get a clearer and broader picture of how nuclear reversal occurs and what can be done to motivate it. With this panoramic view, we begin to see critical patterns emerge. Not all allies are immediately amenable to U.S. pressure. Fierce adversaries may ultimately cave in to an offer of rewards to avoid harsh punishment. Unlikely partners and unforeseen impediments to nuclear decision-making may arise. And the process of nuclear reversal can take from mere months to decades to transpire. For example, recently declassified documents released by the Central Intelligence Agency reveal the rapidity of the U.S. response to the South Korean proliferation attempt in the aftermath of President Nixon's rapprochement with China.[47] While the first round began with an American threat of alliance abandonment and nuclear pursuit by South Korea, the second saw the offer of rewards by the U.S.—the creation of the ROK-U.S. Combined Forces Command in 1978 that essentially ensured U.S. military involvement in a dispute on the Korean Peninsula. This tripwire mechanism assured South Korean President Park Chung-hee of the United States' commitment and persuaded him to abandon their nuclear intentions.

When facing an information disadvantage—the U.S. does not know the true ambitions or extent of the program—it can use its past experience to determine its initial negotiation posture and to differentiate between proliferators that may be more or less committed to the pursuit of nuclear weapons despite the costs of doing so. For allies or friendly states for whom the policy distance to the U.S. is not large, the U.S. may choose to begin with rewards to dissuade nuclear proliferation. States such as Australia or Indonesia may indeed be satisfied with offers of conventional military assistance, armaments, or non-military forms of nuclear technology. For these states, the rewards need not be substantial—allies and states friendly to the United States are unlikely to present a strong resistance to these inducements given their similarity in policy preferences and the risk that rejecting an offer may frustrate or alienate its superpower ally or patron. As they do not differ much from the U.S. in their policy preferences and believe that policy levers offered by the United States are indeed credible, smaller rewards (i.e., guaranteeing a security umbrella, providing military assistance) are sufficient.

That said, the historical record of U.S. and multilateral nuclear negotiations suggests that not all cases of nuclear counterproliferation can be solved with a simple offer of inducements. Some states may be more committed to the pursuit of nuclear weapons and not so easily dissuaded from their ambitions. In these cases, proliferators may ignore attempts at negotiations and continue down the nuclear path. Here, again, the United States' prior experience may influence how it chooses to use other forms of policy instruments to change domestic decision-making. The U.S. may leverage other policy inducements to identify proliferators that are more committed to nuclear weapons and for which the United States is more resolved to end the program—ostensibly, states that may seek to revise and challenge the status quo. The U.S. may opt to employ higher rewards or economic sanctions or both in an attempt to differentiate further among states that are interested in nuclear weapons (even among friendly or allied states) and those that may still be compelled to stop their weapons pursuit if offered the right mix of inducements.

Indeed, it is important to note that negotiation failure may occur even with allies of the United States. France, a U.S. ally and member of NATO, successfully acquired nuclear weapons in the early 1960s, nearly two decades after the dawn of the nuclear age. Motivated by concerns over security and a perceived lack of international reputation in the aftermath of World War II, France began to develop a nuclear program. The U.S. was initially opposed to French proliferation because it was opposed to all proliferation and worked to provide positive inducements to persuade France to abandon its nuclear efforts. However, the U.S. did not have sufficient resolve to try to counter the proliferation attempt potentially through the use of negative inducements or military force, given that France was a staunch ally of the United States and a member of a broader, multilateral alliance (NATO). Without this threat of punishment, the French desire to acquire nuclear weapons was stronger than the United States' willingness to take whatever actions necessary to stop it. Thus, in some instances, we observe that no offer of inducements (or at least the amount that the U.S. is willing to offer) is sufficient to outweigh the benefits states may acquire (or believe they will acquire) from nuclear weapons.

Examining these dynamics provides an important insight into how international pressure and offers of inducements can fundamentally alter nuclear trajectory of a variety of states. To better understand implications of this scope condition, I consider strategic interactions on two core dimensions: (1) the distance or convergence between U.S. policy and that of a proliferator—essentially whether the proliferator can be considered a friend or a foe along this spectrum; and (2) resolve or willingness on part of the U.S. to issue a threat of military force to stop a nuclear weapons program. With these two variables, we can identify important implications for how the U.S. is likely to interact with various proliferators, what we may expect from the bargaining attempts, and ultimately, what types of policy levers are most likely to be effective in inducing nuclear reversal.[48] Table 2.1 below presents the two core dimensions, the implications for bargaining, and exemplar proliferators.

Low U.S. Resolve to Employ Military Force

First, consider a circumstance where the United States has low resolve for forcing a change in nuclear behavior and is unwilling to issue a threat of military force against a proliferator. In the instances where the United States is confronted

Table 2.1 **Role of Resolve and Policy Distance in Nuclear Reversal**

	Small Policy Distance (Friend/Neutral State)	**Large Policy Distance (Foe)**
Low Resolve: Non-Credible Threat of Military Force	– Medium level of rewards (i.e., foreign aid) – Friends may negotiate higher rewards from patron – Nuclear reversal likely – *Examples: India, Taiwan*	– Negotiations include rewards and sanctions – Some proliferators reject negotiations to drive up rewards even if sanctioned – If there is some ceiling effect, proliferation likely (low probability of reversal). – *Examples: China, North Korea*
High Resolve: Credible Threat of Military Force	– Smallest rewards and sanctions – High likelihood of reversal, given that superpower most likely to both threaten destruction and be able to offer appropriate inducements (rewards and sanctions) – Probably a null set in the real world, since the U.S. would likely not threaten to destroy the program of a close friend. – *Example: Likely null set*	– Negotiations include rewards and sanctions – Sanctions are ineffective but serve to screen among proliferators; proliferator may continue nuclear development – Threat to use military force may be issued – *Examples: Libya, Iran*

with a proliferation attempt from a close ally or friend like South Korea and with whom it shares convergent policy preferences, it faces a decision about how best to deter further nuclear development, without endangering an alliance or security commitment, or revealing potential weaknesses in this relationship to adversaries. In many, though not all instances, the use of force is unlikely to be considered or employed because of the costs associated with doing so (likely higher among allies or friends). The U.S. could choose to differentiate among proliferators by threatening punishment including sanctions, or the removal of a security guarantee or extended deterrence but would not be able or willing to issue a threat of military action. In such interactions, the U.S. will likely first offer rewards to prevent these states from continuing nuclear development.[49] In turn, knowing that continued punishments are unlikely, and the use of force is off the table, these proliferators may negotiate to receive higher rewards in exchange for foregoing the nuclear option. The rewards primarily include military or political assistance, although some allies, especially those with significant security threats, may leverage their nuclear reversal to acquire a security guarantee or a defense pact from the United States as their patron. In the event that the negotiations reveal a more committed proliferator that seeks to acquire nuclear weapons despite pressure from the United States, it is possible that the U.S. may then choose to simultaneously impose sanctions or another form of punishment to incentivize the state to accept the negotiated settlement and stop its nuclear weapons pursuit. This dynamic results in the following testable hypothesis.

> *Hypothesis 3 (U.S. Low Resolve/Small Policy Distance)*: For states with convergent preferences to the United States and for whom the U.S. is not resolved to stop their proliferation with force, rewards increase the likelihood of nuclear reversal.

To illustrate this dynamic, consider the case of Taiwan. Taiwan's clandestine nuclear program, confirmed by specialists at Los Alamos National Laboratory who had visited Taiwan, ultimately caught the attention of the U.S. government who began to pressure the Taiwanese to stop pursuit of nuclear weapons and dismantle their existing nuclear facilities. Upon realizing that Taiwan had violated the terms of a security guarantee, the United States aimed to reinstate negotiations to stop further nuclear development. After President Chiang Ching-kuo, long a proponent of nuclear weapons, publicly announced that Taiwan could produce nuclear weapons if they desired, the U.S. significantly increased public and private pressure on Taiwan to end all nuclear-related activities.[50]

This pressure took various forms, including the threat of changing or revoking existing positive inducements and the promise of new forms of positive inducements. If Taiwan agreed to dismantle its nuclear reactor laboratories and processing facilities, return the U.S.-supplied plutonium, and convert the country's main reactor to use low-enriched and natural uranium exclusively (not suitable for weapons), the U.S. would agree to strengthen and more credibly signal its promise to guarantee Taiwan's security. If Taiwan did not accede to these demands, it would face the withdrawal of U.S. support. This new 1979 Taiwan Relations Act (TRA) aimed to codify the role of the U.S. as a security guarantor against "grave concerns," leaving the exact nature of that relationship ambiguous.[51]

The United States offered this reward to the Taiwanese as a way of relieving some of their concerns about security, especially whether the U.S. could be relied upon to protect Taiwan in the event of foreign aggression. Given that regime survival was the primary aim of Taiwan's indigenous nuclear development, Taipei was willing to abandon its nuclear weapons program. In so doing, Taiwan effectively revealed its type: though the Taiwanese wanted an effective nuclear deterrent, they did not desire nuclear weapons *enough* to incur the costs of acquiring them on their own. Repeated negotiations, including threats to withdraw or suspend support, helped reveal Taiwan's preferences. This bargaining demonstrated that Taiwan was amenable to offers of military assistance or security guarantees, rather than risking the costs of coercion in the form of economic sanctions, if they had opted instead to pursue an indigenous nuclear deterrent. This case highlights that the process of negotiation can help the international community, including the United States, identify the most effective policy instrument to incentivize nuclear reversal.

With the promise of a U.S. military commitment to provide security against foreign aggressors such as China, Taiwan ultimately relented. It began to dismantle its nuclear program, including allowing close inspections of nuclear facilities and returning nearly 80 kilograms of spent plutonium to the United States.[52] Taiwan did briefly reconsider a nuclear program in the late-1980s, but again, the U.S. was able to quickly pressure Taipei to re-abandon any weapons-related activities. Indeed, it was ultimately Taiwan's response to the reinstatement of the Taiwan Relations Act, and continued U.S. protection, that helped distinguish Taiwan from other proliferators.

* * *

Alternatively, what happens if the United States has a low resolve for inducing nuclear reversal with force against states that have divergent policy preferences? Again, the United States may be reticent to resort to military force because of the technical, political, and reputation costs of doing so. The U.S. is likely to initially approach negotiations with rewards and sanctions, especially if the proliferator is suspected of violating international law with its nuclear development (more likely in the post-NPT era). If the proliferator is committed to pursuing nuclear weapons, it is not likely to be swayed by the sanctions imposed and rewards offered, as they may not adequately compensate for the loss of an indigenous nuclear weapons program. It is likely to reject the initial U.S. offers of rewards, even if it is targeted with simultaneous or subsequent economic sanctions. The ultimate acquisition of nuclear weapons outweighs the cost of sanctions, particularly if the proliferator is convinced that the United States is unwilling to escalate the costs of punishment to the use of military force. This type of nuclear weapons pursuit may very well culminate in successful proliferation. However, if inducements were to succeed in motivating a nuclear reversal, they would need to be significantly larger and include a variety of short- and long-term benefits.

These may include sanctions relief, foreign aid, and even the allowance of some level of residual nuclear capability that lets the proliferator retain a latent nuclear status.

> *Hypothesis 4 (U.S. Low Resolve/Large Policy Distance)*: For states with divergent preferences from the United States and for whom the U.S. is not resolved to stop their proliferation with force, sanctions *and* rewards increase the likelihood of nuclear reversal.

To illustrate this scenario, one may consider the case of DPRK's nuclear program. The international community was strongly opposed to allowing North Korea to develop a nuclear weapons capability, along with the means to target proximate and distant allies, and potentially even the United States. To influence the North Korean nuclear program, the U.S. has relied on rewards, such as food assistance and medical supplies, along with intermittent and parallel imposition of economic sanctions. These inducements have been unsuccessful in altering the North Korean nuclear intentions. To date, the U.S. has been hesitant to issue credible and consistent coercive threats of military attack or regime-change to North Korea as it may backfire in accelerated nuclear development or a conventional retaliation against regional allies. Given this concern, the North Koreans have persisted in their nuclear course without fearing escalatory punishment or preemptive military action, and a successful counterproliferation strategy remains elusive. The North Korean case is discussed in greater detail, with an emphasis on future policy recommendations, in Chapter 7.

High U.S. Resolve to Employ Military Force

On the other side of the spectrum, how do interactions with proliferators change if the United States *is* willing to consider the use of force to stop a nuclear weapons program? In these instances, the proliferator poses enough of a threat that the United States is willing to pay the costs associated with military force to stop the program. First, I consider how such an interaction may occur in the unlikely scenario where the United States is attempting to counter the spread of nuclear weapons to a friendly state with whom it shares a similarity in policy preferences. Increased military assistance or a new or strengthened security guarantee may be necessary to signal a potential proliferator that, while the United States is willing to employ military force to terminate its nuclear progress, it would prefer to counter the proliferation attempt through other means. This coercive tactic may be especially effective for states that are resolved to acquire nuclear weapons because they face security concerns or existential threats. For states that have demonstrably embarked upon the nuclear path, and for whom the United States is willing to threaten military force, an initial offer of rewards need not be substantial. While highly unlikely in reality, this condition in which the United States can both threaten to end a friendly proliferator's nuclear weapons pursuit *and* offer a sufficient level of rewards will have a high likelihood of success. This approach yields another hypothesis, that while unlikely, can still be tested:

> Hypothesis 5 (*U.S. High Resolve/Small Policy Distance*): For states with convergent preferences to the United States and for whom the U.S. is resolved to stop proliferation with force, rewards increase the likelihood of nuclear reversal.

Lastly, consider what happens in instances where proliferators with divergent preferences from the United States pursue nuclear weapons in an environment where the threat of military force is high. These states may be non-aligned with the U.S. or may be revisionist states whose preferences for the global order differ dramatically from those of the United States and other members of the international system. Importantly, unlike other proliferation cases, the use of force against foes can help facilitate changes in decision-making. And depending on the state in question, the United States may actually consider military action a viable strategy. In this setting, the United States may choose at the outset to offer positive inducements to bring states to the negotiation table. For some of these proliferators, this offer may be sufficient to motivate a change in decision-making. Even leaders of rogue or pariah states may seek to gain the domestic political benefits associated with reaching an agreement and acquire significant benefits from the United States.

However, those choosing instead to continue down the proliferation course may suffer the costs of bilateral or multilateral economic sanctions that were imposed to distinguish among proliferators. In these instances, the U.S. can offer rewards simultaneously with a punishing round of sanctions to coerce the proliferator to reverse its nuclear weapons programs. For revisionist states who remain committed to acquiring a nuclear weapons deterrent, however, economic sanctions are likely to be ineffective since they tend to present no significant technical and financial obstacles to their nuclear development. For persistent proliferators, the United States may need to continue to offer greater rewards and simultaneously threaten/employ further sanctions, to motivate these states to abandon their weapons program to avoid military intervention. For proliferators that may be persuaded, the United States may need to offer substantial rewards to: (1) outweigh the loss of a highly desired nuclear deterrent; (2) provide political cover to the leader of the proliferating state who abandons a lengthy nuclear program; and (3) provide long-term incentives to prevent future nuclear weapons attempts. Among these non-allies or rogue states, rewards and sanctions are mutually reinforcing policy tools that may actually precipitate

nuclear reversal aimed at avoiding being the target of a military strike or externally imposed regime change. This logic yields the final testable hypothesis.

> *Hypothesis 6 (U.S. High Resolve/Large Policy Distance)*: For states with di-
> vergent policy preferences to the United States and for whom the U.S. is re-
> solved to stop their proliferation with force, sanctions *and* rewards increase
> the likelihood of nuclear reversal.

To examine how this last interaction may play out among non-allies or
adversaries of the United States and the broader international community, consider the case of Libya's nuclear weapons program. Libya's proliferation story
is markedly different from other proliferators: during his tenure, Muammar
Qaddafi placed Libya on the map as a pariah state that sponsored terrorism, while
secretly pursuing weapons of mass destruction through foreign assistance.[53]
Despite a strong desire to acquire nuclear weapons, he ultimately decided to accept the deal offered by the United States and Great Britain, and permanently
dismantled Libya's nuclear weapons program. This instance of reversal helps to
illustrate an important distinction among nuclear proliferators: sometimes, even
states that have significant sunk costs after thirty or more years of nuclear pursuit
are *still* susceptible to negotiations. Libya's nuclear pursuit (discussed in detail in
Chapter 4) provides a useful example of one of the most interesting and counter-
intuitive reversal stories. With a looming threat of force, the offer of rewards following a long-standing sanctions regime can coerce even the most committed
and determined of proliferators to abandon a lengthy nuclear program.

Potential Limitations:
Opportunities for Theoretical Extensions

No single theory can explain every case of nuclear reversal; the logic described
in the previous section has limitations and constraints on its scope. In this
section, I discuss four limitations of this theory, and potential solutions and
opportunities for broader theoretical extensions in future work.

Selection Effects:
Negative Inducements on the Toughest Cases

One may be concerned that in my theory, like others on proliferation and counterproliferation, decision-making suffers from potential selection biases. Is it possible, for example, that counterproliferators like the United States only employ

negative inducements against the toughest cases—states whose preferences diverge far from those of the U.S. and who may want to shift the status quo in their favor? Or rather, the U.S. only employs a half-hearted approach against states for whom the likelihood of nuclear reversal is relatively low? These biases cannot definitively be ruled out and may complicate efforts at causal inference.

It is important to note that these are problems inherent in any type of international bargaining. First, consider the use of negative inducements on the toughest cases. If this bias exists, we may expect to see counterproliferation efforts fail for these proliferators. One way to mitigate this bias would be to examine whether other instances of tough cases yield counterproliferation success if targeted with both positive and negative inducements. In the following empirical chapters, I find that even the toughest cases can successfully result in nuclear reversal if proliferators are approached with this strategy. Second, in almost any incomplete-information bargaining model, there will be proposers who know going into the situation that bargaining will fail with reasonable probability and intentionally choose offers that do not maximize the likelihood of acceptance. This maneuvering is likely to occur in nuclear negotiations as well. Even if the United States knows that the bargaining may fail, it may still choose to engage to some degree in the first place. And in accord with prevalent bargaining theory, given that most actors would prefer to reach a negotiated settlement than go to war, we can expect that, even with the likelihood of failure, attempting to negotiate may still be preferable to conflict.[54]

Ally Extortion:
Pursuing Nuclear Development for the Carrots

Patron states such as the United States may be concerned that allies are willing to start nuclear weapons programs simply to reap the benefits of an eventual counterproliferation deal.[55] This is no doubt a theoretical possibility. Allies, given that they do not fear threats of military force or even significant punishments from the U.S., may choose to develop nuclear weapons to later negotiate away for positive inducements. And as my theory would predict, in an effort to limit horizontal nuclear proliferation but lacking the resolve to use force to achieve its aims, the U.S. may be incentivized to simply offer positive inducements to reverse an ally's nuclear endeavor.

Despite this theoretical possibility, there are at least two reasons why this outcome may not occur empirically. First, even the process of beginning sophisticated nuclear activities (enough to cause the U.S. to want to counter the effort) is costly. In addition to acquiring the necessary technology, infrastructure, and fissile materials, states must also invest in the necessary personnel to manage these processes (even if they receive initial sensitive nuclear assistance from the U.S.).[56] As we know from existing scholarship, even states with strong resolve to acquire nuclear weapons may suffer from a lack of human capital to undertake such an enterprise.[57]

Further, even if states are able to adequately invest in technology, materials, and personnel to develop a nuclear weapons program, enough to raise alarm and coerce concessions from the international community, there is still the possibility of being subject to punishments from either the U.S. or other members of the community. Even with allies, the U.S. may decide to approach negotiations for counterproliferation with sticks, not carrots. In addition to complicating relations between ally and patron, engaging in nuclear activity is also likely to frustrate domestic populaces who may not see the value in provoking punishments from the U.S. simply to receive some future concessions. It is equally likely then that allies are not willing to embark upon an insincere nuclear proliferation attempt and suffer the incumbent monetary and political costs.

Assumptions of Credibility

In an effort at simplicity and parsimony, my theoretical framework makes assumptions about the credibility of state actions. Specifically, I assume that offers made during negotiations are credible, that the United States will follow through on providing positive inducements or doling out negative inducements, *and*, importantly, that the proliferator in question will actually reverse its nuclear weapons program as part of a final agreement. I make these assumptions of credibility for two reasons: (1) they generally reflect the existing scholarship on crisis bargaining, both formal and non-formal work, where models can assume some degree of credibility despite commitment problems;[58] and (2) they represent much of the historical record. First, take for example, Debs and Monteiro.[59] In their study, threats of military force play a critical role in understanding why proliferators may choose to forgo or abandon their nuclear weapons programs, especially among non-U.S. allies. And, importantly, the threats are deemed to be credible by both the U.S. and proliferators, when the cost of preventive war is greater than the externalities of proliferation. Second, for the most part, the U.S. has followed through with imposing sanctions and offering foreign aid or other benefits to encourage states to reverse their nuclear weapons programs, while proliferators, to their credit, have generally complied with counterproliferation conditions. While there are obvious counter-examples, including the failure of the 1994 Agreed Framework with North Korea and the Joint Comprehensive Plan of Action with Iran vis-à-vis the United States, these have generally been more anomalous than modal.

However, there are reasons to question, and potentially relax, these theoretical assumptions. First, it is important to consider whether the combined use of negative and positive inducements may affect the credibility of either of them. Would the United States attack a country to which it has just offered military assistance? While there are some combinations of inducements that may seem difficult to imagine, it is certainly possible for the U.S. to issue escalatory threats of punishment (including credible threats to attack a country) after trying to incentivize a state to stop its nuclear weapons program with rewards. There are cases throughout the historical record (including Iran) where the U.S. or other proxies have sought to provide military and economic assistance but have later threatened grave action if the target were to continue down its current path. Iran also serves as a good example of a state who had been threatened with "all options on the table," but was ultimately offered a deal that included a variety of economic and political benefits (including diplomatic reengagement). Even as recently as 2006, policy analysts were suggesting that the U.S. offer Iran a security guarantee while still maintaining a policy where the use of force was an option if a deal was rejected. It is likely that the offer of a security guarantee, in this context, was not seen as credible for a variety of reasons, including concerns from other allies protected under the security umbrella, such as Israel.

Second, questions of credibility and reputation have resurged in the modern geo-strategic era.[60] Decline in U.S. reputation in the twenty-first century has been exacerbated after a series of foreign policy failures (e.g., the Iraq War in 2003, the creation of failed redlines in Syria in 2013), and potentially worse, the idiosyncratic "America First" foreign policy of the Trump Administration that even extols the benefits of nuclear proliferation. If adversaries and allies alike mistrust the United States and its commitment to both the nonproliferation regime and existing alliances, concerns will continue to escalate about whether the U.S. would be willing to actually abide by a nuclear agreement and provide the promised inducements from negotiations or forgo threats of military force if the proliferator actually complies. If proliferators or other actors in the international community doubt the United States' credibility, proliferators on the cusp of nuclear reversal may question whether they should proceed with their planned denuclearization. Future research may choose to relax these assumptions and assess whether the same theoretical mechanisms are as salient in a new geopolitical environment where state (and specifically leader) credibility is up to debate.

Role of Non-U.S. Actors:
Other Superpowers and Regional Adversaries

The theoretical framework in this book focuses primarily on the role of the United States as the key actor involved in nuclear negotiations. This is not without reason. First, its role as the head of the nonproliferation (and thus counterproliferation) regime is generally unequivocal. Since the introduction of nuclear weapons in the international system in 1945 (by the United States), the U.S. scientific and policy communities, as well as policymakers and heads of states, have done their utmost to both manage and curtail the spread of nuclear technology throughout the international system.[61] Second, as discussed throughout this study, the United States has traditionally been both the primary donor of positive inducements and imposer of sanctions and other negative inducements. This is true not just within the nuclear arena but often with regard to human rights violations, terrorism, or other security threats posed by external adversaries. Third, and relatedly, the United States, as the global hegemon, often has the most to lose from proliferation challenges to the status quo. As leader of the international world order, threats posed by proliferators to adapt or alter "the nuclear club" hold significant costs for the U.S., both in terms of security and with regard to its interests globally.[62]

Though the focus on the United State is warranted, the inclusion of other actors in a broader counterproliferation analysis is beneficial. First, in an interconnected global arena—and one where great power competition may be again on the rise—identifying successful partnerships and problematic relationships will be necessary for maintaining the nonproliferation order that has existed since 1968. In particular, should a possible end to the Joint Comprehensive Plan of Action catalyze an Iranian pursuit of nuclear weapons and potentially instigate a new wave of reactionary proliferation, understanding which global levers are available to counter such a trend will be vitally important for crafting U.S. policy moving forward. States are increasingly inter-connected, meaning that U.S. policies cannot be implemented without considering what other states are likely to do. Drafting a plan for economic sanctions on North Korea, for example, would be incomplete without considering what actions China and Russia are likely to take. Also, assessing whether external actors may serve as "spoilers" to undermine nuclear reversal can help improve the manner in which the United States pursues its negotiating strategy. Building a more inclusive analysis that allows for the assessment of global counterproliferation tools will strengthen both academic and policy research, allow for more accurate forecasting and predictions, and yield more productive policy prescriptions.

Second, the ability to design more effective counterproliferation policy can yield changes in line with U.S. national security interests and potentially enhance cooperation among major powers in curbing the spread of both nuclear weapons and technology. Given the current landscape with concerns over both the Iranian and North Korean nuclear programs, these challenges remain and may be joined by additional ones moving forward. Having a deeper understanding of what policies are likely to work, and in conjunction with whom, should help the United States anticipate and counter potential nuclear challenges as they emerge. Especially in an era of fiscal concern, such insights will be critical for instituting smarter and more effective counterproliferation policy as one key piece of a broader American grand strategy. For example, the opportunity to rely on other major powers could help alleviate the burden the United States may face in expending resources, both monetary and political, in incentivizing nuclear reversal. Future research (and data collection efforts) can better answer important questions about the role and importance of other major powers in the counterproliferation equation.

Third, it is similarly important to recognize the role of other actors in the international system, such as the regional rivals or adversaries of proliferators. For example, states that have enduring rivalries with nuclear-armed states might wish to gain nuclear weapons to protect themselves against nuclear blackmail.[63] It is plausible that for similar reasons, states that face security threats, particularly from a rival or adversary, will seek to alter their nuclear decision-making for the potential benefits that a nuclear deterrent may similarly confer. For these states, choosing to reverse their nuclear programs might enable them to similarly deter their opponents from acquiring nuclear weapons.

One may consider Brazil's and Argentina's nuclear trajectories to trace this logic. Brazil's nuclear activity dates back to the 1950s when Brazilian leaders began to receive assistance from the United States. The program became a priority for President Figueiredo during the 1970s, as a result of rivalry with neighboring Argentina (also pursuing a nuclear program). According to scholars, "some analysts believe that Brazil's nuclear program was intended to deter a potential Argentine nuclear weapons program, the technology itself was seen as a 'species of deterrence', the mere capacity to match a potential Argentine bomb was presumed sufficient to deter its construction."[64] An increasingly crowded regional and global nuclear landscape, especially the introduction of a nascent nuclear rival, may have partially motivated Brazil's nuclear pursuit over time. This logic includes the presence of rivals who may have already begun their nuclear weapons activity. It is then plausible that changes in the status of these rivals, including their efforts to denuclearize, may similarly influence whether states alter their nuclear decision-making. However, while this reasoning may be theoretically possible, the influence of regional adversaries is still likely to be less salient than that of major world powers, especially the United States. The alleviation of the motivations behind the initiation of nuclear programs do not necessarily lead to decisions to reverse nuclear programs. And importantly, though we see the alleviation of some enduring rivalries (such as Iran and Iraq), we can test to see whether a proliferator's pursuit of nuclear weapons subsides as a result of such a change in regional dynamics.

Concluding Remarks

External incentives offered by the United States can change nuclear outcomes. To explain patterns of nuclear reversal over time, one must look to the policy tools offered by the United States as a means of changing the calculus behind costly proliferation decisions. Implications from my theory reveal that nuclear reversal can be incentivized by the strategic interplay of rewards and sanctions, and *both* are required to encourage counterproliferation. In isolation, sanctions or rewards may actually have the opposite impact, potentially further encouraging proliferation attempts. Importantly, positive inducements are critical in providing political cover to leaders who are forgoing continued nuclear development in exchange for negotiated settlements with the United States, which, without rewards, could result in challenges to the political survival of leaders in proliferating states.

This research yields important contributions and implications for the scholarship of international relations. While the existing literature has found mixed results with regard to the efficacy of rewards and sanctions in modifying state behavior, this research takes a step forward in addressing this debate and identifies a condition in which the employment of these types of inducements can influence nuclear decision-making. My analysis demonstrates that these tools are most effective when offered in the shadow of a game-ending move, an ultimate strategic action that can compel states to accept a negotiated settlement in lieu of severe punishment. Yet, it is similarly important to note that this condition (when an actor is willing to resort to an act of war) may be constrained to issue areas where the United States or other actors are resolved to actually and credibly employ force to compel changes in behavior. Thus, while a useful strategy for the United States in countering nuclear proliferation, it may have varied effects in other policy areas within international relations. It may be reasonable to expect American leaders to threaten military force to stop the spread of nuclear weapons (i.e., Iran) or to deter domestic policies of ethnic cleansing or genocide (i.e., Yugoslavia), but it is unlikely to be a viable strategy for other issue areas in security or trade crises. And in some contexts, this approach may backfire and further motivate negative behavior. Better understanding of how rewards and punishments can be used to influence decision-making requires further analysis of the strategic interactions underlying international phenomena.

Implications for Counterproliferation Policy

My theory of nuclear reversal provides important implications for U.S. policymakers. First, it is important to note the scope of this research. While this theory reveals the important role that inducements can play in changing domestic political decision-making among proliferating states, it does not make inferences about how the United States (or the international community, more broadly) *chooses* among the available policy levers. Future research will examine the domestic political drivers of how the U.S. chooses to employ particular policy instruments to counter the spread of proliferation. The current analysis only helps to illuminate the complexities of that process and the variety of different factors, for example, the resolve of the U.S. to employ force and the proliferator's relationship to the U.S. among others, in tailoring the counterproliferation process to the state in question.

The Use of Military Force

This research reveals an important additional purpose for the threat or use of military force in nuclear reversal. Thus far, military force has been used to permanently stop nuclear weapons program, as in Iraq and Syria, by destroying suspected nuclear facilities and infrastructure. The framework proposed previously suggests that the *threat* of military force may similarly be an effective bargaining tool that can shape future negotiations with proliferators. The efficacy of rewards and sanctions, especially with more persistent proliferators, is conditional on the ability of the United States or other states in the international community to credibly signal that they will follow through on the use of force if a proliferator does not accept the deal being offered. In this way, the United States' position on the use of force with regard to a particular proliferator can have a dramatic impact on the strategic interaction between the two actors. If the use of force is a politically viable tool and policymakers can credibly signal that it is, it may shape how a proliferator responds to the offer and may stop even the most committed of proliferators.

This, no doubt, is an important implication that demands more in-depth analysis among policymakers and nuclear decision-makers. Threats (or actual use) of military force are incredibly costly. In addition to creating further destabilization in already insecure regional environments, the use of military force also comes with significant domestic political costs for U.S. leaders if they fail to act if a red line is crossed. And, as other scholarship and policy analysis suggest, the use of preventive war to stop nuclear weapons proliferation may exacerbate security concerns, potentially increase the likelihood of retaliation, or generally foster instability and uncertainty between the proliferator and the United States.[65]

How reasonable is it, then, for the United States to threaten a military strike, and thus increase the likelihood of conflict with a potential or de facto nuclear weapons state, to shift the bargaining dynamic between the two states? While research suggests that this strategy is likely to be effective, it is important to assess the long-term, potentially unforeseen, consequences of such a strategy, especially if it becomes necessary to follow through on the threat of military force, that is, by carrying out a preemptive military attack. This finding also runs counter to much of the existing academic scholarship that examines other issue areas in international relations. The U.S. is not likely to consider using military force against states engaging in human rights violations, state repression, or other domestic policy issues that rise to international attention. And while less desirable from an interstate relations perspective, very few other issues rise to the status of nonproliferation where the U.S. may be willing to bear any cost, including war, to change the outcome. Further, this aspect of U.S. foreign policy wanes and waxes in strength and signal in response to the current climate of international relations. Recent conversations with policymakers and advisors in the United States, Iran, and elsewhere suggest that Obama Administration's refusal to militarily intervene despite Bashar Al-Assad's crossing of a "redline"— the use of chemical weapons against his citizens—weakened U.S. credibility in the eyes of allies and non-allies across the world.[66] Analysts engaged in policy decisions about weapons of mass destruction (WMD) within the government and policy communities in the United States, saw a decline in credibility of the United States' willingness and ability to use military force, with potentially far-reaching and lasting repercussions. If the U.S. was unwilling to use military force in the aftermath of a chemical weapons attack on civilians, how credible and strong was the threat to employ military force against a suspected nuclear facility?

Lastly, my research suggests an unfortunate, but relatively unsurprising, implication about global nuclear weapons proliferation: not all instances of proliferation can be prevented. First, despite the U.S. commitment to counterproliferation, there may be instances where the offers of inducements do not sufficiently motivate the proliferator to abandon its nuclear weapons program. The discussion of the Indian nuclear program in Chapter 5 provides a useful case analysis. India ultimately built nuclear weapons, in part because the Indians were not satisfied with the inducements offered by the United States. Thus, it could be that some counterproliferation failure (that results in the acquisition of nuclear weapons) may be the result of missteps in the U.S. foreign policy due in part to domestic political processes within the U.S. Though outside the scope of this project, domestic political fractures, fundamental misunderstandings of an adversary, and adherence to ideology (regardless of evidence) can all contribute to ineffective counterproliferation policy, or as we see today, the decision to abandon effective counterproliferation strategies and negotiations. There is no doubt that U.S. policy has generally improved over time, and this analysis contributes to our understanding of what works and what does not. This historical insight should make policy-making easier and more efficient in the future. But counterproliferation policy (like all policy arenas) is subject to bias, ignorance, inertia—or politics.

This analysis does not imply that rewards will work every time with every proliferator, or that sanctions will always work effectively to screen among proliferators. Either tool may potentially fail in a particular proliferation instance. Despite the best efforts of the international community, especially key member states like the United Nations P-5, it is still possible that a truly committed state will successfully acquire a nuclear weapons deterrent outside the confines of the nonproliferation regime and international law. Though nuclear reversal is almost three times as likely as successful proliferation even in recent times, some nuclear weapons states, such as North Korea, may not be receptive to any inducements employed by the international community. Thus, while it is possible that the nuclear club may continue to expand, it is imperative that we better understand the domestic constraints within the proliferating states, and the complex dynamics between proliferators and the international community when negotiating nuclear reversal.

Overview

Introducing the Evidence

Introduction

This overview accomplishes three tasks. First, I lay out my empirical research design and expand on the utility of mixed-method research design. This step is especially important given the relatively small universe of nuclear reversal cases. Second, I introduce broad characteristics underlying nuclear weapons activity from the historical record. Third, I explain the selection criteria, value, and sources of case studies and how they provide support for my theoretical framework. These cases illustrate how political relationships with the United States influence nuclear decision-making and the likelihood of counterproliferation success and failure, in the shadow of military force.

Empirical Research Design

My research design leverages a mixed-method approach. First, I begin by assessing general patterns and characteristics of nuclear weapons activity over time. These broad generalizations highlight the necessity of conducting a large-*n* quantitative study of the observable implications of my theory. Chapter 3 conducts a battery of statistical tests to establish important empirical relationships over time. Then, in Chapters 4-7, I conduct five historical case studies of successful (and unsuccessful) nuclear counterproliferation. Within each case, I employ a process-tracing analytical approach to show how causal mechanisms derived in my theoretical framework work in reality. I conduct structured case comparisons, both across and within specific case studies, to identify how changes in the independent variables (i.e., the counterproliferation policies enacted by the United States) impact the dependent variable (the likelihood of nuclear reversal).

Delaying Doomsday, Rupal N. Mehta. Oxford University Press (2020). © Oxford University Press.
DOI: 10.1093/oso/9780190077976.001.0001

Conducting a mixed-methods research design allows me to take advantage of an individual method's strengths, while simultaneously overcoming its weaknesses. In statistical models, all cases receive equal weight, meaning there is no need to decide which cases are more or less important prior to analysis. Further, these types of statistical analyses provide important generalizable patterns over time. These characteristics of quantitative analysis also allow me to avoid selecting the dependent variable or biasing the results by examining unrepresentative cases.[1] Instead, quantitative analysis can highlight useful, deviant, or outlying cases on and beyond the general trend lines, which we can subsequently investigate more closely through case analysis.

Whereas quantitative methods are designed to provide evidence of correlation—not causation—and are intended to identify statistical trends across the full population, case studies fill this gap by illuminating causal mechanism(s) that link the independent and dependent variables. Conversely, while case study analysis cannot precisely specify what an independent variable signifies, statistical analysis can. And, while operationalizing and quantifying complex concepts such as nuclear reversal may be difficult to accomplish exclusively with quantitative methods, qualitative analysis allows scholars to investigate complex mechanisms by embracing more nuanced measurements and indicators.

I also conduct process tracing on a representative sample of cases to delve into the results of quantitative analysis and to identify specific causal mechanisms responsible for the correlations we find. In-depth case studies are useful for conducting a "detailed examination of a historical episode to develop or test historical explanations that may be generalizable to other events."[2] Process tracing provides significant advantages for hypothesis testing and theory development. First, case studies allow scholars to qualitatively identify and measure the observable indicators that best represent their concepts (in this case, nuclear reversal). Second, they allow close examination of causal mechanisms by tracing the process linking purported causes to outcomes. And, third, this approach allows us to address potential causal complexity, in which outcomes are a result of numerous interacting causes.[3]

Thus, following the lead of other recent scholarship on nuclear subjects,[4] I leverage this multi-method approach to identify the conditions under which states are willing to reverse their weapons programs. While no theory or analysis can explain every case, this approach provides an avenue by which to better identify and provide support for important trends over time. And together, the evidence offered in Chapters 3-7 leads to an important conclusion: positive and negative inducements *together* can motivate states to alter their nuclear decision-making and abandon nascent (or completed) nuclear weapons programs.

The Phenomenon of Nuclear Reversal:
Exploring the Universe of Cases

Before delving into the empirical tests of the historical data, it is first important to get a sense of the phenomenon of nuclear reversal over the past seventy years. Despite its prominence and visibility in the arena of international relations, the nuclear weapons universe is relatively small. Out of nearly two hundred countries now in the international system, less than 20% have engaged in any nuclear weapons activity. Given the role of the nonproliferation regime, superpower coercion, strict export controls, and prior successes, most countries do not engage in nuclear weapons activity and thus do not appear in my analyses.[5] Among the states that attempted proliferation, the motivations and stated rationale behind their nuclear pursuits are varied and complex. They range from demand-side factors such as threats to security and the search for national prestige, to the supply-side determinants including external assistance and domestic capacity. Indeed, states may be driven by a multitude of important reasons to proliferate, but may ultimately choose to reverse course, only under ideal circumstances.[6]

To get a sense of this phenomenon over time—essentially, trends of when states start and stop their nuclear programs—I begin with a brief description of nuclear weapons activity. Table I.1 presents the start and stop years of global nuclear weapons activity (both proliferation and reversal) from 1945 to 2015.[7] Recall that Figure 1.1 presented a summary of nuclear activity over time in graphical form.

Nuclear reversal occurs in 23 out of 32 states, or about 72% of all instances of nuclear weapons activity. The table reveals a few interesting implications regarding nuclear weapons activity over time. First, a significant portion of proliferation activity occurred in the late 1940s and early 1950s, in the early days of the Cold War, and most likely, as a result of civilian nuclear assistance from the United States and other Western nuclear states through President Eisenhower's Atoms for Peace Initiative.[8] Additionally, a second "wave" of proliferation occurred soon after the NPT went into full force in 1970. Table I.1 also shows that many proliferators opted to dismantle their nuclear weapons programs or stop their nuclear pursuit near the end of the Cold War, and that reversal may be part of a broader international political trend of that era. Lastly, the data reveal the diversity in nuclear experience. While some states maintain nuclear weapons programs for only a few years, many others pursue lengthy and often unsuccessful nuclear programs before choosing to abandon their efforts.

How do nuclear reversers compare to current proliferators? First, and perhaps unsurprisingly, nuclear proliferators have a relatively high industrial capacity ex ante. By examining a measure of latent industrial capacity that incorporates

Table I.1 **Nuclear Activity (1945-Present)**

Country	Start	Stop	Duration (years)
Algeria	1983	1991	8
Argentina	1968	1990	22
Australia	1956	1973	17
Brazil	1955	1990	35
Canada	1944	1969	25
China	*1955*	-	
Egypt	1955	1980	25
France	*1946*	-	
W. Germany	1957	1958	1
India	*1948*	-	
Indonesia	1965	1967	2
Iran	1974	2015	41
Iraq	1976	1995	19
Israel	*1949*	-	
Italy	1955	1958	3
Japan	1945	1970	25
Libya	1970	2003	33
North Korea	*1965*	-	
Norway	1949	1962	13
Pakistan	*1972*	-	
Romania	1985	1993	8
USSR/Russia	*1945*	-	
South Africa	1969	1993	24
South Korea	1959	1978	19
Spain	1959	1975	16
Sweden	1954	1969	15
Switzerland	1946	1969	23
Syria	1976	2007	31
Taiwan	1967	1988	21
United Kingdom	*1945*	-	
United States	*1945*	-	
Yugoslavia	1954	1988	34

technical and production capabilities, we can see that this capacity may be a barrier to entry: if states do not have a high industrial capacity, they may be precluded from even starting down the nuclear path. Moreover, proliferators often require vast economic resources to fund their often-lengthy nuclear weapons programs. Many of these states are OECD (Organisation for Economic Co-operation and Development) countries with high GDP per capita and economic growth rates.

Perhaps contrary to expectations, nuclear reversers generally lack significant conventional military capabilities, an attribute that might predict a propensity for proliferation. If potential proliferators are concerned with external security threats that their limited conventional military resources are unable to counter, they may turn instead to the acquisition of nuclear weapons as a substitutive deterrent against foreign aggressors. However, some of the more recent literature on vertical nuclear proliferation and force structure suggests that strong conventional capabilities are a critical component of a diversified and effective nuclear deterrent, indicating that nuclear deterrent and conventional military capabilities may be more complementary than substitutive.[9]

Selection Criterion and Sources of Qualitative Case Studies

In Chapters 4-7, I analyze a series of cases to examine important patterns of nuclear reversal. Each case study addresses the two main questions posed in this book. First, given the value of nuclear weapons to the proliferator in question, what were the conditions under which they were willing to alter their nuclear trajectories? Second, which policy tools were employed by the United States to incentivize a change in nuclear decision-making? In addressing these issues, I aim to illustrate my theory of nuclear reversal, and to demonstrate the limitations of other theories that espouse alternative explanations.

The evidence used in these cases comes from a detailed review of the historical record. I consulted a variety of primary sources including declassified documents, statements, memoirs, and official reports to examine the decision-making of the important actors. I also relied on secondary literature including seminal and authoritative analyses from existing scholarship. Lastly, to supplement this evidence, I collected original data by conducting several interviews with former and current policymakers in the United States, France, Argentina, Brazil, Pakistan, and Iran.[10] This novel data has helped provide important original context to complex dynamics of nuclear reversal.

Beyond examining the core hypotheses regarding how the United States can offer inducements to motivate nuclear reversal, these case studies examine two other scope conditions that underlie a critical part of my theoretical framework: (1) the role of new leaders, and (2) the relationships between proliferators and the United States. Recall from Chapter 2 that I specify this strategic interaction on two core dimensions: (1) the United States' policy convergence (or divergence) with the proliferator; (2) the United States' resolve or willingness to issue a credible threat of military force to stop a nuclear weapons program.

From this two-dimensional spectrum of Resolve and Policy Distance (depicted in Table 2.1), I identify the following cases for further analysis: Chapter 4 covers two instances of successful and unsuccessful counterproliferation- Libya (1969–2003) and China (1964–present), Chapters 5 and 6 present detailed case studies of India (1974–present) and Iran (1974–2015), respectively, and Chapter 7 concludes with a discussion of North Korea's nuclear endeavor (1959–present). These cases provide two avenues for case comparison. First, India's proliferation trajectory lends itself to an important intra-case comparison design wherein the United States' counterproliferation strategy was initially successful in motivating a freeze and temporary abandonment of India's nuclear program, but ultimately could not stop India from acquiring nuclear weapons. Relatedly, by comparing the Indian and Iranian nuclear programs, we can better understand the conditions under which the U.S. was finally successful in concluding the Joint Comprehensive Plan of Action with Iran in 2015. This research design approach allows me to evaluate decision-making in two closely matched cases: (1) India prior to and after the 1974 Peaceful Nuclear Explosion; (2) the Indian and Iranian decision-making in the lead-up to successful nuclear proliferation and nuclear reversal, respectively.

These cases exhibit variations on a number of salient features described earlier. First, they vary on how the United States has leveraged inducements over time, with the Chinese and Indian cases offering variation in whether the use of inducements actually resulted in changes in nuclear decision-making. Second, they include states that successfully acquired nuclear weapons both before and after the entry-into-force of the Nuclear Nonproliferation Treaty and the Nuclear Suppliers Group, as well as states that reversed their nuclear programs both before and after the end of the Cold War, allowing me to control for the effects of different historical eras. And, finally, there are two other important sources of variation. First, I examine the cases of China, Libya, and Iran (representing states with divergent preferences to that of the U.S.) and India (representing an on-and-off informal ally of the United States though still formally a member of the Non-Aligned Movement). Second, I assess the United States' willingness to employ military force by looking at its approach to the Iranian, Libyan, and North Korean nuclear programs over time.

These case studies no doubt provide important historical context and illustrations of theoretical mechanisms. However, like all methods of empirical inquiry, they too may suffer from limitations. First, this study is focused on understanding changes in decision-making, especially with regard to how leaders, often new leaders, may respond differently to external pressure. As described in the existing scholarship, in most instances of bargaining dynamics, leaders have critical incentives to misrepresent or fail to disclose important information from the historical record. Second, and relatedly, despite my efforts to gather as much evidence as possible to provide an exhaustive analysis of counterproliferation decisions, it is likely that critical information may be missing or withheld. This gap is especially salient when we consider the role of other actors, including other major powers in either aiding or inhibiting nuclear reversal negotiations. Understanding the conditions under which counterproliferation is successful, or not, is an important part of broader U.S. foreign policy.

Proliferation challenges are likely to persist in the future with states developing or acquiring nuclear technology (horizontal proliferation) or advancing existing nuclear capabilities to pursue nuclear weapons (vertical proliferation). By understanding how states in the international system can interact to facilitate cooperation, or spoil attempts to negotiate nuclear reversal, we can better understand how the United States should operate in these interventions to successfully and efficiently counter the spread of nuclear technology. Given budgetary constraints and an evolving foreign policy environment that may be more limited in its attention to the nonproliferation regime, it is important to assess whether, and in what ways, other states may facilitate or hinder these global efforts. Unfortunately, evidence from the USSR/Russia and China on their counterproliferation policies has been scarce. Further, gathering data on the nuclear programs of newer proliferators, such as India, Pakistan, Israel, and North Korea has traditionally been difficult. While scholars, analysts, and observers are working to uncover more evidence from new sources,[11] there is still work to be done to provide a more complete analysis.

Evidence from the Historical Record

Introduction

Proliferators end their nuclear weapons pursuit as a result of inducements provided by key members of the international community, most notably the United States. In particular, I find all types of states respond by reversing their nuclear weapons program when offered both positive and negative inducements. Second, I find limited support for alternative explanations, including the logic that states will abandon their nuclear weapons program when targeted with negative inducements, such as economic sanctions or threats of military force, alone. These theoretical findings hold regardless of how committed a state may be to its nuclear pursuit and its relationship to the United States or other key members of the international community. I test these hypotheses using a battery of statistical analyses on data on nuclear weapons activity described in Appendix 3.1 at the end of this chapter. The findings lend support to my theory of nuclear reversal. First, the main explanatory variable, *Inducements*, is positive and statistically significantly associated with nuclear reversal across a variety of model specifications. Further, when disaggregating this combinative measure to see what types of policy tools appear to have been the most effective, and as a test of some of the alternative explanations, I find that positive inducements (among all policy levers available) are primarily responsible for driving nuclear reversal. On the other hand, negative measures, used in isolation, have a limited impact or no impact on nuclear reversal for most types of proliferators. Yet, to ensure that the proliferators do not take advantage of counterproliferators by driving up the price of deals through rewards-only based agreements *and* to be most effective for the broadest set of states, a combination of these inducements must be used.

A couple of notes are worth stating here. First, although my theory explains the powerful role that positive and negative inducements play in nuclear reversal, it does not predict which counterproliferation tools will be employed by the United States or other members of the international community. The

Delaying Doomsday, Rupal N. Mehta. Oxford University Press (2020). © Oxford University Press.
DOI: 10.1093/oso/9780190077976.001.0001

findings from my theory relay the overall efficacy of these inducements but cannot envisage how the U.S. will choose from among a menu of policy levers. For example, different policy levers may be useful in motivating states to stop their pursuit of nuclear weapons. What works for Canada or Indonesia may not be as effective with Australia or Taiwan, and a tailored approach is critical for successful counterproliferation. In the aftermath of the 1974 announcement of India's "peaceful" nuclear detonation, the United States approached New Delhi with an offer to provide foreign aid, including military and economic assistance, to persuade India to slow its progress in acquiring a nuclear deterrent. As I will discuss in a detailed case study of the Indian nuclear pursuit in Chapter 5, recently declassified documents suggest that the Indians were more interested in strengthening the U.S.-India alliance (perhaps even including a defense pact or security guarantee) and in shoring up Washington's support in response to China's recent nuclearization, and an expected provocative reaction to their own nuclear test from the Pakistanis. While the motivation for choosing this less than successful approach by the United States is important because it allows us to further investigate cases of failed counterproliferation, it falls outside the scope of the theoretical framework discussed in this book.

Second, and more importantly, proliferators' decisions to initiate and end nuclear weapons programs, and the best policy instruments chosen by the United States to counter them are not random or haphazard. Given observational limitations on causal inference in the historical record, it is necessary to identify specific conditions under which we may expect to see the employment of certain policy instruments that are more or less effective, on average. Some barriers to causal inference include alliance dynamics, the perceived credibility of the tool, the latent resolve of the target given its security environment, and its relationship to or dependence on the United States. My empirical analysis attempts to address these and other confounding factors that may challenge inference, while still assessing average effects. In doing so, and to the extent possible given observational data, I find substantial support for my theory that the use of external incentives can indeed motivate even states truly invested in acquiring a nuclear deterrent. Competing explanations do not fare as well. These findings suggest that even more than domestic-level factors, such as bureaucratic inertia or the search for prestige, external inducements in various forms, and used in combination, better explain nuclear reversal. Thus, my analyses can help adjudicate between available policy options to identify the most effective and efficient strategies for inducing nuclear reversal, and isolate important patterns that may assist policymakers in their ongoing counterproliferation efforts.

Dataset and Variables

To test the theory of nuclear reversal outlined in Chapter 2, I construct a cross-national, time-series analysis of the factors that incentivize states to give up their nuclear weapons programs. This quantitative analysis focuses only on states that have begun nuclear weapons pursuit or have engaged in nuclear weapons activity (ranging from exploration to weapons acquisition) from the end of World War II to 2007. Much of the analysis occurs across different types of rewards and punishments that can lead to nuclear reversal, but some of the comparison occurs among proliferator types. Proliferators diverge along two key dimensions: (1) in a minority of cases, states proliferate and do not stop their nuclear programs despite inducements offered by the international community; and (2) among those that do stop, they do so when offered both positive and negative inducements (rather than just one type in isolation). The analysis thus focuses on comparing the likelihood that rewards and punishments are associated with persuading states to reverse their nuclear courses and revert to a non-nuclear status.

The dichotomous dependent variable is whether a state ends its nuclear weapons pursuit in a given year. In accord with the existing literature on nuclear reversal, the dependent variable includes: (1) stopped development of a nuclear program; (2) return of a complete weaponized arsenal or component capabilities which are part of the nuclear fuel cycle; and (3) dismantlement of complete weaponized arsenal. If any of these are observed in the years of analysis (1945–2007), the state in question has reversed its nuclear program in that state-year (value of "1"). If none of these is observed in a given state-year, the dependent variable takes on a "0" value. To code the start and stop years of the program, I use coding rules from three different datasets: Bleek (2017), Way (2012), and Mueller and Schmidt (2008).

To establish the broadest possible list of states that initially explored nuclear weapons, I combine these datasets into a new dataset of nuclear weapons activity. To incorporate these datasets, I follow three primary decision rules that help establish the widest and most useful population to study that is still theoretically supported. First, I exclude cases where states inherited nuclear weapons (including three former Soviet republics). Second, I include all possible cases where there are at least two independent sources to corroborate evidence of nuclear weapons activity (e.g., Spain and Canada's inclusion in Mueller and Schmidt [2008] despite not being included in the Bleek 2017 dataset). There is one case, Chile, which Mueller and Schmidt include in their dataset, but I am unable to find sufficient supporting evidence to include in my own dataset (Bleek similarly does not include Chile in his dataset). Third,

I use Singh and Way (2004) to confirm the dates provided in Bleek 2017 and Mueller and Schmidt 2008 (though many of the date differences, primarily among the current nuclear weapons states, are reflective of the span of the dataset). Table I.1 in the Overview presented the full universe of cases of nuclear pursuit up to 2007 and start/stop (if applicable) dates for each program. The resulting dataset contains thirty-two instances of nuclear weapons activity between 1945 and 2007.

I code several independent variables, which I describe in more detail in Appendix 3.1. The independent variables generally fall under two primary sets—positive or negative inducements—and can be measured in a variety of ways. Both types of inducements are found in most cases, and at least one in all cases. In most model specifications, I include aggregate measures of positive and negative inducements to assess how this combination may impact the likelihood of nuclear reversal.

The international community generally has an array of policy tools with which they can influence the policies of the proliferator. In employing this range of inducements, I echo the substantial literature in political science and economics where rewards are generally organized into three broad categories—political, military, or economic—and punishment is broadly framed in terms of economic sanctions and the use of military force, including attacks on nuclear-related facilities.[1] Appendix 3.1 includes a full description of these constructs and their operationalizations. However, as discussed previously, given that the theoretical model distinguishes outcomes of interest based on the presence of a credible threat of military force by the United States, economic sanctions are the primary punishment examined in these models.[2]

My study emphasizes the prominent role that the United States plays in inducements offered to a proliferator. As noted earlier, this is not without reason. Since the introduction of nuclear weapons in the international system, and indeed since the sole use of nuclear weapons, by the United States in World War II, it has taken on the lion's share of effort in the nonproliferation regime.[3] In addition to striving to curb nuclear weapons through bilateral and multilateral alliances, the U.S. has attempted to limit the opportunity to develop nuclear weapons through export controls and the management of nuclear technology.[4] Similarly, the United States has often been at the forefront of counterproliferation challenges by taking the lead in bilateral and multilateral talks aimed at negotiating a nuclear reversal. Thus, the majority of this study focuses on inducements employed by the United States, from both the positive and negative sides of the ledger. In a series of robustness checks, I also examine how external incentives may impact nuclear decision-making if they are offered by the broader international community instead.

The Determinants of Nuclear Reversal

Inducements and Reversal Conditional on the Threat of Force: Hypothesis 1

First, I examine Hypothesis 1[5] that addresses the impact of inducements on the likelihood that a state reverses its nuclear program. The measure, *Inducements*, is composed of two aggregate variables, *Positive Inducements* and *Negative Inducements*.[6] *Positive Inducements* is an aggregate measure that includes *U.S. Military Assistance, U.S. Economic Assistance, U.S. Security Guarantee,* and *Nuclear Latency*; the measure *Negative Inducements* includes *U.S. Economic Sanctions*. The base analysis (with no covariates), illustrated in Model 1 of Table 3.1, shows that *Inducements* increase the likelihood of nuclear reversal. In Model 2 in Table 3.1, I use *Positive Inducements* and *Negative Inducements* to provide an initial test of the alternative explanations and their comparative impact on nuclear reversal. These findings suggest that, though positive inducements on their own *can* increase the likelihood of nuclear reversal (even without assessing if the U.S. overspent), negative inducements alone do not yield the same results. This affirms the need for a combinative approach that includes *both* positive and negative inducements.

To further test *Hypothesis 1*, I conduct another set of statistical analyses to evaluate support for my argument when accounting for factors that may otherwise contribute to or influence the decision to reverse nuclear weapons programs. Tables A3.7 and A3.8 in Appendix 3.1 present the results of full multivariate regression analyses. In Table A3.7, I include model specifications where I employ an interaction term for the impact of *Inducements*, given the threat of military force. In Table A3.8, on the other hand, I explore how specific variables

Table 3.1 **Inducements and Nuclear Reversal**

	Model 1	**Model 2**
Inducements	0.524***	
Positive Inducements		0.588***
Negative Inducements		0.028
		(0.123)
Time Trends	Yes	Yes
Constant	0.624***	0.568***
Observations	1,272	1,272

Robust Standard Errors in parentheses; *p<0.1, ** p<0.05, *** p<0.01

and alternative operationalizations fare in the analysis. I compare the entire time period 1945–2007, pre-1970, and post-1970 eras, to see how the introduction of the Nonproliferation Treaty (and its subsequent ratification) may have impacted the probability of nuclear reversal. The results shown in Model 1 of Table A3.7 reveal consistent support for my theory of nuclear reversal, specifically for *Hypothesis 1*. External inducements—positive and negative incentives in tandem—have a statistically significant and positive impact on the likelihood of nuclear reversal, given the threat of military force.

Implications of Probabilistic Conditions

Leadership Change and Pressure Campaigns: Hypothesis 2

There is perhaps no more hotly contested foreign policy issue, in recent memory, than the 2015 multilateral agreement to end Iran's nuclear program (the Joint Comprehensive Plan of Action or the JCPOA). Some observers lauded the negotiating skills of the United States team (specifically President Obama, Secretary of State John Kerry, and Energy Secretary Ernest Moniz) for motivating Iran to return to the negotiation table after decades of failed attempts, and for ensuring the success of a landmark deal despite significant opposition in Congress. Senator Charles Schumer (D-NY) stated, "regardless of how one feels about the agreement, fair-minded Americans should acknowledge the president's strong achievements in combating and containing Iran."[7]

Less studied (at least in the academic scholarship to date), however, is how the election of Iranian President Hassan Rouhani in 2013 contributed to the successful conclusion of the JCPOA only two years later.[8] Observers of domestic Iranian politics suggested that it was the presence of Rouhani, especially following the Ahmadinejad administration, that may have provided a useful context for understanding the nuclear agreement. Farzan Sabet states, for example, "Iranian President Hassan Rouhani swept into office in August 2013 with a slim majority built on a message of 'hope and prudence' and an election campaign that promised to end Iran's international isolation, bring economic prosperity, and expand social and political freedoms."[9] According to these experts, Rouhani and Foreign Minister Mohammed Javad Zarif focused on ending the recession that plagued Iran during previous administrations and remained committed to upholding Iran's end of the nuclear agreement once concluded.[10] It is clear that Rouhani's presidency played an important role in highlighting to domestic constituencies the political benefits inherent in Iran's negotiation of its nuclear program. Indeed, in my own conversations in 2017 with Iranian diplomats involved in the JCPOA negotiations, they expressed the complexities of how domestic political changes in leadership influenced the decision to agree to negotiations with the international community. While the Supreme Leader Ayatollah Ali Khamenei is ultimately in control of Iran's political decision-making, the popular election of Rouhani (over more hardliner candidates supported by the Ayatollah) signified the political importance of embracing the nuclear negotiations to the Supreme Leadership Authority. The re-election of President Rouhani in May 2017 further contributes to the probability that the JCPOA continues in the long term in spite of the United States unilaterally pulling out of the agreement in June 2018.

A survey of the historical record reveals that Iran's nuclear reversal following the arrival of Rouhani is not an isolated occurrence. While Brazil's Collor de Mello, Indonesia's Suharto, and Australia's Whitlam, have little else in common, they all opted to abandon their countries' nuclear efforts in the initial months of their rule. As discussed in Chapter 2, many new leaders are able to overcome biases held by their predecessors. These new leaders concluded that the benefits of nuclear weapons did not justify the resources required to obtain and sustain them. With fresh eyes, these leaders are psychologically uncommitted to the nuclear programs and are much more open to reevaluating them. This is especially true given the high costs of nuclear weapons acquisition; despite having committed sizable expenditures, leaders still have limited information about the ultimate success and costs to acquire a functioning capability. The decision to pursue nuclear weapons is wrought with uncertainty: while many leaders truly desire and strive to acquire nuclear weapons, not all succeed because of technological, material, or personnel challenges. New leaders then face a choice. They can either continue investing or cut their losses and abandon the program, with some amount of compensatory, politically face-saving benefits from the United States or the broader international community. These nuclear decisions meet all the criteria for what political psychologists call "escalation situations," instances where losses have been suffered and where there is an opportunity to withdraw.[11] It is in these situations that the U.S. can begin a screening process to determine the right set of inducements to persuade new leaders to abandon their nuclear efforts.

Nuclear reversal following leadership change is a more common occurrence than many people believe. An examination of the data on regime change shows that among the twenty-three states that have started and stopped nuclear weapons activity since 1945, seventeen (including Australia, Italy, and Taiwan) experienced a leadership change within twelve months of the conclusion of negotiations that permanently stopped their nuclear weapons program. These data reveal changes in the "actual effective ruler" for each state and whether the new leader works to reach an agreement to end the nuclear program after being elected. To operationalize *Leader Change*, I use the Archigos dataset on leaders during the period 1945–2004 to identify states that experience a change in head of state (i.e., prime minister, president, or military leader) through either regular or irregular means in the post–World War II era.[12] According to the Archigos data, leader turnover is a somewhat rare event. There are only 412 instances of leader turnover (or 19% of state years), among the 32 states that have engaged in nuclear weapons activity during that period. Not surprisingly, states that experience the highest rates of leader turnover are parliamentary systems; for example, Switzerland changes leadership nearly every year. The states with the least frequent changes in power are authoritarian or military-led dictatorships (e.g., North Korea, Syria, and Libya). To examine the relationship between a new leader's willingness to forgo sunk costs and end a nuclear weapons program, I employ a variable, *Sunk Costs*, that measures the duration of the program. Sunk costs capture financial and political costs already expended in nuclear pursuit. More so than their predecessors who were heavily invested in lengthy and unsuccessful nuclear weapons programs, new leaders may be willing to pull the plug and stop pursuit of nuclear weapons.

Results

The first analysis examines a core relationship between leadership change and international inducements to see whether these factors contribute to the decision to reverse nuclear weapons programs. As before, to evaluate my theoretical expectations, I test the combined measure, *Inducements*, and two aggregate variables—*Positive Inducements* and *Negative Inducements*—to assess their impact on nuclear reversal. Mirroring the model specifications presented earlier, these tests include the background condition of the threat/use of military force. The results provide support for my argument, namely that new leaders have an opportunity to affect foreign policy decisions, including long-standing policies on the acquisition of nuclear weapons, when offered the appropriate incentives to do so. Table A3.12 presents the full set of results from this test, including covariates to control for confounding factors.

In this analysis, the combined variable *Inducements* is positively associated with nuclear reversal. However, when considering the alternative explanations (i.e., whether to use negative or positive inducements in isolation), a different picture emerges. While *Negative Inducements* has no discernible association with the dependent variable, *Positive Inducements* is positively, and statistically significantly, correlated with reversal. These results suggest that new leaders are resistant to policy tools from the negative side of the ledger. On the other hand, new leaders who are approached with positive tools may be persuaded but could inadvertently drive up the cost of the negotiation to extract more concessions from the United States. These findings also support the core implication from the previous empirical tests: rewards and sanctions must be used in combination to incentivize nuclear reversal. This strategy is particularly successful during periods of leadership transition when rewards are especially effective in offering face-saving incentives for new leaders.

Sunk Costs and Nuclear Reversal

To further assess the validity of this probabilistic condition—that new leaders may reverse long-standing, often unsuccessful, nuclear pursuits as they are able to avoid the biases of their predecessor—I examine the impact of sunk costs on these dynamics. The findings again reveal support for the importance of leadership change in the context of nuclear weapons decision-making. Even when handed long-standing programs that may include a predecessor's heavy investment in nuclear weapons infrastructure, new leaders may still be willing to forego continuing these programs in an effort to project an evolving preference and reap the potential benefits associated with nuclear abandonment. To get at this dynamic, I assess the impact of inducements, given the sunk costs of longer-term nuclear programs, when these proliferators experience leadership change. Table A3.15 presents full findings of these tests. As with prior tests, these model specifications include a credible threat of military force. The positive and significant correlation between rewards and reversal during periods of leadership change suggests that even though leaders may be handed long-running programs (with varying degrees of success), they are able to overcome psychological and political biases and reverse their nuclear efforts.

A Not-So New Leader

How, if at all, do these dynamics change over the course of the first few years of a new leader's tenure? I examine the relationships between *Inducements* and nuclear reversal upon a new leader's entry in office, and after three and five years. Table A3.16 presents the results of such analysis. Recall my initial expectations that these relationships are likely to change over time. Once a new leader has signaled their resolve to either reverse or maintain a nuclear weapons program, the effect of inducements is likely to evolve (if not reverse direction) over time.

A more nuanced picture emerges when we look at the impact of inducements on nuclear reversal throughout the first few years of a new leader's tenure. The measure *Inducements* is positively and initially strongly associated with nuclear reversal. However, the impact of inducements attenuates and may reverse over time. After three years in office, "new" leaders are less likely to accept nuclear deals and reverse their nuclear weapons programs; after five years, leaders are even more disinclined to consider inducements. Thus, after a short honeymoon period, new leaders are less likely to reverse their nuclear program, even if offered an agreement that includes compellent rewards and threatens escalatory punishment (such as military force).

This logic is intuitive, and previously understudied. While a new leader coming to power may have a different preference for nuclear weapons than his predecessor, after a few years and no successful agreement with the U.S., a new leader is more resolved to continue down the same proliferation path and may ultimately acquire nuclear weapons. Furthermore, after failing to secure a nuclear reversal agreement when a new leader assumes office, it becomes more difficult to incentivize nuclear reversal using either positive or negative inducements. These findings have critical implications for the U.S policymakers when attempting to negotiate a nuclear reversal. There seems to be a narrow window of opportunity, within a few years of entry into office, when a new leader may be persuaded to give up a nuclear weapons program. After this time period, leaders become increasingly intransigent in their nuclear commitments, even when threatened with military force to stop their nuclear pursuit. These states are then likely to acquire nuclear weapons regardless of the cost of punishment associated with proliferation. What is perhaps more surprising is that this attenuation of the impact of external incentives does not occur in states that do not experience frequent leadership change, that is, in states with long-serving leaders.

Friends and Foes and the Differential Impact of Inducements: Hypotheses 3–6

Existing scholarship and anecdotal examination of the historical record suggest negative policy tools are generally preferred, and often employed, against non-allied foes of the United States. These states are frequently considered to be rogue or pariah states whose preferences and behavior diverge significantly from those of the majority of the international community. It is not surprising that for many scholars, economic sanctions are perceived to be ineffective as they are used, often as a last resort, against truly committed and persistent proliferators, often adversaries of the United States. On the contrary, my research suggests that there may be opportunities to leverage different tools simultaneously against these states, including potentially, the politically distasteful approach of offering rewards to non-allies. Based on the theoretical framework described in Chapter 2, this probabilistic condition yields four testable hypotheses based on the resolve of the United States to use military force (high or low) and its convergence or divergence in policy preferences from the proliferator (friend or foe). I operationalize *U.S. Resolve* as the threat/consideration or actual use of military force to permanently end a weapons program. And I employ a dichotomous variable that distinguishes between proximate or distant *Policy Preferences* with the United States to measure the relationship between the two states.[13] With variation in these two dimensions, I can test the implications of the four hypotheses and related alternative explanations. First, *Hypotheses 3* and *4* examine how the United States' low resolve for forcefully countering proliferation impacts friends and foes, respectively.

Hypothesis 3 expects that with low U.S. resolve for military force, friendly proliferators will reverse their nuclear programs when offered rewards, such as military assistance or a nuclear security umbrella. The results from statistical tests support my expectations. In Table A3.17 Model 1, the coefficient for *Inducements* is positive and statistically significant, while Model 3 presents detailed results for individual inducements. Though I am primarily interested in observing how the combinative measure *Inducements* impacts the likelihood of nuclear reversal, I indicate which individual policy tools appear to be the most effective, given specific geo-political conditions, to assess how alternative explanations fare. This granularity can help us to better understand that specific tools, when used on their own, often have perverse and opposing consequences. Figure 3.1 illustrates the impact of individual rewards and sanctions on friends in a no-threat environment (without covariates or time-trends).

The results shown in Figure 3.1 provide general support for my expectations for a low-resolve environment: friends or states with proximate policy preferences will require larger rewards (i.e., the extension of a *U.S. Security Guarantee*, above and beyond existing alliances) to be persuaded to reverse their nuclear weapons

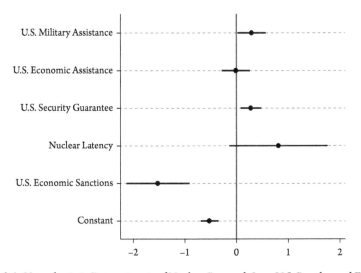

Figure 3.1 Hypothesis 3: Determinants of Nuclear Reversal: Low U.S. Resolve and Friends

programs. In these instances, offers of *U.S. Military Assistance* or *U.S. Economic Assistance*, generally already provided to many of these states within alliance commitments, may not be sufficient for counterproliferation. Indeed, even the opportunity to retain nuclear technology, especially at lower levels of *Nuclear Latency*, may be inadequate for friendly states seeking to compensate for the lost military and reputational benefits of a nuclear weapons deterrent. Figure 3.1 also provides support for my theoretical prediction that friends, especially where there is no possibility of escalation in punishment, may exploit their relationship with the United States to extract a better deal (i.e., seeking a security guarantee over offers of foreign aid or technological assistance). And, as expected, the imposition of *U.S. Economic Sanctions* (if they are subject to punishments at all) decreases the probability of nuclear reversal among friendly states.

On the other hand, *Hypothesis 4* suggests that when the United States is not willing to issue credible threats of force against states with divergent policy preferences (foes), inducements may still increase the likelihood of nuclear reversal but may not always be successful. Models 2 and 4 in Table A3.17 present the results from this test. Negotiations differ when the United States is faced with countering nuclear reversal among foes, where the use of force is not credible or militarily feasible. Model 2 indicates a positive and statistically significant coefficient for *Inducements* under this condition and Model 4 further disaggregates this variable by examining specific types of tools on the likelihood of nuclear reversal among foes with no U.S. resolve to use force.

These findings lend a useful lens with which to assess some of the alternative explanations. In accord with some prior literature, there are fewer possible policy options to alter nuclear decision-making in states with divergent preferences to the United States. Offers of a *U.S. Security Guarantee* have a negative impact on the likelihood of nuclear reversal because they are likely to be deemed less credible. For example, the prospect of the United States extending the nuclear umbrella to cover Iran or Libya as a means of persuading these proliferators to stop their nuclear weapons program would be seen as incredible or worse.

Yet, my theoretical framework still provides avenues by which the United States can incentivize nuclear reversal. For divergent states, offers of foreign aid, including conventional *U.S. Military Assistance* and *U.S. Economic Assistance*, are positive and statistically significantly associated with nuclear reversal. Further, the offer/opportunity to retain *Nuclear Latency* is collinear. The maintenance of this technology may be seen as a useful compromise between the United States and the proliferator who wants to retain access to peaceful nuclear technology. Lastly, as a test of the existing explanations that suggest that foes must be countered with negative inducements, *U.S. Economic Sanctions* alone against these states decrease the likelihood of nuclear reversal. With sanctions alone, foes that are able to observe the United States' low resolve in using military force are unlikely to be deterred from continuing their nuclear programs. In sum, rewards and sanctions, even without the threat of escalatory punishments, are still effective for inducing nuclear reversal, but may not sufficiently incentivize *all* adversarial proliferators to stop their nuclear pursuits. It is in this condition that we are likely to see the highest likelihood of successful proliferation (consider here, for example, China's successful acquisition of nuclear weapons).

On the other side of the spectrum, we consider how these interactions may differ if the United States *is* willing to issue credible threats of military force to persuade states to stop their nuclear pursuits. *Hypotheses 5* and *6* examine how the United States' high resolve for countering proliferation impacts friends and foes, respectively. Table A3.18 presents the full findings of the statistical test. Recall that *Hypothesis 5* predicts that in this environment where the United States can issue a credible threat of force, though unlikely, even smaller offers of rewards and an intimation of sanctions can persuade friends to reverse their nuclear weapons programs. Models 1 and 3 in Table A3.18 examine the impact of inducements under these conditions. In Model 1, a combined *Inducements* variable predicts failure perfectly and Model 3 further disaggregates this variable into individual policy levers.

The results yield interesting implications for my theory, as well as some of the alternative explanations. While seemingly implausible that the United States would consider or use military force against friendly states with whom it shares policy preferences, it can still employ rewards and threat of sanctions to effectively influence nuclear reversal. In this simplified test, rewards such as *U.S. Military Assistance* and the extension of the *U.S. Security Guarantee* are positively and statistically significantly associated with nuclear reversal. Other factors such as *U.S. Economic Assistance* and *Nuclear Latency* operate similarly but are not significant. These results may suggest that even friendly proliferators, when there is the possibility of escalation in punishment, are reticent to push their luck and extort the United States by seeking to extract greater concessions. In the event that such a strategy fails, these states are likely to fear the consequences of the United States' response. Lastly, as anticipated, the imposition of *U.S. Economic Sanctions* against states with a close relationship to the United States, on their own, decreases the likelihood of nuclear reversal. Friendly states are likely to resent the use of these tools especially when they are not coupled with face-saving incentives they can offer to their domestic constituencies.

Lastly, we consider what happens when the U.S. faces states with divergent policy preferences against whom it may consider the use of force. These are

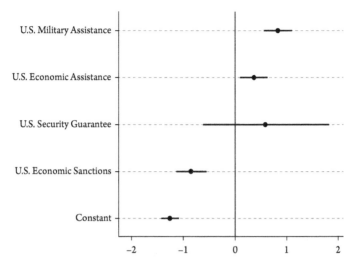

Figure 3.2 Hypothesis 6: Determinants of Nuclear Reversal: High U.S. Resolve and Foes

arguably the cases most debated in policy circles and represent the most concerning challenges to the U.S. counterproliferation policy. Models 2 and 4 in
Table A3.18 test such proliferation cases. Recall, my theory argues in *Hypothesis
6* that if the U.S. has a high resolve for countering the spread of nuclear weapons
against states with divergent policy preferences, rewards and sanctions can
still work to incentivize nuclear reversal. Model 2 from Table A3.18 should
provide comfort for policymakers: even among proliferators in this category,
Inducements has a positive and statistically significant association with nuclear
reversal. A simplified version of this model specification (excluding covariates
and time trends) is presented in Figure 3.2.

The disaggregation of this combined variable provides a useful way to examine
my theoretical priors in comparison to the alternative explanations. While the
conventional wisdom and existing scholarship have often stressed tools from the
negative side of the ledger, often in isolation, the results from my analysis suggest
employing rewards and sanctions in tandem can encourage nuclear reversal. *U.S.
Economic Sanctions* are useful for coercing proliferators previously resistant to
negotiation attempts. However, these tools on their own actually decrease the
likelihood of nuclear reversal, even among states that are facing escalatory punishment of military force. On the other hand, *U.S. Military Assistance* and *U.S.
Economic Assistance*, more so than offers of the *U.S. Security Guarantee* (again,
likely to be seen as non-credible by foes), are positive and statistically significantly associated with nuclear reversal. Lastly, the opportunity to retain *Nuclear
Latency* is collinear with the likelihood of reversal, stressing the importance of a
residual technological capability, among *both* friends and foes. In sum, this set of

tests provides strong support for my theory of nuclear reversal that argues that external incentives contribute to nuclear reversal, among even the most intransigent of proliferators.

Discussion

This empirical evidence yields several important contributions to our understanding of why states end their nuclear pursuits and the conditions under which the use of external inducements is most successful. First, my analysis suggests, in contrast to conventional wisdom and current U.S. foreign policy, that sanctions alone have an undesirable effect of decreasing the likelihood of nuclear reversal. Punishing proliferators without simultaneous rewards may actually work against the broader global interest of curbing nuclear expansion. Further, while our current debates suggest that the only way to effectively deal with a state such as Iran or North Korea is to impose a series of escalating punishments to alter their nuclear decision-making,[14] I find that rewards that are most often reserved for allies can also be successful in some of the difficult proliferation cases. Overall, these findings lend strong support for my theory of nuclear reversal and provide cause for optimism as to the role that the United States can play to more effectively and permanently encourage nuclear reversal.

Second, this research raises questions about the historical policy of treating revisionist, rogue proliferators with policy levers from the negative side of the ledger, especially if the United States is able to project a credible threat of escalatory punishment. Given that one motivation for the pursuit of nuclear weapons can be security concerns (potentially more salient among revisionist proliferators), it seems counterproductive to maintain a policy that endangers the security and stability of proliferating states by continuing to threaten or impose punishments against them to incentivize reversal. It is important to note that the sole use of such coercion had been ineffective against Iran before reaching a watershed agreement in 2015, and to date has not been effective in dealing with North Korea. Though the international community had imposed sanctions and issued threats against both, neither state had been deterred by those policy instruments. In conversations with Iranian and Argentine diplomats involved in the final round of negotiations that led to the signing of the JCPOA in July 2015, it was clear that both Iran and North Korea intensified their efforts in response to negative inducements. Indeed, these diplomats revealed that Iran was more willing to come to the bargaining table when rewards were added to the deal. While the historical record and current foreign policy emphasize the use of coercive measures (especially economic sanctions) against rogue proliferators, my research reveals that it is the promise of face-saving rewards, and the potential for escalatory punishment if they decline, that *ultimately* may be the menu of policy levers that clinches an agreement. A U.S. policy of pressure and engagement must indeed be the future of counterproliferation.

Third, this research reveals an important purpose for the threat or use of military force in nuclear reversal: a credible threat of military force may actually be an effective bargaining tool to help shape future negotiations with proliferators. Until now, military force has been used to stop nuclear weapons programs by destroying suspected nuclear facilities and infrastructure, as in Iraq and Syria. The efficacy of these policy tools, especially with revisionist states, is conditional on the ability of the United States or other states in the international community to credibly signal that they will follow through on the use of force if proliferators do not accept the deal being offered. If the use of force is a politically viable tool and policymakers can signal that the *threat* to use force is a credible one, that threat (in conjunction with rewards and sanctions) may stop even the most committed of proliferators without forcing the United States to resort to military strikes and increase the prospect of conflict.

Finally, the preceding analysis illuminates a consistent pattern whereby seemingly intransigent and hardliner countries may be encouraged to stop their nuclear programs, especially during periods of leadership change. If past behavior is any indicator for the future, successful proliferation is not a foregone conclusion, and bringing a precise mix of inducements to the table, with the emergence of new leaders, may ultimately be an effective approach to curbing the expansion of the nuclear club.

Policy Implications

What are the implications of the historical patterns presented in this chapter for dealing in the future with countries with ambitions for nuclear weapons? I focus on two aspects of this analysis that bear the most on current policy debates: (1) the use of military force in counterproliferation; and (2) how evolving domestic politics, such as leadership change, alter the counterproliferation equation. First, how reasonable is it for the United States to threaten a military strike, and thus increase the likelihood of conflict with a potential nuclear weapons state, to shift the bargaining dynamic between the two states? This question is especially salient when this option is likely to be used against committed proliferators that may also be perceived by the U.S. to be revisionist states. It is important to assess the long-term consequences for international relations and for the U.S. decision-makers that must convey the seriousness and credibility of such a threat, while simultaneously offering a more diplomatic and peaceful solution in its stead. While academic and policy debates over reputation and credibility may persist, adversaries such as North Korea, and allies such as Japan and South Korea are looking to past actions, leader-specific traits, and policy consistency to make inferences about the strength of U.S. credibility.[15] If, for example, the U.S. had opted to continue to abide by the JCPOA, this may have set a useful precedent for North Korea or other potential proliferators attempting to assess the U.S. credibility in negotiations or military action.

Second, this analysis does not presume to say that nuclear reversal always occurs alongside leadership changes in a proliferating state. Opportunities for a successful nuclear reversal are generally present within a couple of years of a new leader coming to power. A few years after entering office, new leaders may be resistant to nuclear reversal and resolved to continue down the nuclear path, even with subsequent offers of military assistance and other rewards. It may be prudent for the international community to capitalize on these narrow windows of opportunity to initiate negotiations and stop proliferation. Yet, while some leaders like Hassan Rouhani use their new position to successfully negotiate a nuclear reversal, others like Kim Jong-Un may use their rise to power for other purposes. These leaders may choose to shore up domestic support (or clamp down on internal dissent), advance or modernize their nuclear arsenal, and further antagonize adversaries in the international community. While effective policy levers against some proliferators are more tractable, it does not rule out the potential need for stronger policy options. Perhaps most importantly, this research does not suggest that external/foreign-imposed regime change or overthrow is an effective inducement for nuclear reversal. The fear or threat of externally instigated overthrow, or a dangerous security environment, is often a primary motivation for seeking nuclear weapons in the first place and may prolong proliferation. Indeed, some attribute Muammar Qaddafi's persistent intent on acquiring nuclear weapons as a possible deterrent to be a direct response to what Saddam Hussein experienced during the 1991 Gulf War and the Iraq War of 2003. The threat of foreign-imposed regime change may actually work to exacerbate or encourage further nuclear proliferation.

Finally, this research yields an unfortunate implication for global nonproliferation regime: not all instances of nuclear proliferation may be prevented. While rewards can work even on the most committed and persistent of states that want to avoid the use of military force against them, there are still likely to be some proliferators that will ultimately be successful in acquiring nuclear weapons. Despite the best efforts of the international community and the United States, it is still possible that some states will successfully acquire a nuclear weapon despite attempts at nuclear negotiation.

Appendix 3.1

Dataset

I employ a time-series, cross-sectional data structure for nuclear activity during the period 1945 to 2007, where the unit of analysis is the state-year. I include all states in the international system that have engaged in nuclear weapons activity within this time period. These states are identified based on previous large-n analyses of nuclear weapons activity, and include approximately 1800 observations, depending on model specification.

Independent Variables

My theory of nuclear reversal predicts that states that are offered external inducements are more likely to reverse their nuclear weapons programs. To capture the spectrum of inducements, I employ both positive and negative inducements (rewards and punishments). And as described earlier, I focus on the role of the United States as the primary offeror of rewards and punishments to proliferators. Thus, the variables employed are mainly those contributed or imposed by the United States (though I also consider alternative operationalizations). Positive inducements include military, economic, or political incentives. The United States may extend a military reward such that a proliferator may be more willing to forego its nuclear weapons program. To measure the effect of a military reward, I include both a binary variable that indicates whether the proliferating state received *U.S. Military Assistance* in a state-year, and a continuous variable, *Percent Change of U.S. Military Assistance*, that measures annual changes in military aid.[16]

Next, to assess how the international community can incentivize nuclear reversal through economic means, I consider measures of economic rewards, such as U.S. economic aid, entrance into economic organizations, and economic openness (the degree to which the proliferator is part of the broader global market). Assistance from an international organization or a specific state may be necessary for domestic stability, and disruption or loss of such foreign aid may prove to be costlier than what the state could expect to receive from an operational nuclear weapons program. To best measure positive economic influence, I include both a binary variable that indicates whether the proliferating state received *U.S. Economic Assistance* in a state-year, and a continuous variable, *Percent Change of U.S. Economic Assistance*, that measures annual changes in economic aid.[17]

Political rewards can take on the form of entrance into, or membership in, trade or regional organizations, or international organizations; the (re)instatement of diplomatic relations; or the establishment of a defense pact or security guarantee.[18] The United States may be able to persuade states to abandon an early nuclear program by offering them protection or other political benefits that they may otherwise not have been able to acquire. To capture this construct of political rewards, I include a representative variable, *U.S. Security Guarantee*, that is coded as "1" if the state has a security guarantee in a given state-year, and "0" otherwise. This variable may include adjustments or additions to existing defense pacts (such as South Korea's Mutual Defense Treaty originally signed in 1953) or the establishment of new defense pacts or treaties that ensure the protection offered by the United States to the proliferator. Given these important distinctions, this variable aims to see how an offer of either an enhanced or a new form of security assurance influences a proliferator's willingness to reverse its nuclear weapons program, above and beyond the parameters of a normal alliance (described later).

Lastly, to capture a form of technological inducement, I include data on *Nuclear Latency*, specifically dual-use enrichment and reprocessing technology.[19] Such capacity can be used for civilian energy purposes or can be manipulated to produce components of the nuclear fuel cycle needed for nuclear weapons. Importantly, the United States may offer this as an inducement, that is, the retention of this capacity as a means of incentivizing a state to abandon their nuclear *weapons* program while continuing to pursue a civilian nuclear program. I also examine the role of *Nuclear Cooperation Agreement* and *Sensitive Nuclear Assistance*, technological assistance offered by the United States, on the likelihood of nuclear reversal.[20]

In contrast, the U.S. may impose some form of negative economic pressure to encourage states to stop or abandon their proliferation attempt. To avoid punishing civilians, economic sanctions are primarily directed at state-level elites or may impose bans on specific goods or technology. In the existing literature and available datasets, sanctions have several forms, including total embargos, blockades, asset freezes, the termination of foreign aid, or the suspension of economic agreements.[21] To capture economic punishment, I include a dichotomous measure of the presence/absence of *U.S. Economic Sanctions*. While there is some data from Hufbauer et al. 2008 and Reardon 2010 that suggest the projected costs of the sanctions, the most useful data from these datasets and the Threats and Implementation of Sanctions (TIES) rely primarily on binary assessments of whether sanctions were imposed in a given state-year.[22] Other cross-national studies on nuclear decision-making, including Miller 2014/2018, similarly rely on this dichotomous data.[23]

This variable, as measured, raises the question about how sanctions and rewards relate to one another. If the United States asserts that it is imposing sanctions because of a state's nuclear program, it is also saying that if the state stops its nuclear program, the U.S. will likely lift the sanctions. The removal of sanctions could be seen as a reward. To some analysts, this appears to be the case in the recent negotiations with Iran, for instance. This is an important point but unfortunately, there is little consensus among scholars or policymakers. Some argue that the lifting of a cost can be seen as a perk while others contend that actors may require actual benefits to compensate for the loss incurred by a sanction.[24] While theoretically more ambiguous, recent empirical analyses suggest that the lifting of sanctions is not necessarily seen in the same light as the extension of assistance or other carrots. Indeed, even in the context of the Iran deal, the Iranians required additional benefits, beyond just the removal of sanctions and the lifting of the oil embargo. While sanctions were seen as unprovoked punishments, their removal was not seen as sufficient. In this analysis, I focus on sanctions imposed by the U.S. because the literature on economic sanctions suggests that collective or multilateral sanctions may be less effective than unilateral sanctions due to free riding or selective reneging. Further, there are far fewer instances of multilateral sanctions to examine.

Lastly, to assess the conditional impact of the threat or use of military force on other available policy levers, I incorporate a measure of militarized action taken against target states. There are relatively few instances of the use of military force against proliferators. Perhaps the most famous example of the use of force to stop nuclear pursuit occurred in 1981 with Israel's attack on the Osirak nuclear facility in Iraq. To get at this conditionality, I include the credible threat or use of *Military Force*.[25] I use data from the Fuhrmann and Kreps analysis on attacks on nuclear facilities. Despite the concerns noted earlier about this measure, it is still the best available option to capture the external threat or use of military force against a nuclear program.

Data on the positive inducements are collected from existing cross-national datasets, including the Correlates of War (COW), Alliance Treaty and Obligations Provisions project (ATOP), Jo and Gartzke nuclear data, Singh and Way nuclear data, and the *Journal of Conflict Resolution* Special Issue 2009 nuclear data. To code some new measures, such as economic and military assistance, I collected data from the U.S. Agency for International Development (USAID) on U.S. foreign assistance from 1945 to 2007. Additionally, I use data from the Hufbauer Economic Sanctions dataset, and data on militarized interstate disputes from the COW dataset, to capture the spectrum of negative inducements. These variables are operationalized as the presence or absence ("1"/ "0") of the inducement in a given state-year unless otherwise specified.

Covariates

To control for other factors that may influence both the dependent variable directly and the independent variable through another, unobserved mechanism, I refer to the existing literature to identify variables that are correlated with nuclear weapons activity in other studies.

Capability

To account for the overall capabilities of states, I use the *Conventional Capability* (Composite Index of National Capability (CINC)) scores for each state.[26] States that have significant conventional capabilities may decide that they do not need the additional advantages of a nuclear deterrent. By including a measure of conventional capacity, I can better assess the role that inducements play above and beyond a state's underlying technical capability to produce nuclear weapons.

Domestic Factors

I also control for a series of domestic-level factors that may play a role in the process of nuclear decision-making. I control for the *Regime Type (Polity)* of the proliferator using data from the Polity IV project, including a polity score that measures regime type on a -10 to +10 scale.[27] I include a logged measure of *GDP per Capita* to control for the effect of economic capacity and relative power.[28] I consider a measure of the proliferator's relationship with the United States, or *Affinity with the United States*, over time using an average of the affinity index that captures the distance in interests from the least (-1) to the most similar (+1).[29] I adapt an existing policy measure scale for the ease of modeling in this analysis: states whose relationship and preferences strongly diverge from those of the international community, especially the United States, compared to states who are more closely aligned with the U.S. If the average is greater than 0.5, it is coded as a "1" in a given-state year, indicating that the state's preferences are similar to those of the U.S. If the average is less than 0.5, it is coded as a "0," indicating that the state's preferences are dissimilar. This variable allows me to get a sense of proliferator type and differentiate between states whose preferences strongly diverge from the United States (foes) and those who more closely align with the U.S (friends).[30]

Similarly, I include a measure of *Alliances* to see how, if at all, nuclear reversal is conditioned by an alliance with the U.S. This covariate is included to ensure that the association between inducements and reversal is not being driven by a proliferator's, or specific leader's, relationship with the U.S. Further, it is aimed at mitigating selection biases, where some inducements are directed at certain proliferators or leaders. To capture potential motivations for the initial pursuit of nuclear weapons that may affect a decision to reverse a nuclear weapons program, I include a dichotomous variable of *Rivalry*, which measures whether the proliferator has a rival.[31] The presence or removal of a rival may wield independent influence on nuclear decision-making. I also include a dichotomous *Cold War* variable to see how these dynamics change between the Cold War and the post–Cold War eras.[32] Relatedly, in some model specifications, I test these dynamics prior to and after *1970*, a key nuclear structural break in the international system with the ratification of the Nonproliferation Treaty.

These covariates help provide a more constrained analysis that allows us to assess how these policy tools impact the likelihood of nuclear reversal, given the stochasticity in international relations.[33] Counterproliferation policies, like most foreign policies, are not chosen at random. A particularly salient concern, it seems, is that sanctions or other negative inducements may only be applied in the "hardest" cases. That might explain, for example, the negative sign on the coefficient for the *U.S. Economic Sanctions* variable in some of the bivariate and multivariate analyses. The inclusion of confounding variables in these analyses help assess how these tools, beyond existing biases in interstate relations (such as alliances, existing rivalries, or even temporal selection effects), impact the likelihood of nuclear reversal.

Method

To test the core hypotheses, my empirical strategy examines the impact of external inducements on the likelihood of nuclear reversal. I primarily employ a probit model. To address concerns about the independence of observations, I add three smoothing functions, *time, time²*, and *time³* since the last event, to the specification. Since observations may be related by state, I cluster standard errors (when applicable) to address any idiosyncrasies among states in the sample. Variables with positive coefficients are associated with an increased likelihood of reversal, while negative coefficients imply the opposite.

The Determinants of Nuclear Reversal

Base Bivariate Analyses:
Testing the Alternative Explanations

As a first step, I examine how alternative explanations fare. From a theoretical standpoint, I argue that the decisions underlying nuclear reversal are likely to be different for several potential reasons. First, proliferators may decide to reverse their nuclear weapons programs not because a security threat from a foreign aggressor has been resolved or the search for prestige has faded, but because the United States may provide a security guarantee or allow for the retention of a civilian nuclear program. Second, the decision to reverse a program may be made by a different actor than the one who started the program. In that case, the motivation for reversal may be orthogonal to the reasons a predecessor started a program with (especially if it was the result of bureaucratic pressures that differentially impacted the predecessor).

To empirically test these implications, I examine the underlying conditions for nuclear pursuit to see how, if at all, they influence the decision to reverse a nuclear weapons program. I expect that some of these original motivations may be present but do not explain each nuclear reversal decision in full. Thus, my theory about the utility of inducements in the shadow of military force makes a clear and compelling addition to these narratives. Tables A3.1–A3.6 present bivariate regressions that can provide a preliminary, though incomplete, look at the determinants of nuclear reversal. I first analyze how "opportunity factors" influence nuclear reversal. Table A3.1 shows the impact of *Nuclear Cooperation Agreements (NCAs)* and *Sensitive Nuclear Assistance* on nuclear reversal. Next, Table A3.2 shows the impact of *Nuclear Latency*, that is, the retention of dual-use technology that can be used for civilian purposes as well as military uses, on nuclear reversal. The United States, and other nuclear suppliers, may allow a proliferator to acquire or retain a latent capacity for foregoing nuclear weapons development. Further, these results

Table A3.1 **Nuclear Cooperation Agreement / Sensitive Nuclear Assistance and Nuclear Reversal; Substantive Effects**

	Coefficient	Standard Error	z	P-Value	95% Confidence Interval (Low)	95% Confidence Interval (High)
NCA on Reversal	0.385	0.309	1.25	0.213	−0.223	0.992
Substantive Effects	0.097	0.086	1.25	0.213	0.193	0.266
Nuclear Assistance on Reversal	Collinear					

Table A3.2 **Nuclear Latency and Nuclear Reversal; Substantive Effects**

	Coefficient	Standard Error	z	P-Value	95% Confidence Interval (Low)	95% Confidence Interval (High)
Reversal	1.24	0.395	3.14	0.002	0.466	2.0136
Substantive Effects	0.464	0.125	3.14	0.002	0.218	0.710

Table A3.3 **Rivalry and Nuclear Reversal; Substantive Effects**

	Coefficient	Standard Error	z	P-Value	95% Confidence Interval (Low)	95% Confidence Interval (High)
Reversal	−0.263	0.063	−4.15	0.000	−0.388	−0.139
Substantive Effects	−0.087	0.205	−4.15	0.000	−0.127	−0.047

Table A3.4 **Nonproliferation Treaty and Nuclear Reversal; Substantive Effects**

	Coefficient	Standard Error	z	P-Value	95% Confidence Interval (Low)	95% Confidence Interval (High)
Reversal	−0.160	0.063	−2.55	0.011	−0.283	−0.037
Substantive Effects	−0.053	0.021	−2.55	0.002	−0.094	−0.013

Table A3.5 **U.S. Economic Sanctions and Nuclear Reversal: Substantive Effects**

	Coefficient	Standard Error	z	P-Value	95% Confidence Interval (Low)	95% Confidence Interval (High)
Reversal	−1.158	0.117	−9.85	0.000	−1.389	−0.928
Substantive Effects	−0.272	0.017	−9.85	0.000	−0.306	−0.236

Table A3.6 **Threat or Use of Military Force and Nuclear Reversal; Substantive Effects**

	Coefficient	Standard Error	z	P-Value	95% Confidence Interval (Low)	95% Confidence Interval (High)
Reversal	−0.863	0.296	−2.92	0.004	−1.442	−0.282
Substantive Effects	−0.207	0.0429	−2.92	0.004	−0.291	−0.122

also include the substantive effects of each variable on the likelihood of nuclear reversal. For example, receiving a nuclear cooperative agreement may increase the likelihood of nuclear reversal by nearly 10%.[34] And, the opportunity to retain a nuclear latent capacity may increase the likelihood of nuclear reversal by 46%, indicating that an opportunity to retain nuclear latency represents a substantial incentive to reverse a nuclear weapons program.

Next, I consider how "willingness factors" fare in impacting nuclear reversal by looking at two additional variables in what follows. In Table A3.3, I include a measure of *Rivalry*. The results show that when states have rivals, there is a negative and significant association with nuclear reversal. If states continue to face rivals, they are willing to continue their nuclear programs to counter these threats. This suggests that security-based explanations may play a role in nuclear reversal decision-making and must be controlled for in broader multivariate tests.

Further, in Table A3.4, I look at the impact of the *Nonproliferation Treaty* (NPT) on nuclear reversal. Here, again, we see a negative and statistically significant association with the likelihood of nuclear reversal. This correlation suggests that in contrast to some of the existing literature, the NPT has not had a compelling effect on nuclear decision-making.

On the other side of the policy ledger, Tables A3.5 and A3.6 examine the relationships between negative inducements—*U.S. Economic Sanctions* and *Military Force*—and nuclear reversal.[35] Both analyses reveal negative and statistically significant associations between these negative inducements and nuclear reversal. Furthermore, when examining their substantive effects on the probability of nuclear reversal, I find that *U.S. Economic Sanctions* reduce the likelihood of nuclear reversal by 27%. Similarly, *Military Force* reduces the likelihood of nuclear reversal by nearly 21%. These preliminary findings run counter to much of the existing scholarship in the academic and policy communities that highlight sanctions as an effective policy tool for motivating changes in nuclear decision-making *once* states have started down the nuclear path.

It is clear that Kenneth Waltz's fateful prediction that states cannot be deterred from acquiring nuclear weapons may have been premature.[36] The United States can indeed influence nuclear decision-making to prevent nuclear proliferation—with an ideal set of inducements. These simple bivariate regression analyses, and related substantive effects, provide an initial set of interesting results that demonstrate that positive inducements have a significant positive impact on states opting to reverse their nuclear course and stop weapons pursuit. Negative inducements, equally importantly, have the opposite impact. Furthermore, these results contribute to the debate in international relations on the efficacy of rewards and sanctions as useful tools for compellence and coercion in counterproliferation.

Such simple analyses are informative for two reasons. First, if one were to simply look at the effects of these tools in isolation, it would not reflect real-world negotiations where the tools are generally used in some combination. By demonstrating that these results are only part of the story (and contrary to conventional wisdom), my analyses suggest that more work needs to be done to understand the utility of these tools. Second, these simple bivariate analyses contradict some of the existing explanations that highlight the efficacy of punishments alone as potential policy tools. Yet, these results clearly do not depict the entire story. The next step is to assess whether these relationships persist with the inclusion of potential confounding variables that may independently impact the likelihood of nuclear reversal.

Inducements and Reversal Conditional on the Threat of Force (Hypothesis 1)

Tables A3.7 and A3.8 examine the core hypothesis of this study: how inducements, given a credible threat of military force, impact nuclear reversal, across time (both prior to and after the ratification of the NPT). The demarcation of NPT in the

Table A3.7 **Inducements and Nuclear Reversal: Interaction Term (Conditional on Threat of Force)**

	Model 1: (1945–2007)	Model 2: (pre-1970)	Model 3: (post-1970)
Inducements*Military Force	3.449***	+	2.564***
	(0.452)		(0.519)
Inducements	0.514***	1.21***	0.422**
	(0.098)	(0.200)	(0.173)
Military Force	−4.385***	Collinear	−4.165***
	(0.741)		(0.629)
Controls	Yes	Yes	Yes
Constant	−0.121	1.109	2.924***
	(0.817)	(1.877)	(1.257)
Observations	1,604	607	957

Robust Standard Errors in parentheses; *p<0.1, ** p<0.05, *** p<0.01; +: *Predicts Failure Perfectly*

Table A3.8 **Determinants of Nuclear Reversal (Conditional on Threat of Force)**

	Model 1 (pre-1970)	Model 2 (post-1970)
U.S. Military Assistance	1.837***	1.530***
	(0.492)	(0.252)
U.S. Economic Assistance	0.309	−0.132
	(0.574)	(0.194)
U.S. Security Guarantee	7.650***	0.302
	(0.781)	(0.250)
Nuclear Latency	Collinear	2.375***
		(1.004)
U.S. Economic Sanctions	0.813	−0.638**
	(0.783)	(0.262)
Controls	Yes	Yes
Time	−2.327***	−0.675***
	(0.650)	(0.069)
Time²	0.194***	0.029***
	(0.067)	(0.004)
Time³	−0.004**	−0.000***
	(0.002)	(0.000)
Constant	8.762***	−0.140
	(3.033)	(0.961)
Observations	618	1,600

Robust Standard Errors in parentheses; *p<0.1, ** p<0.05, *** p<0.01

history of nuclear proliferation and reversal is important. It helps reveal whether inducements have variable effects prior to the creation of the NPT (when nuclear proliferation was not illegal), and after its ratification. In Table A3.7, the findings from this interaction model show the positive and statistically significant association between inducements and reversal. Model 1 presents the results for the full sample for the period 1945–2007. Model 2 presents the results for nuclear reversal cases prior to 1970 and Model 3 covers those after 1970 (the ratification of the NPT). These analyses reveal similar effects prior to and after the implementation of the NPT, though the majority of these observations occurred after 1970. These results again support *Hypothesis 1*: inducements, conditional on military force, are positively associated with nuclear reversal.

Table A3.8 shows results from a similar test but disaggregates *Inducements* to look at the independent impact of each policy tool—again for periods prior to and after the nonproliferation regime in 1970. These results provide a useful lens with which to examine some of the alternative explanations found in the existing scholarship.

Positive inducements, on their own, are generally effective both before and after 1970. This suggests that for many proliferators, inducements that privilege rewards are attractive in nuclear reversal. Interestingly, we see important variation across both eras with regard to the efficacy of the *U.S. Security Guarantee*, which loses significance in its association with nuclear reversal post-1970. This finding could suggest that for states that pursued nuclear reversal in contravention of international law (post-NPT), and faced escalatory punishment, do not view security guarantees as credible. Given the influence of Cold War dynamics in establishing "spheres of influence" among allies and other states, these proliferators may require other viable inducements to abandon their nuclear programs. Instead, they may turn to other policy levers like military assistance or technological capabilities to serve as face-saving incentives. Lastly, prior to 1970, on their own, *U.S. Economic Sanctions* have no discernible impact on nuclear reversal but in the post-NPT era, their isolated use decreases the likelihood of nuclear reversal. This result makes sense: given that nuclear pursuit was not illegal prior to the creation of the NPT, the United States would likely find it politically challenging to sanction states (often friends or allies) legally pursuing their right to nuclear weapons. These mixed effects over time reiterate the need for a combinative approach of rewards and sanction to incentivize counterproliferation.

Robustness Checks

Robustness Check 1: Effects of Rewards Conditional on Sanctions Being Instituted

In this section, I consider two robustness checks to ensure the strength of my results across a variety of model specifications. First, to examine the effects of rewards conditional on sanctions being instituted, I interact positive and negative inducements measures which allows me to evaluate whether rewards are more effective conditional on the presence of negative inducements. This test includes relevant covariates and time trends, along with the threat of military force. Table A3.9 presents the results from this robustness check that demonstrate that positive inducements, when interacted with negative inducements, are positively and statistically significantly associated with nuclear reversal.

Table A3.9 **Effects of Inducements Conditional on Sanctions Being Instituted**

	Model 1
Positive Inducements*Negative Inducements	0.271***
	(0.084)
Regime Type (Polity)	0.018
	(0.012)
Conventional Capacity (Composite Index of National Capacity, CINC)	−4.255
	(2.685)
Rivalry	−0.413***
	(0.133)
Allies	−0.028
	(0.783)
GDP per Capita	0.035
	(0.096)
Cold War Era	1.659***
	(0.138)
Time	−0.626***
	(0.074)
Time^2	0.028***
	(0.084)
Time^3	−0.000**
	(0.000)
Constant	0.419
	(0.802)
Observations	1,600

Robust Standard Errors in parentheses; * $p < 0.1$, ** $p < 0.05$, *** $p < 0.01$

Robustness Check 2: Alternative Specifications for Military Force Condition

To ensure the validity of the empirical results for my base model, I include two more robustness checks. The findings are presented in Tables A3.10 and A3.11. These analyses include interaction terms that allow me to model how sanctions and rewards shape the probability of nuclear reversal with and without a

credible threat of military force. The first test includes interaction terms measuring the relative impact of positive, negative, and combined inducements in
the presence of a threat of military force. Table A3.10 presents the findings from
this analysis.

Table A3.10 **Inducements and Nuclear Reversal: Interacted with Military Force**

	Model 1: Positive	Model 2: Negative	Model 3: Combined
Positive Inducements*Military Force (Interaction)	2.947***		
	(0.246)		
Positive Inducements	0.571***		
Negative Inducement*Military Force (Interaction)		+	
Negative Inducements		−0.523*	
		(0.244)	
Combined Inducements*Military Force (Interaction)			3.449***
			(0.452)
Combined Inducements			0.514***
			(0.098)
U.S. Military Force	−3.515***	−0.338	−4.385***
	(0.346)	(0.269)	(0.741)
Regime Type (Polity)	0.028**	0.023**	0.027**
	(0.013)	(0.012)	(0.013)
Conventional Capacity (CINC)	−5.569*	−5.740***	−5.625***
	(3.161)	(1.704)	(2.805)
Rivalry	−0.393***	−0.367***	−0.383***
	(0.136)	(0.129)	(0.135)
Alliances	−0.244	0.130	−0.223
	(0.165)	(0.141)	(0.164)
GDP per Capita	0.029	−0.019	0.063
	(0.103)	(0.089)	(0.099)

Table A3.10 **Continued**

	Model 1: Positive	Model 2: Negative	Model 3: Combined
Cold War Era	1.626***	1.671***	1.634***
	(0.148)	(0.132)	(0.149)
Time	−0.653**	−0.634***	−0.644***
	(0.076)	(0.076)	(0.075)
Time^2	0.029***	0.028***	0.028***
	(0.004)	(0.004)	(0.004)
Time^3	−0.000***	−0.000***	−0.000***
	(0.000)	(0.000)	(0.000)
Constant	0.153	0.892	−0.121
	(0.849)	(0.748)	(0.817)
Observations	1,604	1,666	1,604

Robust Standard Errors in parentheses; * $p < 0.1$, ** $p < 0.05$, *** $p < 0.01$; ⁺: *Predicts Failure Perfectly*

The results in Model 1 reveal the positive and significant association between the extension of positive inducements, interacted with military force, on the likelihood of nuclear reversal. Model 3 shows a stronger positive and significant association between combined inducements and nuclear reversal, given the threat of military force. In contrast, in Model 2, negative inducements, when interacted with military force, predict failure.

A second test examines these interactions when the threat of military force is not present. In Table A3.11 , I examine the impact of aggregate measures of inducements on the likelihood of nuclear reversal, absent a threat of military force. In Model 1, I focus solely on *Positive Inducements*, in Model 2, solely on *Negative Inducements*, and in Model 3, I consider the measure of *Combined Inducements*.

Combined Inducements is positive and significantly associated with nuclear reversal without a threat of force. Interestingly, the coefficient for *Positive Inducements* is also positive and significantly correlated with nuclear reversal, again with no threat of military force. This result suggests that for some subset of the universe of proliferators, the extension of positive inducements may be sufficient to incentivize nuclear reversal, even without an underlying threat of force. In the following sections, I move beyond testing the core hypotheses and begin examining the probabilistic conditions of leadership change and the proliferator's relationship with the United States.

Table A3.11 **Inducements and Nuclear Reversal: No Threat of Military Force**

	Model 1: Positive	Model 2: Negative	Model 3: Combined
Positive Inducements	0.563***		
	(0.124)		
Negative Inducements		−0.118	
		(0.139)	
Combined Inducements			0.494***
			(0.123)
Regime Type (Polity)	0.024	0.024	0.017
	(0.016)	(0.016)	(0.014)
Conventional Capacity (CINC)	−6.808*	−7.086*	−5.659*
	(3.402)	(3.681)	(3.216)
Rivalry	−0.379***	−0.372***	−0.426***
	(0.136)	(0.129)	(0.135)
Alliances	0.033	−0.005	0.397**
	(0.213)	(0.219)	(0.195)
GDP per Capita	0.078	0.038	0.074
	(0.126)	(0.132)	(0.119)
Cold War Era	1.535***	1.534***	1.544***
	(0.183)	(0.183)	(0.182)
Time	−0.717**	−0.730***	−0.707***
	(0.099)	(0.101)	(0.100)
Time²	0.033***	0.034***	0.033***
	(0.005)	(0.005)	(0.005)
Time³	−0.000***	−0.000***	−0.000***
	(0.000)	(0.000)	(0.000)
Constant	−0.310	0.010	0.133
	(1.021)	(1.068)	(0.986)
Observations	1,154	1,154	1,172

Robust Standard Errors in parentheses; * $p < 0.1$, ** $p < 0.05$, *** $p < 0.01$

Implications of Probabilistic Conditions

Leadership Change and Pressure Campaigns: Hypothesis 2

To test *Hypothesis 2* which examines the first scope condition of the impact of leadership change and inducements on nuclear reversal, I employ a set of cross-sectional, time-series analyses. Specifically, I use data on nuclear weapons activity and U.S. policy levers, and the Archigos dataset on leaders from 1945 to 2004.[37] In accord with previous work on nuclear proliferation,[38] I use a probit model to analyze these effects. I employ clustered standard errors that address heteroskedastic error variance, in addition to correcting for temporal dependence using splines.[39]

Additional Independent Variable

To operationalize *Leader Change*, I use the Archigos dataset on leaders, originally from 1875 to 2004, to identify states that experience a change in head of state (i.e., prime minister, president, or military leader) through regular or irregular means in the post–World War II era.[40] The variable is coded dichotomously, where an observation coded "1" has a new leader enter into office in that state-year, and "0" otherwise.

Base Model: Inducements, Leadership Change, and Nuclear Reversal

Table A3.12 shows the estimated relationship between inducements and leadership change on nuclear reversal, using a probit model. As in prior model specifications, this model includes the condition of the threat of military force. In Model 1, the coefficient estimate on *Inducements* indicates support for the core hypothesis. During periods of leadership change, *Inducements*, is positively and significantly associated with the likelihood that the state will reverse its nuclear weapons program. Further, in Model 2, while *Positive Inducements* increase the likelihood of nuclear reversal, *Negative Inducements* have no discernible impact.[41]

Leadership Change and Nuclear Reversal Among Allies vs. Non-Allies

In Table A3.13, I examine the interaction effect between inducements and changes in leadership, for allies and non-allies. Model 1 examines the impact of *Inducements*, conditional on changes in leadership among U.S. allies while Model 2 looks at non-allies. The results reveal a weak positive association between *Inducements* and nuclear reversal among allies during periods of leadership change. Yet, they also suggest that these tools can potentially backfire against

Table A3.12 **Hypothesis 2: Inducements and Nuclear Reversal,
During Leadership Change (Conditional on Threat of Military Force)**

	Model 1	Model 2
Inducements	0.298**	
	(0.151)	
Positive Inducements		0.485**
		(0.159)
Negative Inducements		0.160
		(0.167)
Regime Type (Polity)	0.033*	0.042**
	(0.017)	(0.018)
Latent Industrial Capacity	−0.049	−0.053
	(0.058)	(0.057)
Conventional Capacity (CINC)	−3.573	−2.727
	(3.096)	(3.164)
Rivalry	−0.405**	−0.353*
	(0.191)	(0.191)
Affinity w/ U.S.	−0.368	−0.522*
	(0.238)	(0.255)
Alliances	(0.139)	−0.053
	(0.236)	(0.254)
GDP per Capita	0.434***	−0.453***
	(0.111)	(0.111)
Cold War Era	1.615***	1.622***
	(0.194)	(1.193)
Constant	−4.517***	−4.792**
	(1.044)	(1.041)
Observations	332	332

Robust Standard Errors in parentheses; * $p < 0.1$, ** $p < 0.05$, *** $p < 0.01$

non-allies. This may be because non-allies experiencing leadership change may view the extension of inducements as intrusive and potentially threatening to the new regime. Importantly, this model includes no background threat of military force. This may help explain why among non-allies, the inducements offered to new leaders (without the fear of military force) decreases the likelihood of nuclear reversal.

Table A3.13 **Inducements, Leadership Change, and Nuclear Reversal**
           (Allies and Non–Allies)

	Model 1: Allies	Model 2: Non–Allies
Inducements*Leader Change	0.032	−0.607**
	(0.272)	(0.243)
Inducements	0.226	1.060***
	(0.146)	(0.161)
Leadership Change	−0.269	0.463
	(0.403)	(0.361)
Regime Type (Polity)	0.012	0.052***
	(0.023)	(0.017)
Conventional Capacity (CINC)	1.245	−9.682**
	(6.307)	(4.819)
Rivalry	−0.579***	−0.433*
	(0.181)	(0.227)
Alliances	0.092	−0.246
	(0.299)	(0.234)
GDP per Capita	−0.202	0.157
	(0.211)	(0.103)
Cold War Era	1.560***	1.848***
	(0.182)	(0.267)
Time	−0.755***	−0.549***
	(0.018)	(0.095)
Time^2	0.034***	0.023***
	(0.006)	(0.005)
Time^3	−0.000***	−0.000***
	(0.000)	(0.000)
Constant	2.657	−1.503*
	(1.779)	(0.875)
Observations	752	752

Robust Standard Errors in parentheses; * $p < 0.1$, ** $p < 0.05$, *** $p < 0.01$

Leadership Change and Nuclear Reversal: Substantive Effects

When we compare the substantive effects of leadership change separately, we see a significant difference. Table A3.14 presents the substantive
effects: *Leader Change* increases the likelihood of nuclear reversal by 6.5%
while *Positive Inducements* and *Negative Inducements* increases the likelihood
by up to 15%. This provides support for my theory that external inducements,
over other alternative explanations emphasizing solely domestic factors, such
as regime change, are influential in nuclear decision-making during leadership change.

Leadership Change and Nuclear Reversal: Sunk Costs

In Table A3.15, I address another important dynamic: how new leaders respond when faced with ending long-running nuclear weapons pursuits. These
models include the full host of covariates to control for the impact of any other
confounding factors affecting nuclear reversal. Model 1 presents the results
from the analysis with no lag in the dependent variable while Models 2 and
3 include a dependent variable lagged by three and five years, respectively. It
is possible that the political impact of ending a long-running nuclear program
that incurred heavy sunk costs is likely to evolve over time. These results suggest that an initial impact is likely to dissipate (or potentially reverse) with
time. New leaders may be increasingly disinclined to reverse inherited nuclear
programs the longer they are in power.

The results in Model 1 provide support for this logic. The coefficients for
Inducements and *Sunk Costs* are positive and statistically significant. This finding
suggests that even with long-running programs, the introduction of a new leader
is positively associated with nuclear reversal. Further, this relationship attenuates
over time as leaders continue in office. Once new leaders decide to continue
their inherited nuclear program, they are impacted by the biases of sunk costs
and less amenable to nuclear reversal.

Leadership Change and Nuclear Reversal: Time in Office

Additionally, Table A3.16 examines the impact of combined inducements on
nuclear reversal in the same three models (upon entry into office, and three and
five years after a leadership change occurs), under the conditional threat of military force. Again, the results from Model 1 reveal the positive, but attenuating,
impact of *Inducements* on the likelihood of nuclear reversal, after three years
(Model 2) and five years (Model 3).[42] If inducements are not initially offered,
new leaders may resist further efforts to negotiate nuclear reversal, even if faced
with escalatory punishment if they persist.

Table A3.14 **Inducements, Leadership Change, and Nuclear Reversal (Substantive Effects)**

	Model 1	Model 2
Leader Change	0.065**	
	(0.032)	
Positive Inducements		0.154**
		(0.060)
Negative Inducements		0.090
		(0.066)
Regime Type (Polity)	0.004**	0.016**
	(0.002)	(0.007)
Latent Industrial Capacity	0.012	−0.010
	(0.007)	(0.022)
Conventional Capacity (CINC)	−0.753**	−0.489
	(0.346)	(1.163)
Rivalry	−0.103***	−0.077
	(0.085)	(0.069)
Affinity w/ U.S.	−0.007	−0.176*
	(0.033)	(0.096)
Alliances	0.024	−0.061
	(0.024)	(0.097)
GDP per Capita	0.046***	0.159**
	(0.016)	(0.040)
Cold War Era	0.707***	0.704**
	(0.030)	(0.059)
Time	−0.008	−0.010
	(0.006)	(0.016)
Time^2	0.000*	0.001
	(0.001)	(0.001)
Time^3	−0.000***	−0.000
	(0.000)	(0.000)
Observations	1,596	329

Robust Standard Errors in parentheses; $^*p < 0.1$, $^{**}p < 0.05$, $^{***}p < 0.01$

Table A3.15 **Leadership Change, Sunk Costs, and Nuclear Reversal (with Lags)**

	Model 1: No Lag	Model 2: 3-yr Lag	Model 3: 5-yr Lag
Inducements	0.321**	−0.076	−0.134
	(0.146)	(0.137)	(0.123)
Sunk Costs	0.136***	0.052*	0.051*
	(0.025)	(0.027)	(0.027)
Polity	0.052***	0.015	0.015
	(0.017)	(0.015)	(0.015)
Latent Industrial Capacity	−0.019	−0.011	−0.061
	(0.069)	(0.062)	(0.063)
Conventional Capacity (CINC Score)	−0.756	2.934	4.734
	(3.363)	(3.415)	(3.206)
Rivalry	−0.318	−0.212	−0.119
	(0.205)	(0.202)	(0.199)
Affinity w/ U.S.	−0.322	−0.029	−0188
	(0.259)	(0.222)	(0.227)
Alliances	−0.058	0.104	0.018
	(0.249)	(0.207)	(0.209)
GDP per Capita	0.404***	0.343***	0.263**
	(0.119)	(0.108)	(0.106)
Cold War Era	2.473**	2.434**	0.263**
	(0.317)	(0.292)	(0.266)
Time	0.012	−0.059	−0.057
	(0.045)	(0.045)	(0.043)
Time^2	−0.001	0.002	0.001
	(0.002)	(0.002)	(0.002)
Time^3	−0.000	−0.000	−0.000
	(0.000)	(0.000)	(0.000)
Constant	−4.613**	−3.227***	−2.259**
	(1.135)	(1.029)	(1.021)
Observations	329	329	329

Robust Standard Errors in parentheses; $^*p < 0.1$, $^{**}p < 0.05$, $^{***}p < 0.01$

Table A3.16 **Inducements (Combined) and Nuclear Reversal (with Lags)**
(Conditional on Threat of Force)

	Model 1:	Model 2: 3-yr Lag	Model 2: 5-yr Lag
Inducements	0.394***	0.230***	0.086
	(0.102)	(0.108)	(0.110)
Regime Type (Polity)	0.018	−0.001	−0.025
	(0.017)	(0.020)	(0.020)
Latent Industrial Capacity	−0.077	−0.024	−0.114[†]
	(0.065)	(0.069)	(0.067)
Conventional Capacity (CINC)	2.204	9.437[†]	13.458**
	(6.055)	(5.114)	(4.891)
Rivalry	−0.132	−0.113	−0.181
	(0.206)	(0.218)	(0.243)
Affinity w/ U.S.	−0.098	0.200	0.664*
	(0.305)	(0.322)	(0.306)
Alliances	−0.421	−0.281	−0.446
	(0.275)	(0.296)	(0.303)
GDP per Capita	0.312**	0.288[†]	0.332**
	(0.141)	(0.134)	(0.147)
Cold War Era	2.485**	2.374**	2.653**
	(0.335)	(0.321)	(0.334)
Time	−0.014	−0.031	0.003
	(0.046)	(0.043)	(0.046)
Time^2	0.002	0.001	−0.002
	(0.002)	(0.002)	(0.002)
Time^3	−0.000	−0.000	0.000
	(0.000)	(0.000)	(0.000)
Constant	−2.978**	−2.056*	−2.538[†]
	(1.335)	(1.282)	(1.410)
Observations	338	338	338

Robust Standard Errors in parentheses; * $p < 0.1$, ** $p < 0.05$, *** $p < 0.01$

Friends and Foes and the Differential Impact
of Inducements: Hypotheses 3–6

Recall that *Hypotheses 3* through *6* test the probabilistic conditions derived in Chapter 2 that describe how two factors—the resolve of the United States to employ military force and its relationship with the proliferator—influence nuclear reversal decisions. My theory suggests that under the threat of military force, inducements should incentivize nuclear reversal even among proliferators with divergent preferences to the United States. States with similar preferences to those of the U.S. should be motivated by an offer of rewards, even if force is not on the table.

Tables A3.17 and A3.18 present the results from the tests on four hypotheses. These analyses include the full hosts of covariates to ensure that they mitigate the effects of confounding variables on the likelihood of nuclear reversal. Table A3.17 examines if states with proximate or divergent policy preferences to the United States respond differently when the United States is *not* willing to employ force to stop the proliferation attempt (*Hypotheses 3–4*). Table A3.18 presents the results of such analyses when the U.S. *is* willing to credibly threaten the use of military force to terminate a proliferator's nuclear weapons program (*Hypotheses 5–6*). In both tables, Models 1 and 3 examine states with proximate policy preferences (friends) and Models 2 and 4 focus on states with divergent policy preferences (foes).

In Table A3.17, we first examine how these relationships may evolve when the U.S. has a low resolve for permanently ending a proliferator's nuclear program through military force. In Models 1 and 2, the coefficients for *Inducements* are positive and statistically significant for both friends and foes. When disaggregating this measure to see which policy tools are more or less useful, the results reveal important differences across proliferator types. In Model 3, when considering states with convergent policy preferences, *U.S. Military Assistance* and *U.S. Economic Assistance* are positive but not significantly associated with nuclear reversal. Also, *U.S. Security Guarantee* seems to have negligible effect in motivating friendly states to reverse their nuclear programs. These results suggest that states with close relationships to the United States are not always persuaded by these types of rewards, but may instead require different or more substantial compensation for forgoing their nuclear weapons programs. On the other hand, the positive and statistically significant coefficient on *Nuclear Latency* suggests that this is an especially useful tool for states that are already aligned with the United States. The opportunity to retain nuclear technology for civilian energy purposes, in line with NPT obligations, may be especially salient in compensating states that are willing to forgo pursuing an indigenous nuclear weapons program. Further, this result supports some of the findings from the existing literature: providing nuclear assistance or allowing

Table A3.17 **Hypotheses 3–4: Determinants of Nuclear Reversal with Low U.S. Resolve (No Threat of Force): Friends and Foes**

	Model 1: Friends	Model 2: Foes	Model 3: Friends	Model 4: Foes
Inducements	0.254**	0.889***		
	(0.126)	(0.139)		
U.S. Military Assistance			0.273	1.726***
			(0.169)	(0.204)
U.S. Economic Assistance			0.007	0.578***
			(0.180)	(0.252)
U.S. Security Guarantee			0.005	−1.269***
			(0.143)	(0.591)
Nuclear Latency			1.264***	Collinear
			(0.458)	
U.S. Economic Sanctions			−0.902***	−0.939***
			(0.329)	(0.252)
Regime Type (Polity)	0.013	0.058***	0.011	0.086***
	(0.023)	(0.016)	(0.011)	(0.014)
Conventional Capacity (CINC)	1.588	−8.974***	13.461***	−15.163***
	(5.529)	(4.286)	(4.453)	(6.108)
Rivalry	−0.570***	−0.570**	−0.345***	−0.872***
	(0.175)	(0.238)	(0.108)	(0.180)
GDP per Capita	−0.172	0.212**	0.075	0.135**
	(0.201)	(0.103)	(0.104)	(0.099)
Cold War Era	1.577***	1.779***	2.119***	2.670***
	(0.186)	(0.256)	(0.166)	(0.217)
Time	−0.745***	−0.545***	−0.032	−0.120***
	(0.116)	(0.097)	(0.026)	(0.038)
Time^2	0.034***	0.024***	0.01	0.006***
	(0.006)	(0.006)	(0.001)	(0.002)
Time^3	−0.000***	−0.000***	−0.000**	−0.000***
	(0.000)	(0.000)	(0.000)	(0.000)

(continued)

Table A3.17 **Continued**

	Model 1: Friends	Model 2: Foes	Model 3: Friends	Model 4: Foes
Constant	2.321	−1.746**	−1.407	−2.145***
	(1.711)	(0.886)	(0.935)	(0.896)
Observations	752	852	752	850

Robust Standard Errors in parentheses; * $p < 0.1$, ** $p < 0.05$, *** $p < 0.01$

states to retain a latent capacity can play an important role curbing proliferation.[43] Lastly, it is important to note that without the fear of escalatory punishment, these states may seek to push their luck and attempt to extract more concessions from the United States.

In Model 4, however, an interesting picture emerges. The positive and statistically significant coefficients for U.S. *Military Assistance* and U.S. *Economic Assistance* among states with divergent preferences suggest that these may be useful policy levers to encourage states that have previously not received these types of rewards. Adversarial proliferators may want to receive conventional arms, or other forms of military assistance, as well as various types of economic aid, from the U.S. as compensation for not pursuing a nuclear weapons deterrent. The negative and significant coefficient for U.S. *Security Guarantee* suggests that states with divergent policy preferences may not be convinced by this reward and may consider it non-credible. This doubt may be due to the costs and constraints associated with extending the nuclear umbrella by the United States.[44] Indeed, this thinking was evident during the Iranian negotiations. Iranian diplomats did not believe that offers to include Iran, a state with tense relations with the United States, in the U.S. security umbrella were credible given the United States' other alliance commitments (to Israel, for example). These states may seek to extract other forms of concessions because they do not fear an escalation in punishment if they were to prolong nuclear negotiations. Lastly, the negative and significant coefficient for U.S. *Economic Sanctions* reaffirms a core finding from this book. Punishments alone are insufficient and must be coupled with positive inducements to favorably impact the likelihood of nuclear reversal. On their own, they have the opposite impact in decreasing the likelihood of nuclear reversal.

Table A3.18 examines how these relationships may change when the United States *is* willing to employ military force to achieve nuclear reversal. To test these propositions, I employ an interaction term in Models 1 and 2 to examine impact of *Inducements*, given the threat of military force.

While *Inducements* predicts failure perfectly for friends, it has a positive and significant impact on the likelihood of nuclear reversal for foes. The coefficient on the use of *Military Force* is negative and statistically significant. This result

Table A3.18 **Hypotheses 5–6: Determinants of Nuclear Reversal with High U.S. Resolve (Threat of Force): Friends and Foes**

	Model 1: Friends	Model 2: Foes	Model 3: Friends	Model 4: Foes
Inducements*Military Force	+	3.408***		
		(0.494)		
Inducements	0.254***	0.881***		
	(0.126)	(0.139)		
Military Force	+	−4.123***		
		(0.779)		
U.S. Military Assistance			0.272	1.731***
			(0.168)	(0.206)
U.S. Economic Assistance			0.006	0.562**
			(0.180)	(0.253)
U.S. Security Guarantee			0.003	−1.264**
			(0.143)	(0.594)
Nuclear Latency			Collinear	Collinear
U.S. Economic Sanctions			−0.850**	−0.919***
			(0.388)	(0.254)
Regime Type (Polity)	0.013	0.057***	0.011	0.085***
	(0.023)	(0.016)	(0.011)	(0.014)
Conventional Capacity (CINC)	1.579	−9.291***	13.358***	−15.037***
	(5.528)	(4.377)	(4.449)	(6.064)
Rivalry	−0.569***	−0.545**	−0.341***	−0.870***
	(0.175)	(0.244)	(0.108)	(0.181)
GDP per Capita	−0.172	0.216**	0.075	0.136
	(0.201)	(0.104)	(0.104)	(0.099)
Cold War Era	1.577***	1.784**	2.120***	2.656***
	(0.186)	(0.257)	(0.167)	(0.219)
Time	−0.745***	−0.549***	−0.032	−0.123***
	(0.116)	(0.098)	(0.026)	(0.039)

(*continued*)

Table A3.18 **Continued**

	Model 1: Friends	Model 2: Foes	Model 3: Friends	Model 4: Foes
Time^2	0.034***	0.024***	0.001	0.006***
	(0.006)	(0.006)	(0.001)	(0.002)
Time^3	−0.000***	−0.000***	−0.000**	−0.000***
	(0.000)	(0.000)	(0.000)	(0.000)
Constant	2.320	−1.776***	−1.415	−2.136***
	(1.710)	(0.896)	(0.936)	(0.898)
Observations	743	852	744	823

Robust Standard Errors in parentheses; * $p < 0.1$, ** $p < 0.05$, *** $p < 0.01$; ⁺: predicts failure perfectly.

suggests that on its own, the use of force is not an effective strategy for foes but, in combination with inducements, provides a powerful incentive. This finding stands in contrast to historical approaches that argue for military force to incentivize nuclear reversal among adversaries. Instead, I find that military force against adversarial proliferators decreases the likelihood that they will abandon their nuclear weapons programs.

In disaggregating these policy tools, I can assess how some of the alternative explanations fare. First, I again note the negative role of *U.S. Economic Sanctions* without simultaneous rewards. For both friends and foes, sanctions when used alone reduce the likelihood of nuclear reversal. Frequently employed rewards such as *U.S. Military Assistance* and *U.S. Economic Assistance* are not effective with friends. These states may instead require more significant concessions from the United States, such as the retention of *Nuclear Latency*, that compensate for a lost nuclear deterrent. The results also indicate that the use of rewards such as military or foreign aid can still be an important tool in nuclear reversal for states with divergent preferences to the United States. In fact, when confronting adversarial proliferators, most rewards, except *U.S. Security Guarantee*, are positively associated with nuclear reversal. The negative coefficient on this variable suggests that states with divergent preferences to the U.S. may not find offers of security guarantees credible.

Alternative Operationalizations of Inducements

The broader international community no doubt plays an important and influential role in the global nonproliferation regime, especially in managing the spread of nuclear technology and encouraging states from *initially* starting down the nuclear path. With both the ratification of the Nonproliferation Treaty in 1972 and the creation of the Nuclear Suppliers Group (a regulatory body aimed at limiting the availability of nuclear materials and technology that could be used for nuclear weapons), the international community has focused its attention on providing incentives, and disincentives, to those seeking to acquire a nuclear weapons deterrent. For example, as I discuss further in Chapter 4, part of Muammar Qaddafi's decision to stop Libya's pursuit of nuclear weapons was driven in part by a desire to end decades of political isolation and the promise of international reengagement, as well as a part of a related agreement with the United Kingdom regarding the downing of Pan Am 103 in Lockerbie in 1988.[45]

In some instances, major powers can help provide the necessary bargaining leverage to help negotiate an agreement to end a nuclear weapons program. On other occasions, states can play a more complicated role in counterproliferation. The People's Republic of China (PRC) and the Democratic People's Republic of Korea (DPRK) exchanged diplomatic recognition in 1949 soon after the division of the Korean Peninsula. This relationship prompted the establishment of the Sino-North Korean Mutual Aid and Cooperation Friendship Treaty that remains the cornerstone of the PRC-DPRK alliance. As part of this relationship, China (and also Russia) have historically presented significant obstacles to international cohesion on imposing United Nations or multilateral sanctions against the DPRK. However, despite China's role as North Korea's primary ally and economic supporter, recent tensions caused by ballistic missile tests and the purported testing of a hydrogen bomb have worsened the PRC-DPRK alliance. These provocations have actually encouraged China to take on a broader role in the international community's counterproliferation efforts with North Korea. This mixed approach of the Chinese toward DPRK—often ally, sometimes annoyed patron—may help explain why the international community has been unsuccessful in dealing with the North Korean nuclear issue. Further, the lack of unanimity or consistency in approach (with some states acting as spoilers against agreements or the imposition of costs) helps justify the role of the United States as the foremost actor in counterproliferation.

In order to explore these dynamics further, I examine several new measures that account for the role of the broader international community in counterproliferation. While the U.S. is generally the main actor in counterproliferation agreements, other members of the nonproliferation regime or the broader international system may sometimes play an important role in nuclear negotiations. To account for this possibility, the tests that follow focus on the role of the international community in inducing nuclear reversal. This section includes analyses with select alternative operationalizations of the independent variables, as well as related covariates.

I examine alternative political rewards that indicate whether the proliferator can enter into specific international institutions or organizations with high barriers to entry. For example, it is unlikely that a state such as Sweden could be persuaded to abandon its nuclear effort with the promise of ease of entrance into the United Nations and the broader political system. It is, however, more likely that such an incentive could be sufficient for a state such as Libya or Iran that seeks to enter/re-engage the international community. To analyze the effects of organizational membership on proliferators, I include *Entry to WTO* in my analysis.[46]

In the same vein, I include alternative measures of economic and military benefits. To account for an alternative type of military support, I include a binary variable, *Entry to NATO*, that indicates whether the proliferator can enter NATO or is extended a defensive alliance commitment from a member of the international community.[47] Second, I capture economic interdependence or emergence into the global economy with a variable that measures *Economic Openness* or the amount of imports and exports as a share of GDP.[48]

On the other side of the spectrum, I include alternative operationalizations of negative inducements. It could be that a potential proliferator may be influenced by sanctions imposed by the United Nations, perhaps seen as a signal of international condemnation. To account for this possibility, I include a measure of *UN Economic Sanctions*.[49] To determine whether the proliferator is affected by the threat of military force, I include an alternative measure, *Security Environment*, a five-year moving average of militarized interstate dispute involvement.[50] It may be the case that a proliferator is not just the target of blatant threats or the use of force by the United States, but rather from instances of smaller threats or coercion from a broader network of adversaries. This is certainly a noisier measure than that of the threat of military force against nuclear facilities from the Fuhrmann and Kreps dataset. However, it does allow us to examine a broader range of threatening military action (including actual disputes). Table A3.19 presents these alternative operationalizations.

Table A3.19 **Determinants of Nuclear Reversal: Alternative Operationalizations**

Construct	Alternative Measure	Source
Positive Military Reward	*Entry to NATO*	Correlates of War 2004
Positive Economic Reward	*Economic Openness*	Singh and Way 2004
Positive Political Reward	*Entry to WTO*	Leeds et al. 2002
Negative Economic Inducements	*UN Economic Sanctions*	Hufbauer et al. 2007
Military Force Condition	*Security Environment*	Correlates of War 2004

To assess the overall impact of these alternative inducements, I create an aggregate measure *Alternative Inducements*. In Table A3.20, I assess the impact of this measure on the likelihood of nuclear reversal. This model specification includes relevant covariates, time trends, clustered standard errors, and the conditional threat of military force (herein measured by *Security Environment*).

The results show the positive, statistically significant association between *Alternative Inducements* and nuclear reversal. Yet, in comparing the substantive effects of *Inducements* versus *Alternative Inducements*, a different picture emerges.

Table A3.20 **Alternative Inducements and Nuclear Reversal**

	Model 1
Alternative Inducements	0.011***
	(0.004)
Regime Type (Polity)	0.020
	(0.013)
Conventional Capacity (CINC)	−3.344*
	(1.775)
Rivalry	−0.390***
	(0.141)
GDP per Capita	−0.111
	(0.112)
Cold War Era	1.689***
	(0.138)
Alliance	0.334*
	(0.158)
Time	−0.597***
	(0.081)
Time^2	0.026**
	(0.004)
Time^3	−0.000***
	(0.000)
Constant	1.109
	(0.864)
Observations	1,380

Robust Standard Errors in parentheses; * $p < 0.1$, ** $p < 0.05$, *** $p < 0.01$

In accord with my theoretical framework which focuses on unilateral rather than multilateral counterproliferation strategies, *Inducements*, given a threat of military force, increases the likelihood of nuclear reversal by nearly 5% for all proliferators. Importantly, *Alternative Inducements* has no statistically significant substantive effect.

4

Success and Failure in Nuclear Reversal

Archetypes of Nuclear Reversal

To better understand the impact of inducements and to get a broader sense of the process of nuclear reversal, I present two short tales of nuclear proliferation. These cases distinguish the nuclear reversers from the current proliferators, allies from adversaries, those that tried and succeeded decades ago, and those that remained committed for decades with a failing program and ultimately reversed their nuclear course. These illustrative vignettes of success and failure help to delve deeper into the nuclear reversal process, to get a better understanding of how states embark on and end the pursuit of nuclear weapons. More importantly, these cases reveal the importance of the two core elements of my theory: a combinative strategy of rewards and sanctions (based on the proliferator's relationship with Washington), and the threat/use of military force to incentivize nuclear reversal. In the Libyan case, where the use of military force was deemed a credible option given its less than friendly relationship with the West (especially the United States and the United Kingdom), after years of costly sanctions, Muammar Qaddafi reversed Libya's nuclear program in exchange for a set of rewards—including an assurance that the United States would not actively encourage regime change in the aftermath of the Arab Spring.[1] In contrast, when examining the United States' approach to the prospect of a nuclear Red China, the United States wavered in its willingness to threaten military force (especially without a buy-in from the USSR). The decision to not actively counter Chinese proliferation with inducements, given that the use of military force was not on the table, contributed to China's successful acquisition of a nuclear weapon in the 1960s.[2] While not representative of every nascent proliferator, tracing these cases and the decision-making both in the United States (as the primary nuclear negotiator) and the proliferators in question reveal important patterns and provide critical support for my theory of nuclear reversal.

Delaying Doomsday, Rupal N. Mehta. Oxford University Press (2020). © Oxford University Press.
DOI: 10.1093/oso/9780190077976.001.0001

Libya (1969–2003):
Three Phases of Libya's Nuclear Pursuit

Libya's remarkable attempt at procuring a nuclear weapon began similarly to many states in the region—with the signing and ratification of the Nonproliferation Treaty in the period 1969–1970. By the beginning of the 1970s, however, Libya had already begun its nuclear pursuit, when Qaddafi approached China to purchase a nuclear weapon.[3] Determined to focus its energy overseas rather than on indigenous production, Libya continued to approach nuclear technology suppliers, hoping to acquire anything that would be considered part of a civilian nuclear energy program. This ranged from uranium mining and enrichment to research reactors to plutonium reprocessing capability. During this initial period, Libya's progress was thwarted by the reluctance of many states (including Argentina, France, and Egypt) to supply sensitive nuclear technology or equipment, thus forcing Qaddafi to turn to the Soviet Union and Pakistan for assistance.[4]

The limited progress made during the 1980s, with the assistance of the Soviets and the Pakistanis, came to a halt in the early 1990s. The secret work conducted during this time on plutonium separation, uranium conversion, and gas centrifuges exemplify Libya's difficulties in acquiring nuclear technology and training from reluctant nuclear suppliers.[5] Despite significant efforts, the Qaddafi regime remained relatively frustrated by the lack of progress. According to a report published by the United States Department of Defense, by the early 1990s, the Libyans had spent millions on a failing nuclear program. The report stated that the Libyan program "lacks well-developed plans, technical expertise, consistent financial support, and sufficient support from foreign suppliers."[6] The report went on to say that despite significant obstacles to their progress, the Libyans seemed intent on continuing their nuclear program and upgrading their infrastructure using both indigenous and exogenous production avenues. The report concluded, "[Libya] continues to send scientists abroad for training and actively recruits foreign nuclear scientists and technicians."[7] Interestingly, the report argued that despite their dedicated efforts, Libya posed no short- or medium-term threat as a nuclear proliferator.

The second phase of the Libyan nuclear program began in the early 1990s with the establishment of the Tajoura Nuclear Research Center (TNRC) and its IRT-1 reactor, a 10MW light-water research reactor, with assistance from the Soviet Union/Russia.[8] From here, the Libyans began their long-term clandestine effort to build a nuclear weapon by working on uranium conversion (gas-centrifuge enrichment), and plutonium separation. While beginning experiments on plutonium separation at TNRC, Libya continued its efforts abroad, receiving only limited help in uranium enrichment from an Eastern European country, most likely Yugoslavia.[9] However, two observations emerge: first, states were generally unwilling to work with Qaddafi because of concerns of his nuclear weapons pursuit, and Libya's terrorist activities and sponsorship; and second, proliferators committed to acquiring a nuclear weapon are difficult to deter, even with tight restrictions on nuclear materials and technology, ostensibly to be used for civilian purposes.

The final phase of the Libyan nuclear program began in 1995 when Qaddafi focused efforts on uranium enrichment, leading to the reduced role of the TNRC research reactor. According to reports at the time, "Libya reportedly seeks to purchase weapons-grade fissile material on the black market to restart or accelerate its nuclear weapons program."[10] This one last push at acquisition also marked the beginning of Libya's collaboration with AQ Khan and his associates in Europe.[11] The Khan network provided Qaddafi with assistance on developing a gas-centrifuge uranium enrichment capability, overseas training for Libyan nuclear personnel, acquisition of sensitive materials and equipment, and supplier contacts. The Qaddafi regime placed orders with Khan who, serving as a middleman, procured the requested components from suppliers before reshipping them to Libya. By 2002, Libya had also successfully acquired design and manufacturing instructions for a 10-kiloton implosion device (based on a 1960s Chinese design), suitable for delivery by aircraft or ballistic missile.[12] This resurgence of nuclear ambitions, from the mid-1990s onward, cost somewhere between $100 and $500 million.[13] With such an investment, it was becoming increasingly clear that Qaddafi remained committed to acquiring nuclear weapons. More importantly, Qaddafi was willing to incur great costs to do so, despite the economic sanctions and international reprobation imposed by the United Nations and the United States.

What was driving this intense desire to acquire nuclear weapons? Because of its behavior and reputation in the international system, the regime "became afraid that Libya would become the main target of the Middle East region for the United States."[14] Despite Qaddafi's long-standing desire to acquire nuclear weapons, he was first and foremost concerned with maintaining his position and not being the victim of a forcible regime turnover. Qaddafi observed what happened to heads of state who were suspected of pursuing nuclear weapons programs and realized that there was little difference between him and Saddam Hussein from the perspective of the United States. Further, regional security concerns, specifically Israel's nuclear weapons program and the belief that a nuclear deterrent would elevate Libya both regionally and internationally, provided a strong foundation for a costly and lengthy nuclear pursuit. According to Qaddafi, ". . . we did not reflect on where or against whom we could use the nuclear bomb. Such issues were not considered. All that was important was to build the bomb."[15]

Nuclear Dismantlement:
Behind the Technical and Political Processes

The Libyan nuclear reversal case provides clear insight into how the international community can influence nuclear decision-making even among the most committed of proliferators. Further, analysis of the U.S.-led dismantlement process in Libya provides a clear snapshot of the most permanent and satisfying type of nuclear reversal: complete elimination of nuclear and missile programs. The primary objective of the United States was to remove the most sensitive aspects of the WMD and missile programs. This priority initiated the airlifting of nearly 55,000 lbs. of documents, materials, and parts from Libya's nuclear and ballistic missile efforts to the United States. This haul included containers of uranium hexafluoride (used for enrichment), two P2 centrifuges that originated in AQ Khan's labs, and other centrifuge-related documents, materials, and equipment.[16]

The dismantlement process continued for the next several months. In addition to removing sensitive nuclear materials and technology, the Organization for the Prohibition of Chemical Weapons (OPCW) monitored the destruction of more than 3,000 unfilled shells that could be used for chemical weapons.[17] Over the course of the next year, more than 1,000 tons of other centrifuge parts, as well as parts for missiles (including five Scud-C missiles), missile launchers, and associated equipment were shipped from Libya to the United States. Further, Russia removed nearly 15 kilograms of unused, 80% highly enriched uranium (HEU) that the Soviet Union had initially supplied in the 1980s for the research reactor at Tajoura.[18]

The dismantlement process also revealed some crucial intelligence about the nature of the Libyan nuclear pursuit. At the time that Libya ultimately gave up its nuclear weapons program, Qaddafi seemingly had most of the technical pieces required for successful weaponization. However, there remained significant roadblocks to nuclearization—including the absence of a high-technology industrial and scientific base that resulted in a lack of qualified expertise to actually run and operate nuclear technology.[19] Yet, the question remains—why did Qaddafi ultimately decide to stop this decades-long pursuit after such high sunk costs, given the potential benefits to be gained through a nuclear weapons deterrent?

The answer to this question is driven by the international community's strong desire to prevent a nuclear Libya and its willingness to "up the ante" on Qaddafi. Throughout Libya's nuclear story, the U.S. and other members of the international community opted to try to coerce Libya to abandon its nuclear program through bilateral and multilateral sanctions, without a parallel rewards strategy. Ultimately, sanctions had limited negative impact on Libya's proliferation process. Libya's nuclear program initially blossomed under sanctions though later evidence suggested that they may have posed some financial or technical impediments to the country's decades-long acquisition attempt. Libya was able to compensate for the costs of sanctions by turning to state and non-state allies for economic and technological assistance, which only seemed to grow in the midst of international sanctions. The cohort of "rogue" actors, including AQ Khan and North Korea, rallied together to help Qaddafi acquire nuclear weapons, seemingly undeterred by multilateral efforts to impose heavy, and hopefully prohibitive, costs on Libya. Rather, U.S. and U.N. sanctions were useful in identifying Libya as the type of state that required a different, potentially more aggressive, approach to counterproliferation.

The failure of a series of sanctions required the United States and the United Kingdom to begin to look at other available options to motivate a change in Qaddafi's decision-making. Libya's interest in nuclear weapons had presented a significant challenge to the international community, due in no small part to Qaddafi's status in the international system. During his tenure, Qaddafi placed Libya on the map as a pariah state that sponsored terrorism, while secretly pursuing weapons of mass destruction through foreign assistance. Interestingly, it is Libya's status as a revisionist state whose preferences differed dramatically from those of the United States and other members of the international system that made the prospect of war and foreign-imposed regime change credible.

Thus, after months of secret meetings and negotiation attempts (some initiated by Libya), officials from the United States and the United Kingdom first began to inspect Libyan nuclear weapons sites and laboratories that were used for the nuclear program, and other military facilities. These initial visits provided concrete evidence that the Libyans had engaged in a far more extensive WMD effort (both nuclear and chemical weapons) than was previously concluded.[20] Further, these inspection visits coincided with further evidence that the sanctions may finally have had an effect on the progress of the Libyan nuclear program. In 2003, while U.S. and U.K. officials were conducting their visits, a shipment bound for Tripoli that was carrying uranium enrichment centrifuge equipment was interdicted in Taranto, Italy.[21]

Tracing the Theoretical Mechanisms

What eventually was successful in accomplishing the seemingly impossible? My theory of nuclear reversal identifies two primary reasons why Libya ultimately reversed its nuclear course. First, Libya was offered a set of political, economic, and military inducements, including the partial lifting of previously applied sanctions, to encourage negotiations. Second, bargaining with Libya occurred with a background threat of a military attack, already made credible given the Bush Administration's decision to invade Iraq over concerns over Saddam Hussein's WMD program. Qaddafi was faced with a critical choice. Rather than continue to invest in a desired but unsuccessful nuclear program and face escalatory punishments, he could stop the program and receive the resulting political and economic benefits.

This choice ultimately prompted Qaddafi to reassess his nuclear ambitions and respond to international pressure, primarily through negotiations with the United Kingdom and the United States on how to settle the Pan Am bombing dispute. Trilateral bargaining provided Libya with the opportunity both to rehabilitate its international image and to address the proliferation issue more concretely. According to the agreement, Libya was to admit responsibility for the Lockerbie bombing and pay compensation to the families of the victims. In exchange, the U.S. cancelled sanctions against Qaddafi, announced the resumption of full diplomatic relations with Libya, and removed it from a list of states that sponsored and supported terrorism.[22] Perhaps most importantly, however, the agreement provided the perfect context for negotiating Libya's nuclear reversal. Libya's promise to abandon its nuclear pursuit, and surrender nuclear-related equipment and ballistic missiles with ranges greater than 300 km to the U.S., facilitated the initial Lockerbie negotiations and resulted in Libya's reemergence into the international community.[23] The promise of economic assistance, international recognition, and re-entrance into the international system, coupled with the assurance that his regime would survive, prompted Qaddafi to renounce his nuclear ambitions and reverse the weapons program.

The United States' actions in Iraq in the recent past played a significant role by projecting a grim future for Qaddafi and Libya if the U.S. chose to continue its counterproliferation efforts through force in the region. If the U.S. was ostensibly willing to engage in costly military action to forcibly stop Iraq's purported nuclear weapons, they would certainly be willing to do so in Libya—or so Qaddafi thought. Fearing that his regime may soon be the target of preemptive military action from the United States as part of a broader counterproliferation strategy (as was the pretext for the Iraq War where the United States argued that use of military force was justified to stop Iraq's development of weapons of mass destruction), Libya ultimately reversed its nuclear program. For Qaddafi, a military strike against Libya suddenly became a very real possibility—one that conditioned how both Libya and the United States approached negotiations for nuclear reversal. Again, as my theory would predict, the fear of a military attack, as a means to permanently end a weapons program, operated in the background to encourage Qaddafi to negotiate ending the nuclear program and ultimately dismantle decades worth of effort.

Despite Libya's commitment to the acquisition of nuclear weapons, Qaddafi ultimately decided to accept a negotiated settlement offered by the United States and Great Britain to permanently dismantle Libya's nuclear weapons program. This instance of nuclear reversal helps to illustrate an important distinction among nuclear proliferators: sometimes, even states that have significant sunk costs after thirty or more years of nuclear pursuit are *still* susceptible to nuclear negotiations. This case also marked a significant success for the nonproliferation regime. According to Qaddafi's son Seif al Islam, British Prime Minister Tony Blair pleaded with Gaddafi to not delay the deal, stating, "please, we are in a hurry. It is a big success for all of us."[24] Libya's nuclear tale provides a useful example of one of the most interesting and counter-intuitive reversal stories. An effective counterproliferation strategy coerced one of the most determined, and adversarial, of proliferators to abandon a lengthy nuclear program.

Thus, this case provides important support for a core theoretical implication of this book: all types of proliferators *can* be incentivized to abandon their nuclear efforts. Second, the Libyan nuclear counterproliferation case highlights my findings regarding the limitations of alternative explanations, such as the use of economic sanctions or threats of military force used in isolation. When used without a parallel rewards strategy, Qaddafi remained unconvinced about abandoning his decades-long nuclear pursuit. Yet, by tracing both the technical and political processes by which the Libyans reversed their nuclear program, I find further causal support for my core argument (and related probabilistic condition). Even states with divergent preferences to the United States can be persuaded to abandon their nuclear weapons programs if approached with both positive and negative inducements, in the shadow of military force. In the next case study, I examine what happens when some of these conditions are not present.

China (1955–Present): Opportunity and Willingness

China's path to proliferation is different from that of Libya or of other proliferators within the nuclear club. The Chinese faced very little overt opposition in their nuclear trajectory. While the use of military force was briefly considered by the United States as a means to counter China's proliferation, the U.S. did not believe that they could successfully coerce the Chinese without the support of the Soviets—a cooperative overture that seemed improbable. With no clear U.S. counterproliferation strategy, the Chinese successfully acquired nuclear weapons.

The People's Republic of China first publicly announced its decision to pursue nuclear weapons in 1955 under the guidance and direction of the Soviet Union. There is some evidence to suggest that the Sino-Soviet nuclear relationship actually began in 1951 when the two states signed an agreement in which China provided uranium ore in exchange for Soviet assistance in pursuing a nuclear weapons program. Yet, most observers attribute the start of the program to the Chinese decision to develop a strategic nuclear force under the guise of pursuing peaceful uses of nuclear energy.[25] The program was included in a Twelve-Year Science Plan that would establish the Ministry of Nuclear Industry which would immediately begin the construction of a gas-diffusion uranium enrichment plant for producing weapons-grade uranium. Indeed, the evidence suggests that initially, acquiring a nuclear weapons deterrent was not necessarily their highest priority. As Peking (now Beijing) pursued nuclear weapons without significant opposition from the international community, Chinese leaders did not necessarily see the initial development of the nuclear arsenal as integral to their security and survival.

China's initial desire to acquire nuclear weapons was in part to augment their conventional capability and to protect against the unknown possibility of a U.S. strike during the Korean War. Further, the Chinese were seemingly motivated by the 1954–1955 confrontation with the United States over the Quemoy and Matsu Islands in the Taiwan Strait.[26] Concerns about a growing American presence in its neighborhood, as well as an interest in growing China's status as a regional and major world power, prompted Mao Zedong to begin to consider a modest nuclear capability. By January 1955, in the midst of the crisis in Taiwan Strait, Mao ordered a full-scale effort to establish China as a nuclear power.[27] A removal of these security concerns could conceivably have persuaded the Chinese to focus their resources and energy on strengthening conventional capabilities and to abandon their nuclear program. Despite their status as a growing regional power, Chinese officials saw nuclear weapons primarily as a means to a strategic end. While Mao believed that nuclear weapons could help China's international status, an analysis of the historical record reveals that China saw other advancements, particularly in military modernization and power projection in space, as similarly important contributions to Chinese prestige.[28] Thus, evidence suggests that China's proliferation was due to both "opportunity" and "willingness."

Indeed, the Chinese program began because of offers of assistance and guidance from the Soviets as part of the growing relationship between the two Communist states. In the 1950s, the Chinese and Soviets signed an agreement that provided the Chinese with new technology and a guarantee of Soviet nuclear assistance in designing and manufacturing nuclear weapons, in addition to supplying a sample atomic bomb.[29] While the overwhelming Soviet support for the Chinese has been attributed to "Nikita Khrushchev's romantic belief in world socialist revolution, and the strength of the Sino-Soviet alliance," recent evidence suggests that the Soviets, though initially hesitant to help Chinese proliferation attempts, were persuaded by the post-Stalin power struggle that required support from Mao.[30] As a result, the Soviets helped construct a research reactor and a cyclotron, assisted in cooperative uranium prospecting and mining, and helped establish the Eastern Atomic Energy Institute in nuclear technology training.[31] This type of support continued through 1957 when the Soviets supplied the Chinese with a host of sensitive nuclear assistance—in uranium enrichment, plutonium reprocessing, warhead design and production, and missile development—in exchange for Mao's continued support for Khrushchev. In addition, the Second Taiwan Strait Crisis in 1958 reaffirmed Mao's belief that his decision to wholeheartedly pursue a nuclear deterrent was the right decision. Within the next few years, Mao had established the Beijing Nuclear Weapons Research Institute (similar to Los Alamos Scientific Laboratory in the U.S.) as well as beginning construction of Baotou Nuclear Fuel Component Plant and Lanzhou Gaseous Diffusion Plant which helped produce an indigenous supply of enriched uranium.[32] Further, the Chinese began developing a plutonium reprocessing complex with Soviet assistance. Recently declassified documents reveal that by February 1960, "ground was broken for construction of a plutonium production reactor at the Jiuquan Atomic Energy Complex, which also contained key facilities involved in the final stages of producing China's atomic weapons."[33]

By the early 1960s, the United States was concerned that the Chinese were developing a nuclear weapons program. The efforts of the United States intelligence community indicated that while they knew about the construction of some of the facilities and nuclear activities, the extent of their progress was unknown. For example, according to declassified documents, while the U.S. intelligence community had photos of the Lanzhou plant in September 1959, and limited satellite imagery, the intelligence was far from specific.[34] This limited evidence was coupled with virtual silence from the Chinese about their nuclear infrastructure. Thus, the National Intelligence Estimate published in 1960 stated, "our evidence with respect to Communist China's nuclear program is fragmentary as is our information about the nature and extent of Soviet aid."[35]

Sino-Soviet relations began to cool during the next few years, eventually resulting in the withdrawal of Soviet advisors and the complete termination of nuclear assistance in the early 1960s.[36] President Kennedy hoped to use this wedge to reach out to Moscow to assess whether there may be opportunities for cooperation to restrain or reverse China's nuclear pursuit. However, when Premier Khrushchev arrived at a summit in June 1961 in Vienna, he seemed disinterested in working with the Americans on managing "Red China," perhaps hopeful that there may be an opportunity for reconciliation with China in the future.[37]

China, by then determined to pursue nuclear weapons, relied on domestic know-how and the indigenous development of facilities and acquisition of materials to build a viable weapons program. China successfully exploded its first atomic bomb in 1964 and launched its first nuclear missile in 1966. For the past half-century, the Chinese have proceeded to develop a highly advanced nuclear weapons program. And despite a brief slow-down in production during the Cultural Revolution, the Chinese have recently invested more capital into modernizing their arsenal, including the implementation of a sea-based nuclear force and warhead miniaturization.[38]

Why were the Chinese successful in their nuclear pursuit when so many other proliferators have not been? The historical record suggests that the U.S. was unwilling to approach the Chinese with an adequate set of rewards and sanctions. This position was exacerbated by the lack of a credible threat of military action if the Chinese persisted. This half-hearted counterproliferation approach by the U.S. did not sufficiently disincentivize Beijing from pursuing a nuclear weapons program. Recently declassified documents from the Kennedy and Johnson administrations, acquired from the National Security Archives, reveal the ambivalence and "policy of non-action" that the United States chose in addressing the increasingly likely Chinese acquisition of nuclear weapons.[39] The evidence suggests that although U.S. intelligence was relatively confident that China would successfully conduct a nuclear test in the early 1960s, it was much less certain about the appropriate course of action to contain or neutralize a Chinese nuclear capability.[40] Further, declassified documents from the Kennedy Administration reveal that given other priorities, such as Cuba and Berlin, that ranked higher on the administration's agenda, a nuclear-armed China was a less significant concern.

The Failure of the U.S. Approach: Why Counterproliferation Was Unsuccessful

In January 1963, advisors to President Kennedy suggested that the U.S. cooperate with Moscow to "compel China to stop nuclear development." The concern was that a nuclear China, and the potential threat of a nuclear Germany, would form the basis for an anti-U.S. alliance. For a state like China, for whom nuclear weapons were desired but not required, the use of military force would likely have promptly and permanently shut down the program. Yet, for the United States, the leader in counterproliferation at the time, military intervention was clearly not an option. Without at least implicit international support, ideally from the Soviets, the U.S. could not undertake a strategy that would involve a military strike on Chinese nuclear facilities. This option was deemed to be too costly and, in the end, the U.S. maintained the status quo by opting to do nothing.

After months of inaction and ambivalence about how to manage the Chinese nuclear pursuit—whether to use military force or enter into a tenuous political alliance with the Soviets—the administration began to entertain the hope that a nuclear China may not act as recklessly or belligerently as predicted.[41] Rather, the United States became focused on attempting to mitigate the *consequences* of a Chinese nuclear deterrent. While agreeing that the successful "attainment of a nuclear capability will have a marked impact on the security posture of the United States and the Free World, particularly in Asia," it was not immediately clear what the U.S. strategy was toward China. For the most part, the U.S. was focused on the potential domino effects of Chinese proliferation and whether "other nations might enter the field if only to counter the power and prestige which their rivals or their enemies might gain."[42] Recently declassified CIA documents suggest that Washington was concerned that "even a small increase in the number of nations possessing nuclear weapons will add to the dangers inherent in critical situations when they arise," potentially incentivizing irrational or risky behavior throughout the international system.[43] Thus, by 1964, the United States had ostensibly run out of time to prevent Chinese proliferation and had "fully anticipated the possibility of Peking's entry into the nuclear weapons field and had taken it into full account in determining our military posture."[44]

My theory of nuclear reversal is helpful in understanding why proliferation was successful in China. First, perhaps as a result of poor intelligence or more pressing priorities, the United States failed to propose a coherent, comprehensive strategy to deal with the nascent Chinese nuclear program. Recently declassified documents reveal that as late as February 1963, the Assistant Secretary of Defense for International Security Affairs, Paul Nitze, requested a study for how to employ "persuasion, pressure, or coercion" to induce China to sign a test ban treaty (effectively precluding the possibility of China verifying its nuclear capacity). By April, the Joint Chiefs of Staff at the Pentagon replied with a report on some possible measures, both direct and indirect (like diplomacy and propaganda) that could be used to induce China to abandon its nuclear effort. However, while the study was being assembled, some intelligence sources reported that the Chinese were already close to a successful detonation. CIA analysts believed that the Chinese were likely to have a successful nuclear test as early as 1964 or 1965 (if there were any normal delays in the process).[45] The CIA report also raised the possibility of another undisclosed plutonium reactor that could allow the Chinese a successful "first detonation at any time."[46] Yet, despite this mounting evidence of successful Chinese nuclear proliferation, the U.S. failed to develop an inducements-based strategy that could coerce or compel the Chinese to stop its nuclear pursuit.

Second, despite earlier considerations of the use of military force (primarily with Soviet assistance), the United States failed to credibly signal that they were willing to attack Chinese nuclear facilities to forcibly stop their nuclear progress. According to declassified documents, President Kennedy and other senior administration officials "were considering how to rein in, even 'take out,' China's nuclear program. With Sino-Soviet hostility increasing, Kennedy hoped that he could enlist Khrushchev's support."[47] Yet, there was significant doubt from the Joint Chiefs of Staff (JCS). Acting Chairman, Curtis LeMay, argued that it is "unrealistic to use overt military force against China" and even if an agreement could be reached after an attack, there was little to suggest that the Chinese would actually abide by it.[48] The JCS report also warned about the ramifications of unilateral military force (ranging from blockades to air strikes). This type of action could prompt retaliation or escalation against U.S. bases in Taiwan and would elicit international outrage. Soviet cooperation on U.S. air strikes against Chinese nuclear facilities may "well be the difference between escalation and quick acquiescence by the Chicoms."[49] Throughout 1963 and early 1964, the U.S. continued to reach out to the Soviets to assess their temperature on a joint Soviet-U.S. response to the Chinese nuclear threat. Despite some initial interest from Premier Khrushchev, it was clear that the Soviets were ultimately not interested. Thus, a viable plan never emerged, and U.S. policymakers were left to identify the costs and benefits of pursuing a unilateral military approach. An Office of Policy Planning and Coordination study, led by Robert Johnson (one of the leading China experts during the Kennedy and Johnson administrations), summarized the analysis by arguing that preventive military force against the Chinese nuclear weapons program was "dangerous and likely to fail and that it could hurt the United States' image and weaken its prestige, the intangible assets of world power."[50] The report concluded that preventive military force was "undesirable except possibly as part of general action . . . in response to major ChiCom aggression."[51] Within the next few months, the issue was moot. By the end of 1964, China successfully verified its nuclear capability with a detonation.

Though outside the scope of this study, another important question emerges: why did the U.S. not develop an effective strategy to deal with the Chinese nuclear threat before it was too late? There are several reasons why the United States failed to articulate a coherent plan. First, it is likely that the U.S. delayed acting to stop China's acquisition of nuclear weapons technology because it lacked a strong ally in the Soviet Union and did not want to engage China without assistance from the Soviets (who at the time of China's proliferation would also have preferred to shut the door on the nuclear club). Second, the evidence further suggests that, although the U.S. was concerned about the prospect of a nuclear-armed China, it was also worried about the proliferation repercussions throughout Asia. A nuclear China could provoke India to seek the bomb (as turned out to be the case a decade later in 1974) or could help provide order and peace to the region by discouraging arms races and deterring reactive proliferation. And lastly, the emergence of China as a de jure nuclear weapons state and a new leader in the international community prompted other states to balance China's growing power by acquiring nuclear weapons, sparking an arms race in East and South Asia. Intelligence documents indicate that United States Air Force planners advocated dispersing nuclear weapons to U.S. allies and potential allies in the region, including India, in contravention to the Johnson administration's growing policy preference for global nonproliferation.[52] This inherent policy tension, and the lack of viable partners with whom to cooperate to incentivize reversal, may have stunted and ultimately prevented the U.S. and other members of the international community from effectively responding to the increasing likelihood of a nuclear China.

Though an unknown counterfactual, one could argue that it may have been possible that a commitment by the United States to help strengthen conventional forces or address regional tensions could have slowed Chinese proliferation or potentially stopped it altogether. Instead, it is likely that the U.S. inadvertently fueled these security concerns by extending a nuclear umbrella to some of China's regional opponents, strengthening Chinese claims that their need for nuclear weapons was truly motivated by hostile neighbors and all but ensuring China's continuation to a nuclear weapons state.[53]

What then can we glean from the analysis of the Chinese nuclear case? My theory provides a useful means with which to explain why the Chinese were able to successfully acquire a nuclear deterrent without exogenous pressure from the international community. It is possible that if the U.S. had pursued nuclear negotiations using a combinative strategy of both positive and negative inducements, it may have been able to prevent China from acquiring nuclear weapons—even if the U.S. was unwilling to resort to the use of force to do so without Soviet assistance. Historically, this counterproliferation failure stems from an oft-incorrect conventional wisdom that adversaries should primarily receive the negative end of the inducements stick and that coercion must be at the top of the menu of options to deal with these proliferators. Yet, from recently declassified documents, a different picture emerges. It is conceivable, though impossible to test, that if President Kennedy or President Johnson had followed through on suggestions from analysts and policymakers within the administration to establish a China counterproliferation strategy that privileged the use of both positive and negative inducements (including the possibility of issuing a credible threat of force), things may have turned out differently. This type of counterproliferation approach, useful for both friends *and* foes, could have influenced nuclear decision-making and prevented the Chinese acquisition of nuclear weapons.

Concluding Remarks

It is no surprise that the paths to pursue and relinquish nuclear weapons are varied and somewhat idiosyncratic. However, by examining key archetypes of nuclear reversal, both successes and failures, we may begin to see a broader picture of the role of the international community in incentivizing states to renounce their nuclear ambitions. In this chapter, I presented two descriptive case studies to explore how coercive rewards and punishments have shaped two states' proliferation and reversal histories. Using the theoretical framework presented in Chapter 2, I examine cases in which states with divergent preferences to that of the United States, chose to reverse or maintain a nuclear pursuit. In one case (Libya), the potential for military force against its nascent nuclear program was present and proved useful in counterproliferation. With the Chinese case, I analyze the other side of the spectrum where the U.S. lacked the resolve to issue a threat of game-ending military force to effectively persuade the proliferator to accept the negotiated settlement and end its nuclear program. Some interesting implications emerge from these two vignettes.

First, there is wide variance in the types of states that start and reverse their nuclear programs. Each state has different motivations for its initial proliferation decisions and the conditions under which it is willing to abandon its efforts. Surveying the historical record provides a useful baseline by which to see how inducements, threats of military force, and the proliferator's relationship with the U.S. work to reverse nuclear weapons programs. Here we see that, without the threat of military force looming in the background of negotiations, inducements offered may not yield the same political weight as if the U.S. were able to threaten preventive war if the state were to continue to proliferate.

Second, and relatedly, these illustrations highlight the need for a combinative approach of positive and negative inducements to persuade leaders, even those as intransigent as Muammar Qaddafi. These inducements both serve as compensation for stopping their weapons program as well as necessary political cover for leaders, even autocrats like Qaddafi, who still require domestic victories to retain power.

Lastly, theoretical considerations and empirical evidence help us to understand instances of counterproliferation failure. Unlike other theories of proliferation and counterproliferation, my theory of nuclear reversal helps analysts and policymakers better understand why attempts to persuade leaders to abandon their nuclear programs may fail and to learn from these historical anomalies. Lessons from the Chinese proliferation case, for example, suggest that if the United States feels ambivalence or is unwilling to fully commit to stopping nuclear weapons programs through any means necessary (i.e., military force or even siding with political opponents), there is a greater likelihood of successful proliferation.

The next three chapters further explore these dynamics in some of the most interesting and important proliferation cases from the historical record: the Indian, Iranian, and North Korean nuclear programs. In each, the theoretical framework presented in Chapter 2 provides a crucial vantage point from which to understand why nuclear negotiations were ultimately unsuccessful in India but proved successful in Iran. It concludes with an examination of the North Korean case, which remains the greatest nonproliferation challenge that the international community faces today.

India: Erstwhile Ally and Nuclear Reversal

Introduction

The analysis in this book thus far has centered on examining broader patterns among the universe of states that have pursued nuclear weapons programs and the external inducements most useful in motivating nuclear reversal. While such analysis of the historical record is helpful as we attempt to understand the full scope of nuclear weapons activity and abandonment, it is necessary to investigate individual cases in depth to identify causal mechanisms at play and to ensure that this study and its findings pass the burden of proof in critical cases.

In Chapters 5-7, I delve into three specific cases, the Indian, Iranian, and North Korean nuclear programs, to examine these processes in detail. I consider these cases for several reasons. First, India provides the opportunity for an intra-case comparison. I can examine India's program prior to the Peaceful Nuclear Explosion (PNE) in 1974, upon which the United States was successful in motivating India to halt its nuclear progress, and in the lead-up to the 1998 nuclear tests that announced India's successful proliferation. This form of comparison provides a quasi-matched design approach that allows me to examine two closely related instances of Indian decision-making and to determine why the extension of inducements, despite initial success, ultimately failed to prevent India's acquisition of nuclear weapons.

Second, despite key distinctions described in what follows (including the fact that Iran signed the Nonproliferation Treaty while India did not), India and Iran have similarities that enable an inter-state comparison. First, both countries' pursuit of nuclear weapons was similarly driven by external security concerns, by a desire for regional hegemony, a search for national prestige and a military-bureaucratic complex. While keeping other potential domestic factors that may have independently impacted the likelihood of nuclear reversal "constant," these historical narratives are able to illustrate the causal mechanisms at play in

Delaying Doomsday, Rupal N. Mehta. Oxford University Press (2020). © Oxford University Press.
DOI: 10.1093/oso/9780190077976.001.0001

actual strategic interactions between the United States and these proliferators. In doing so, we can better understand how the international community provided inducements to persuade proliferators to give up their nuclear weapons programs, and why these strategies worked in one instance and failed in the other.

Third, analyses of the Indian, Iranian, and North Korean cases represent three of the core types of proliferators examined in my theoretical framework. India represents a friendly, erstwhile ally (officially neutral) state against whom the United States had little desire to use military force to address its proliferation concern, despite the potential for diffusion to other states in the region. Iran illustrates how a perennial adversary to the United States, if offered a combination of rewards and sanctions, with a looming threat of military force, can still be persuaded to abandon its weapons program. And finally, North Korea represents one of the most challenging cases that the United States (and the broader nonproliferation community) has faced: an adversary who is unpersuaded by multiple packages of inducements offered by the U.S. over time, and who faces no viable threat of military force.

Lastly, these cases signify some of the most salient examples for policymakers in the United States, and the international community more broadly, since the introduction of nuclear weapons in the international system. India's nuclear proliferation is considered one of the biggest failures for the global nonproliferation regime, especially given its immediate domino effect on Pakistan's proliferation. Iran's recent nuclear agreement may signify the most important (temporary) success in counterproliferation in recent memory while North Korea's belligerence in light of decades of effort by the U.S. to reverse its nuclear course remains the greatest challenge to the nonproliferation regime.

These case studies rely on both primary- and secondary-source data collected through archival research and interviews. Specifically, I use new archival data gathered from documents at the National Security Archives, the Foreign Relations of the United States, the U.S. Department of State, and other primary-source archival sites. These primary-source documents are supplemented with secondary-source literature and historical evidence on these countries and their relationships with the United States. The interview-based data come from extensive interviews I conducted in 2017 and 2018 in Vienna, Paris, and Washington, D.C., with policymakers from Iran, Pakistan, Argentina, and the U.S.; officials associated with the International Atomic Energy Agency (IAEA); and American and European analysts that were integral to the JCPOA negotiations during the period 2013–2015, as well as ongoing discussions with North Korea.[1] I also rely on various methodological tools to further evaluate the large-*n* statistical findings in order to assess the causal mechanisms outlined in Chapter 2.

What follows is the first of these critical cases: the successful Indian program to acquire nuclear weapons after a quarter-century-long hiatus and a temporary success in counterproliferation. The nuclear weapons test in May 1998, cele-brated throughout the country, came as a shock to the United States. There had been some indications that India was interested in acquiring a nuclear capability ever since it conducted a Peaceful Nuclear Explosion in 1974 after two decades of pursuing a primarily civilian nuclear program. But the United States' strategy for countering India's proliferation was at times half-hearted, though still aimed at ensuring a nuclear-free South Asian subcontinent.

Yet, if examined in the context of my theoretical framework, the fact that India did in fact succeed in acquiring nuclear weapons may not be that surprising. An analysis of the Indian case allows us to delve deeply into one of the four core types derived in the theoretical framework presented in Chapter 2. In this type of proliferation with low U.S. resolve for military force, the size of rewards and scope of punishments necessary to incentivize nuclear reversal should be con-siderable, in dealing with friendly states which do not expect escalatory punish-ment if they persist. In theory, they could have been adequately incentivized to reverse or abandon nuclear programs given their proximate relationships with the United States and their satisfaction with a U.S.-led international system. Under this logic, India represents an important counterproliferation failure.

Importantly, however, the first half of the Indian case operates as my theory predicts. The Indians began to engage in nuclear weapons activity, as part of Eisenhower's Atoms for Peace program that eventually raised concerns and suspicions in the American intelligence community that the Indians might be moving toward a weapons option. After the PNE in 1974, a confirmation of India's mixed intentions, the U.S. responded with a strategy of rewards and lim-ited sanctions—without a background threat of military force if the Indians con-tinued. And as my logic suggests, the Indians were willing to, and did for almost a quarter century, abandon their nuclear efforts out of fear of endangering an already tense relationship with the United States.

However, despite this initial success, the story did not end happily. The Indians opted to restart and ramp up their nuclear weapons pursuit in the early 1990s. While India's relatively friendly relationship with the United States had not dramatically evolved, its relationship with neighbors had heightened its se-curity concerns and the U.S. offer of rewards were not sufficient to compensate for a lost nuclear deterrent. And without a credible threat of an attack on their nuclear facilities or other escalatory punishments, economic sanctions alone, es-pecially without parallel rewards, no longer intimidated Indian leaders. Within the decade, India progressed to a de facto nuclear weapons state, with a series of nuclear tests in May 1998. The United States' inability to counter India's prolifer-ation attempt stems from two key factors: (1) insufficient rewards and sanctions, especially during frequent leadership changes throughout the 1980s and early 1990s; and (2) relatively low resolve to effectively counter the spread of nuclear weapons to the subcontinent. Indeed, India's successful nuclear weapons acquisition and its rise to prominence as a de facto nuclear weapons state—in contravention to the nonproliferation regime and the NPT—represents one of the biggest failures in global counterproliferation policy. India ultimately was able to build nuclear weapons because the United States did not pursue the necessary dual-track strategy of engagement and pressure. Indeed, this case exemplifies an important and unfortunate implication when examining the universe of nuclear reversal: not all nuclear proliferation can be prevented.

In this chapter, I examine efforts by the United States to pressure the Indians to alter their nuclear intentions through the offer of rewards and the threat of punishments. This analysis yields support for my theoretical framework: a combinative strategy of rewards and sanctions successfully influenced India's path to proliferation by inducing a temporary delay in nuclear development. This within-case analysis allows me to rule out the null hypothesis—that the international community cannot impact domestic nuclear decision-making—as well as some alternative explanations. It also provides support for my core logic in that rewards and sanctions contributed to a pause in India's nuclear development from 1974 to 1998.

This intra-state variation case study also provides an in-depth, nuanced analysis of the causal mechanisms at play in the international community's application of pressure in the lead-up to India's successful acquisition of nuclear weapons in 1998. Through this analysis, we can examine why the United States' subsequent attempt to discourage India from acquiring nuclear weapons, when there is no option to employ a credible threat of military force, was unsuccessful. As the U.S. would not resort to the use of force (given its strategic interests in India in attempting to sway India to become an ally during the Cold War), and did not offer an appropriate package of rewards and sanctions to compensate for a lost nuclear deterrent, India felt little pressure to comport with the United States' lukewarm tactics. Ultimately, the United States' half-hearted strategy for inducing nuclear reversal led to nuclearization in both India and Pakistan, a significant blow to the nonproliferation regime. I conclude with the implications of this counterproliferation failure with some thoughts on the future of U.S.-India relations.

India's Nuclear Rise

In Search of an Indian Bomb: 1948-1974

India's early nuclearization was the result of both external conditions and domestic pressures to build an effective nuclear deterrent against foreign aggressors. As a new nation with rivalries on borders with China and Pakistan,

India's decision to pursue nuclear weapons seemed unsurprising. The scholarship on the causes of India's nuclear proliferation suggests that states searching to maintain their security and survival might pursue nuclear weapons to ward against the potential for foreign aggression or assist in the event of conflict with an adversary, especially if they have the latent capacity to do so.[2] India's ultimate decision to develop a nuclear capability, no doubt, was fueled in part by a desire to protect its sovereign territory from potential incursions by China and Pakistan, with whom it had a history of tension and conflict.[3]

Though not existential to India's survival, the threats from its neighbors played a key role in the decision to move from a strictly civilian program to a weapons program. Analysis of Indian nuclear decision-making reveals that New Delhi's decision to pursue nuclear weapons was clearly influenced by China's rise as a regional nuclear power in Asia. Indeed, it was during this time that the growing threat from China (especially in the wake of the Indo-Chinese border war of 1962) prompted the Indians to reexamine their decision to remain a solely civilian nuclear power, and to seriously, though secretly, embark on a nuclear weapons program. According to Brahma Chellaney, one of the authors of India's nuclear doctrine, "the humiliating rout in the 1962 war with China is deeply embedded in the Indian psyche. No other event in independent India has cast so much influence on national planning or on the shape of long-term goals and strategies."[4] China's growing territorial threat, and its rapid military buildup and modernization in the nuclear era sparked urgency among Indian military planners to accelerate their work on a nuclear program to better counter Chinese capabilities.[5]

Furthermore, Pakistan's presence on the western border posed a risk to India's security that was not to be underestimated. Pakistan represented an equally proximate threat to India's security, especially given its history of rivalry and militarized disputes with India, and its own political and military instability. India's desire to deter continued aggression that could have potentially devastating consequences for the subcontinent, prompted the move from a civilian nuclear energy program to one that sought to develop nuclear weapons that would deter territorial threats from its neighbors. Thus, after making the decision to transition to a weapons program, India established the nuclear explosive design group, Study of Nuclear Explosions for Peaceful Purposes (SNEPP), an India-based organization that was dedicated to developing a nuclear explosive device that would use plutonium from a newly constructed separation and reprocessing plant.[6]

There were other factors that helped the Indians in their pursuit and eventual acquisition of a nuclear device. In addition to a strong technological infrastructure that facilitated the quick and sustained development of a civilian, and then weapons program, the Indians had early assistance from the international community, primarily existing nuclear weapons states like the United States, the United Kingdom, and France. The origins of India's nuclear weapons program began with the establishment of the Tata Institute for Fundamental Research (TIFR) in December 1945 and formalized with the Atomic Energy Act of 1948.[7]

This domestic initiative was heavily influenced and supported by President Eisenhower's Atoms for Peace Plan which began as a bold endeavor to "hasten the day when fear of the atom will begin to disappear from the minds of people" and to encourage the spread of nuclear technology and fissionable materials to build nuclear power reactors under adequate IAEA safeguards.[8] Indeed, South Asia became Washington's top priority in curbing nuclearization through the promotion of peaceful nuclear energy. Two National Security Council policy directives, NSC 5409 (U.S. Policy Toward South Asia) and NSC 5507/2 (Peaceful Uses of Atomic Energy), simultaneously aimed to support strong stable governments in a key Cold War battleground (the South Asian subcontinent) and would be instrumental in promoting global and regional interests of the United States by providing sensitive nuclear assistance. With this U.S. policy, India became one of the first recipients of nuclear technology under the Atoms for Peace Plan with the purchase of ten tons of heavy water for use in the CIRUS reactor.[9] The United States remained eager to please the Indians as "the USSR and Communist China will focus increasing attention on India in an effort to insure [*sic*] at least its continued neutralism, and if possible to bring it closer to the Communist Bloc."[10]

Despite Prime Minister Jawaharlal Nehru's role as a key leader of the nuclear disarmament movement, he refused to foreclose the nuclear option. Instead, he moved the nuclear program in the direction that would ultimately lead to the development of a nuclear weapons arsenal, ironically with the assistance of the United States. By 1955, with additional assistance from the British and the Canadians, India had built two research reactors. The CIRUS reactor, purchased from the Canadians, marked a turning point in India's nuclear program and for international proliferation more broadly. Though it was meant for peaceful purposes, the transaction took place before the establishment of any international policies to regulate technology transfer or to set provisions for inspections. To ensure independence, India created a program to manufacture natural uranium fuel for the CIRUS reactor indigenously and maintain complete control of the production cycle.

Over the next decade, the United States remained India's leading supplier of nuclear technology and materials—over $93 million in loans and grants through Atoms for Peace program—after persistent lobbying by Dr. Homi Bhabha.[11] Yet, this relationship was not without its challenges. Bhabha often rejected U.S. assistance in order to bargain for more advanced technologies from them (or other nuclear suppliers). Requests for sensitive nuclear assistance, including the joint development of uranium resources, became more frequent until the United States ultimately declared that it was "emphatically not interested" in helping the Indians expand into a weapons program.[12] Indeed, during the early era of sensitive nuclear assistance, the U.S. never suspected that the Indians were trying to produce a nuclear device or that they were well on their way to being able to do so by 1974.

During this period, the United States was focused on arms control and curbing the Soviet sphere of influence. Offering civilian nuclear assistance around the world was a means of accomplishing these goals. Evidence supports much of the existing literature on the role of sensitive nuclear assistance, by the Americans and the Canadians, as a means to providing civilian nuclear cooperation in lieu of military assistance. This support was also aimed at preventing the Soviets from providing nuclear reactors that would have moved India from a non-nuclear state to a proliferator interested in acquiring nuclear weapons.[13] Though this program predated the "grand bargain" of the Nonproliferation Treaty, it aimed to fulfill the same promise. If states would forgo the pursuit and acquisition of nuclear weapons, they would receive nuclear power technology, materials, and assistance from the existing nuclear weapons powers, such as the United States and United Kingdom. President Eisenhower stated,

> The more important responsibility of this Atomic Energy Agency would be to devise methods whereby this fissionable material would be allocated to serve the peaceful pursuits of mankind. Experts would be mobilized to apply atomic energy to the needs of agriculture, medicine, and other peaceful activities. A special purpose would be to provide abundant electrical energy in the power-starved areas of the world. Thus, the contributing powers would be dedicating some of their strength to serve the needs rather than the fears of mankind.[14]

The exchange of materials, technology, and expertise between the U.S. and India was specifically designed to prevent the spread of nuclear weapons technology. But as is often argued, the transfer of civilian nuclear technology actually worked to reduce the costs of proliferation to recipients of the Atoms for Peace program.[15] In the case of India and the United States, the agreement to help develop a civilian nuclear program, in exchange for not pursuing nuclear weapons, was first challenged when India sought to purchase nuclear materials from other suppliers by circumventing the assistance arrangement with the United States. Nuclear cooperation was aimed to be a form of nonproliferation concession meant to prevent India from seeking a nuclear weapons deterrent. Unfortunately, this was not a successful strategy.

While this cooperation was not taken as an indication at the time of India's potential interest in acquiring dual-use technology for the purpose of acquiring nuclear weapons, India, from among the cohort of other recipients of Atoms for Peace program, may have set itself apart by revealing information about its preferences. In the midst of the Cold War and Prime Minister Nehru's stance on remaining non-aligned, the U.S. aimed to maintain India's support, even though they remained hesitant to assist the Indians in their nuclear development. A report of the Gilpatric Committee on Nuclear Proliferation advised a strong stance on nonproliferation, even with strategic allies, to President Johnson in 1965.[16] While nonproliferation had been a key aspect of U.S. foreign policy, it came distinctly second to strengthening the defenses of key non-communist nations (through, for example, a Multi-Lateral Force proposal to share nuclear weapons with NATO allies). The United States' and the broader international community's dual and perhaps conflicting preferences (nonproliferation and winning over the non-aligned) indeed may have contributed to India's decision to begin an indigenous weapons program with limited assistance from other states such as France and Canada.[17]

Additionally, these competing preferences signaled the first signs of what would be the United States' approach in curbing proliferation in the subcontinent. Through these interactions, New Delhi was beginning to learn that the United States would never consider nor use military force to stop India's nuclear program—the Indians were far too important in the fight against the Soviet Union—and that the U.S. was resolved to provide some degree of incentives to prevent India from going down the nuclear weapons path. These lessons structured the ensuing strategic interactions between New Delhi and Washington. With little fear of severe punishment from the United States, the Indians were able to continue their efforts relatively unencumbered. Indeed, by the time the NPT was created and ratified by a vast majority of nations by the early 1970s, India refused to sign it and was well on its way to its first nuclear test.

Rise, and Temporary Fall, of the Nuclear State: 1974–1998

Despite early ambivalence about the value of nuclear weapons (and delays in production during the Lal Bahadur Shastri administration), India turned a corner in its nuclear intentions by the early 1970s. Growing tensions with Pakistan, especially after the war with West Pakistan in 1965 and the Indo-Pakistani War of 1971, led the new Indira Gandhi regime to a resurgence in India's desire to proliferate.[18] This renewed interest was facilitated by the Tata Institute for

Fundamental Research, established in 1945, to conduct scientific research on nuclear weapons; the creation of the Trombay Atomic Energy Establishment in 1954 that began to examine weapons design and production; and the Bhabha Atomic Research Centre tasked with manufacturing and testing a nuclear device. Ultimately, after more than thirty years of changing regimes and nuclear exploration, India finally entered the nuclear weapons club with a Peaceful Nuclear Explosion or PNE, named "Smiling Buddha."[19] On May 18, 1974, the Indian Department of Atomic Energy secretly detonated a nuclear device underground. The device was designed and manufactured by Indian scientists using facilities and materials in India, outside of international safeguards. According to the Indian government led by Prime Minister Indira Gandhi, it was also completely peaceful—it had no military or political implications for Pakistan or the international community more broadly.[20]

India's first public intimation of its nuclear intentions, following the 1974 Peaceful Nuclear Explosion, came at an unfortunate time for international nonproliferation efforts—only four years after the Nonproliferation Treaty (NPT) went into effect. Following in the path of the Atoms for Peace program, the NPT was designed to provide incentives for continued nonproliferation among nonnuclear weapons states. In particular, the "Grand Bargain" of the NPT had been designed to prevent further proliferation. In exchange for non-nuclear weapons states agreeing to forgo the acquisition of nuclear weapons and placing their facilities under international safeguards, they would receive limited assistance from nuclear weapons states for peaceful purposes. Article III Section 2 of the NPT specifies,

> The safeguards required by this article shall be implemented in a manner designed to comply with Article IV of this Treaty, and to avoid hampering the economic or technological development of the Parties or international cooperation in the field of peaceful nuclear activities, including the international exchange of nuclear material and equipment for the processing, use or production of nuclear material for peaceful purposes in accordance with the provisions of this article and the principle of safeguarding set forth in the Preamble of the Treaty.[21]

The nonproliferation regime, including the existing nuclear club, felt assured that if non-nuclear weapons states, such as India, Pakistan, or Israel, among others, were given the opportunity to develop a civilian nuclear energy program, they would be disinclined to pursue nuclear weapons indigenously and clandestinely. Within half a decade of the introduction of the NPT into the international system, the belief was that technology and materials control, and the denial of weapons-grade supplies, would not only deter the spread of weapons capability but also work to satisfy even the most interested and capable of potential proliferators (notwithstanding India's acquisition and test of a nuclear device).

India had opted not to sign or ratify the NPT, perhaps another sign of its less than benign intentions. India's transition from a civilian nuclear state to a nuclear weapons explorer, marked with the 1974 PNE, sparked alarm within the international community. Specifically, the United States became concerned about the continued proliferation of nuclear weapons to non-nuclear states within the confines of the nonproliferation regime, and alarmingly, with assistance from key nuclear suppliers.[22] India had not signed the treaty for what it claimed were political reasons. New Delhi argued that the treaty, by construction, created nuclear "haves" and "have-nots." The suddenness of Smiling Buddha suggested the possibility that the "grand bargain" of the NPT may not actually deter states from proliferating from even within the regime and that access to civilian nuclear technology was not a sufficient nonproliferation lever.

Indian diplomat Rikhi Jaipal argued at the time, that despite evidence to the contrary with the nuclear test, there was no reason to believe that India would seek to acquire nuclear weapons or would become a threat to any other country in the international community. He stated, "every Prime Minister of India since independence has reaffirmed India's opposition to the manufacture and use of nuclear weapons and has reiterated that India has no intention of manufacturing them. This is an important, well-established and consistent policy of the Indian Government, and it should be taken seriously."[23] The immediate response from New Delhi was that the international community should not fear India as a new nuclear weapons state but rather to take it in good faith that this nuclear detonation would not lead to the production of nuclear weapons. The Indians further argued that while the test may be surprising to the international community, it was actually not in violation of any international law or safeguards agreement. While they had been consistent recipients and beneficiaries of civilian nuclear technology, India had not signed or ratified the 1970 Nonproliferation Treaty that prohibited the development of nuclear weapons.[24] Because of this legal technicality that seemingly inoculated India from international reproach and punishment, and New Delhi's public declaration of its peaceful intentions, India was deemed to be a non-NPT nuclear weapons aspirant in 1974. According to the Indian Government, India had transitioned from a purely peaceful, civilian nuclear power to a state that was exploring ways to harness nuclear explosive power for peaceful *and* military purposes.

Not surprisingly, the international community did not perceive India's intentions to be quite so pure. The Smiling Buddha test had done little to instill confidence among the Pakistanis, the Chinese, or the international community that India had no ill-intentions and was not well on its way to becoming a full-fledged nuclear state with a growing arsenal and the capacity to deliver warheads against adversaries. Islamabad, for example, did not view the test as peaceful and canceled a series of talks planned to discuss normalization of relations between the two states. According to Prime Minister Zulfikar Ali Bhutto, "India's so-called Peaceful Nuclear Explosion (PNE) is tested and designed to intimidate and establish 'Indian hegemony in the subcontinent,' most particularly Pakistan."[25] The test appeared to heighten tensions on the subcontinent and threaten Pakistan's sense of survival. Furthermore, members of the Pakistani military-industrial complex, including Pakistan Atomic Energy Commission Chairman Munir Ahmed Khan and Pakistan's leading nuclear physicist, Pervez Hoodbhoy, argued that Smiling Buddha clearly and definitively nudged Pakistan into the nuclear arena, prompting Islamabad to develop and test its own nuclear bomb.[26]

The U.S. response was similarly skeptical. Prior to the test, the State Department's Bureau of Intelligence and Research (INR) as well as much of the intelligence community believed that an Indian nuclear program was a low priority that conveyed "no sense of urgency."[27] For nearly two years before the test, the topic "fell off the radar" in the U.S despite the fact that the INR bureau had predicted that India would be able to conduct an underground test without detection by the U.S. intelligence community.[28] This lack of attention to the Indian nuclear program reflected the interests and priorities of the American policymakers. The Nixon White House was primarily focused on the Vietnam War and maintaining a grand strategic advantage over both China and the Soviet Union. Gathering and analyzing intelligence on nuclear proliferation on the South Asian subcontinent was a lower priority. The United States preferred to maintain strong relationships with non-aligned states like India, despite their proliferation attempts, as a hedge against the USSR and China.

The Peaceful Nuclear Explosion in 1974 significantly damaged U.S.-India relations and the United States' relatively sanguine attitude toward nuclear development in South Asia. The response from Washington now included a series of punishing actions, including a ban on nuclear trade through the Nuclear Non-Proliferation Act of 1978 and the constitution of the Nuclear Suppliers Group, and a set of crippling sanctions.[29] However, the Carter Administration attempted to mute these punishments with civilian nuclear and conventional military assistance. President Jimmy Carter and Prime Minister Morarji Desai signed a Joint Communique outlining continued Indo-U.S. nuclear cooperation to support nonproliferation and disarmament. This deal was meant to encourage New Delhi to sign the Nonproliferation Treaty. In exchange for signing the NPT and stopping its nuclear program, the U.S. would assist India in developing its Tarapur atomic power station and would agree to sell anti-tank missiles worth $32 million. As a blow to both the Carter Administration's and the international community's hopes of countering the spread of nuclear weapons to the subcontinent, India famously resisted this attempt. New Delhi announced a "refusal to fall in line with President Carter's global crusade for 'full-scope' nuclear safeguards aborted much of the visit's expected success" during Carter's India visit in 1978.[30] Frustrated by this rebuff, "President Carter's disappointment at Desai's firm stand was given wide and embarrassing publicity following the leak of a recorded private conversation between President Carter and his Secretary of State, Cyrus Vance. President Carter was recorded as saying: 'When we get back, I think we ought to write him (Desai) another letter, very cold and very blunt.' "[31]

Furthermore, other evidence suggests that some within the U.S. government sought to mitigate India's concerns and provide assurances *in addition* to threats as potential means for achieving nuclear reversal.[32] Fearful of the potential implications of India's formal nuclearization on the subcontinent, U.S. policymakers began to discuss other possible avenues for approaching India to encourage nuclear reversal. For example, after China's first nuclear test in 1964, India suggested that if the Chinese failed to ratify the NPT, it would seek security guarantees from the United Nations, not the U.S. or the Soviet Union. While neither Washington nor Moscow was particularly interested in guaranteeing the security of non-nuclear states at that time, the U.S. did seek to assure the Indians that the U.S. would come to their aid in the event of a conflict with the Chinese (which coincided with American interests more broadly).[33] According to Secretary of State Dean Rusk,

India should know that possession of a nuclear weapons capability by Communist China will have no effect on readiness of U.S. to respond to Indian requests for help in dealing with Chicom aggression. We will meet our defense commitments to India. . . . Obviously we do not intend to stand by and watch India be threatened with nuclear destruction. U.S. support to India over the years against Communist China is well documented. President Eisenhower assured Prime Minister Nehru of our support when he visited New Delhi in 1959. Our response to India's request for help in 1962, with which you were clearly associated, speaks for itself. As Prime Minister is aware, following Nehru's request for U.S. manned aircraft to help India meet Chicom attack, U.S. carrier with attack aircraft was en route to Bay of Bengal when fighting ended in November of 1962. Our Air Defence Agreement of July 1963, in which we agreed to consult with [Government of India] GOI in the event of Chicom attack on India, is earnest of our intentions in future. So is agreement of November 1962 under which we currently are providing military assistance to India.[34]

Hindered by the sanctions imposed following the 1974 test, the restrictions on nuclear collaboration from the United States, and fearful of losing American support, Prime Minister Indira Gandhi rejected attempts to ramp up nuclear development and conduct another nuclear test. For example, during his visit to the U.S. to discuss the delivery of nuclear fuel for the Tarapur reactor, Foreign Minister M.K. Rasgotra was blindsided by the revelation of U.S. intelligence on future test preparations.[35] The U.S. made it clear that there would be additional economic reprisals if the Indians continued to conduct new nuclear tests. When briefed about this meeting and the U.S. intelligence on an upcoming test, Gandhi rescinded her approval of the test and refused to revisit the issue despite growing concerns from the military on the situation with Pakistan and their desire to focus on the nuclear option.[36]

This evidence also rules out some potential alternative explanations for nuclear reversal. India still faced growing security threats from Pakistan. The military-industrial complex continued to clamor for a nuclear deterrent and presented a unified front to the Prime Minister. And, the weapons establishment's obsession with nuclear technology for an indigenous nuclear program as a symbol of national pride persisted in spite of these obstacles. Yet, India stopped its nuclear development. My theory provides an explanation for this behavior and predicts that a proliferator like India would be receptive to incentives from the United States to discontinue its nuclear weapons program. As a friendly state with similar (though not necessarily convergent) preferences to the United States, where the use of military force was not truly a viable option, India should be motivated by a combinative strategy of rewards and sanctions. And in accord with this logic, the U.S. approach did successfully halt India's nuclear development, at least temporarily. Gandhi, and her short-term successors, suspended future nuclear development for nearly a decade for fear of the United States' unfavorable response.

Renewed Effort and the Path to Operation Shakti

Yet, by the early 1990s, India had renewed its nuclear weapons program and was rapidly approaching an operational nuclear weapon. The transition from Smiling Buddha to Operation Shakti marked a second critical moment in the United States' strategic interaction with New Delhi. During this interim period, India experienced several changes in leadership, with some leaders only lasting two years in office. While my theory would suggest that the U.S. take advantage of these leader transitions by offering inducements to stop their nuclear program, Washington did not approach the new prime ministers during this period to attempt to alter their nuclear decision-making. And upon Indira Gandhi's return to power in the mid-1980s, that door had seemingly closed. New Delhi expanded the scope of the nuclear program, ultimately confirming its nuclear intentions in 1986. Indira Gandhi's successor, her son Rajiv Gandhi, formally authorized India's nuclear capability in the wake of the 1986–1987 Brasstacks crisis (which included advances in Pakistan's efforts to acquire nuclear weapons and Islamabad's veiled nuclear threats). This formal announcement of India's burgeoning nuclear program finally moved India from an explorer to a full-fledged proliferator with the capability to produce an operational nuclear arsenal.

India became a declared, de facto nuclear weapons state with a second series of nuclear tests in May 1998. Again, India had managed to conduct another round of underground nuclear tests under absolute secrecy. Only subsequent geospatial analysis helped to identify the times and place for the tests.[37] The first of the Pokhran-II tests, or *Operation Shakti*, consisted of detonations of three fission and one fusion bombs; two days later on May 13, 1998, India detonated two additional fission devices. Shortly after the tests, Prime Minister Atal Bihari Vajpayee issued a statement announcing India's entrance into the nuclear club, stating,

> Today, at 15:45 hours, India conducted three underground nuclear tests in the Pokhran range. The tests conducted today were with a fission device, a low yield device and a thermonuclear device. The measured yields are in line with expected values. Measurements have also confirmed that there was no release of radioactivity into the atmosphere. These were contained explosions like the experiment conducted in May 1974. I warmly congratulate the scientists and engineers who have carried out these successful tests.[38]

After its sudden announcement of nuclear intentions, India quickly moved to further develop its program through advances in technology, and acquisition of materials and supplies necessary to build a larger nuclear arsenal. By 1998, India had become only the sixth known country to test nuclear weapons and enter the relatively elite club of nuclear weapons possessors; Indian society was delighted with this new status and associated prestige.[39] The response from the international community was decidedly less positive. Almost immediately (fewer than ten days later), the Pakistanis conducted their own underground nuclear tests, *Chagai-I*, in the Balochistan Province. It is without question that these first public nuclear tests were in direct response to Operation Shakti. Prime Minister Nawaz Sharif stated, "today, we have settled a score and have carried out six successful nuclear tests."[40] The Pakistani Atomic Energy Commission (PAEC) carried out five or six nuclear tests using fission devices, at the Chagai test site on May 28, 1998. Pakistani scientists responsible for the tests earned national renown and helped launch the state into the selective nuclear club as its seventh member.

The United Nations condemned both states' nuclear tests with the UN Security Council Resolution 1172. The resolution began by denouncing the proliferation of nuclear weapons to the subcontinent, stating that increases in nuclear weapons in the international system posed a threat to international security and peace, and would, at the minimum, spark an arms race in South Asia. The UNSC Resolution also demanded that both India and Pakistan immediately cease their nuclear tests and demanded that the two states show restraint, refrain from provocative moves, and resume dialogue.[41] In addition, both countries were to stop their proliferation and reverse their nuclear programs, and cease development of fissile materials.[42] And, in accord with international law and their own domestic laws, the international community, especially the United States, opted to impose economic sanctions on India and Pakistan. According to then-Undersecretary of State Strobe Talbot,

> The sanctions imposed [on India and Pakistan] were necessary for several reasons. First, it's the law. Second, sanctions create a disincentive for other states to exercise the nuclear option if they are contemplating it. And third, sanctions are part of our effort to keep faith with the much larger number of nations that have renounced nuclear weapons despite their capacity to develop them.[43]

In the United States, the 1998 nuclear tests triggered the provisions in the Glenn Amendment to the Arms Export Control Act of 1994 that required the president to initiate the following seven sanctions against a target state:

(a) suspend foreign aid except for humanitarian assistance, food, medicine, or other agricultural commodities;
(b) terminate sales of military items;
(c) terminate other military assistance;
(d) stop credits or guarantees to the country by U.S. government agencies;
(e) vote against credit or assistance by international financial institutions;
(f) prohibit the U.S. from making loans to the foreign government concerned;
(g) prohibit exports of goods and technology with civilian and military nuclear uses.

Additionally, the United Nations, Japan, and a host of European states, imposed sanctions on India, primarily in the form of suspension of foreign aid to India and government-to-government credit lines.[44] The effects of these negative economic inducements on India's ultimate nuclear development were negligible but their overarching impact on India's economy and her standing in the international community were stark. For example, the suspension of bilateral loans was costly but the decline in lending from international institutions, foreign direct investments, and capital flow were significant for India.[45] Analysis from the World Bank reveals that the sanctions imposed on India had a "modest but measurable adverse effect on India's economy,"[46] mostly due to globalization's ripple effects that led to reduced capital flow to India. United States law, under the Glenn Amendment, required the termination of bilateral aid programs that were substantial in size, but miniscule relative to India's blossoming public sector. U.S. sanctions prompted fourteen other states to impose sanctions against the Indians, again to varying degrees of efficacy. Interestingly, the real impact of U.S. sanctions was indirect and had an effect on India's economy through three distinct means: "(1) changes in financial flows from bilateral creditors and agencies; (2) changes in flows from the international financial institutions (IFIs), especially the IMF and the World Bank; and (3) changes in private capital flow as a direct or indirect response to the presence of the official sanctions."[47] While these related costs on India were temporarily significant, there is no doubt that these effects on the Indian economy would have been far more dramatic if they had been in place longer. In 2001, the Bush administration decided to drop all sanctions on India and reversed the whole series of negative inducements imposed on India after the 1998 nuclear tests.

Despite these heavy financial costs, the international community's response to the Indian nuclear tests did little to slow India's nuclear advancement and modernization or alter the security dynamics on the subcontinent. Within ten years of Operation Shakti, India had been involved in three major disputes/militarized incidents with Pakistan, fueled in part by the parties' new nuclear status and the belief that nuclearization may actually prevent full-scale war between the two long-time rivals.[48] Additionally, India's rapid nuclear development resulted in vertical proliferation (growth of the nuclear arsenal) and diversification of delivery systems for nuclear weapons (the development of air-, sea-, and land-based platforms).[49]

India's path to proliferation raises additional questions about the options that the members of the international community, especially the United States, may have had with regard to countering or reversing its second push to acquire nuclear weapons in the 1980s and 1990s. While it is impossible to know what would have happened if the United States or other members of the international community had opted to respond to India's proliferation with combined rewards and punishments, it is clear that, on their own, economic sanctions and other negative inducements were ineffective and, indeed, counterproductive. In isolation, sanctions did little but momentarily slow the Indian economy. This result validated the ruling Bharatiya Janata Party (BJP) and increased Indian populace's support for nuclearization. Indeed, without any face-saving incentives, punishing India had the opposite effect as intended and may have further motivated them to continue down the path to proliferation.[50]

Understanding the U.S. Failure to Offer the Necessary Inducements

Were there missed opportunities for the United States to influence India's transition from potential proliferator to nuclear weapons state? And equally importantly, what lessons can we learn from the United States' failure to permanently stop India's nuclear progress? To answer these questions, I return to my theoretical framework to determine what we may predict from this strategic interaction. One reason for failure against some proliferators, including U.S. allies, is that the United States may have lacked the resolve to offer the appropriate set of inducements. While a discussion of *why* the United States chooses certain tools to offer from a set of inducements is necessarily outside the scope of this project, we can consider what ensued when the U.S. was not able to effectively negotiate an end to India's nuclear weapons program.

India's relationship with the United States continued to grow toward the end of the Cold War, after decades of its close military relations with the Soviet Union. By the early 1990s and the period of nuclear resurgence in India, New Delhi began to seek increased political, economic, and military cooperation with the United States, as both democracies shared preferences for maintaining the post–Cold War status quo in the international system. India had shifted from neither an ally nor an adversary to a friendly state to the U.S. And due, in part, to this evolving relationship and the United States' substantial strategic interests in the region, there was virtually no consideration of military force as a way of permanently ending India's nuclear program. Under these conditions, my theory would predict that the U.S. could incentivize India's nuclear abandonment with sufficiently large rewards and the imposition of escalatory sanctions.

The historical record reveals the United States undertook a different counterproliferation approach that may explain its ultimate failure. In the twenty-five years between Smiling Buddha and Operation Shakti, the international community adopted an ineffective approach to stopping further nuclear proliferation in South Asia. Primarily, however, the strategy was motivated not only by growing concerns about New Delhi's continuing nuclear program and how to negotiate an end to it, but also for the fear that it would stoke further proliferation in the region. The United States' counterproliferation strategy was motivated by a related concern: deterring Pakistan from acquiring nuclear weapons, by continuing to provide aid and assurances, potentially even security guarantees.[51]

While Pakistan's alliances with the U.S. and China had developed prior to India's 1974 PNE, Washington's clear "tilt" toward the Pakistanis could no longer be ignored.[52] The U.S., for example, had secretly supplied military equipment during the Cold War to the Pakistanis despite Congressional objections. Declassified CIA documents suggest that the United States' interest in assisting Pakistan came from a concern that "India intended to dismember Pakistan and destroy its armed forces, a possible loss of a U.S. ally in the Cold war [sic] that United States cannot afford to lose."[53] This Western pivot toward Pakistan, plus the growing alliance between the Chinese and the Pakistanis, renewed Indian security concerns that made the development of nuclear weapons even more attractive. Indian strategists argued in defense of further nuclearization, "all in all, the broader geopolitical situation had deteriorated for India."[54]

This ambivalent strategy, maintaining some alliances while pitting regional rivals against one another, reflected the United States' ambiguous preferences and signaled to India a weak U.S. preference for preventing nuclear proliferation on the subcontinent. The United States' relationship with Pakistan was seen as threatening. By following a strategy that fueled India's concerns about its security against a neighboring aggressor that now had the support and military assistance of a nuclear state, the United States' behavior persuaded New Delhi to continue its nuclear weapons program for its own security and stability. India, facing a threatening regional security environment actively supported by a global superpower, may indeed have seen the decision to pursue a nuclear program as a necessity to protect itself against both a regional adversary and its superpower patron.

Examination of the Indian nuclear case suggests the United States was perceived to be playing both sides in the India-Pakistan rivalry and allying with whatever state provided more benefits to the United States in its global fight against encroaching Soviet influence. When both Nehru and to a lesser degree, Indira Gandhi, for example, sidled up to the Soviet Union, the United States turned to Pakistan for assistance in containing Soviet power. Alternatively, when the United States believed that India, as a founding member of the Non-Aligned Movement, could be a stronger ally, Washington began to cozy up to New Delhi and turned away from their partnership with Islamabad.[55] Indeed, one side effect of the United States' "security-first narrative" regarding proliferation in South Asia prompted both India and Pakistan to believe that the United States saw them as "pawns" in the broader context of the Cold War.[56] The Indians, especially, saw this instrumental approach to nuclear negotiations as distasteful and began to further distrust American nonproliferation intentions (the Indians already saw the nuclear club as being unfairly exclusive). Thus, according to the Indians, rather than opting to mitigate India's concerns about security and prestige both regionally and globally, the United States' policy toward nuclear proliferation in the subcontinent exacerbated India's hesitance to come to the table and leverage their only bargaining chip, a nascent nuclear weapons arsenal.[57]

Indeed, the United States' actions seemed to have the opposite effect as intended: India continued to develop its nuclear program, primarily indigenously (given restrictions on bilateral and international nuclear assistance), with growing domestic political support.[58] India's initial decision to pursue a nuclear program was in part due to national prestige and a growing desire to be a regional power, in defiance of the international community.[59] This motivation only grew as the United States, and other Western powers, began to ally with India's neighboring rival. Indeed, the decades between Smiling Buddha and Operation Shakti saw the emergence of a hard-lining, hawkish political party, the Bharatiya Janata Party (BJP), that was committed to displaying national power and prestige, where it was becoming clearer that the nuclear program was to be made a national priority.[60] Brajesh Mishra, Prime Minister Vajpayee's national security advisor, said, "I have always felt that you cannot in today's world be counted for something without going nuclear."[61] Nuclear weapons, to Vajpayee and the BJP, instantly provided power and status, the capability to protect oneself against foreign threats, and the opportunity to alter the status quo if desired. The international community's opprobrium and negative reaction to the 1974 PNE only inflamed India's desire to improve its status through nuclear weapons.

Domestically, this stance was an effective political strategy for the BJP-led government. According to Vajpayee, his administration, unlike others before, was willing to incur whatever domestic and international costs would be associated with additional tests if they demonstrated India's resolve to acquire nuclear weapons and enter the main stage in the international community. He stated, "I had faith in the country's inherent strength to withstand any difficulties that may arise out of the test. The fundamentals of the economy were strong, and on such issues, I believe our people are ready to make any sacrifice for the security of the country."[62] With the revelation of India's hardline nuclear persona, through additional tests or high-level declarations, the ensuing international condemnation that the test would trigger—isolation, sanctions, or military action—could only help the BJP's case with the public. The Indian populace, whatever its feelings about nuclear weapons, would support the BJP's risky decision to challenge the international community, especially the United States, and continue down its nuclear path. This domestic calculus only helped to further encourage internal investment in the ongoing nuclear weapons program that resulted in the 1998 nuclear tests. It is important to note that if the United States had been able to offer a deal to motivate India to reverse its nuclear program, it would have needed to provide face-saving political rewards to the BJP to compensate for a potential domestic political loss.

The United States' actions—support for a regional rival that threatened Indian security, threats to revoke economic assistance, and challenges to national prestige—were meant to address India's nuclear program and hopefully persuade the Indians to abandon their nuclear program before full nuclearization. Instead, they made acquiring nuclear weapons significantly more appealing for India. The then-U.S. Ambassador to India sent a memo to Indian Prime Minister's office outlining, and threatening, the very serious consequences associated with a second round of nuclear tests. A State Department document, entitled "Preventive Diplomacy—Indian Nuclear Test Preparations," revealed the Ambassador's memo to the Indian Foreign Ministry.[63] It stated,

> We have urged India not to conduct a test, and have laid out the serious consequences a test would have for India. In addition to the likely international and regional ramifications, we stressed the great damage a test would do to our bilateral relations. We explained that an immediate consequence would be Glenn Amendment sanctions, under Section 102(b) of the Nuclear Proliferation Prevention Act of 1994 (which amended the Arms Export Control Act), and that the U.S. would be required to terminate most forms of economic assistance, defense sales and services, and credit guarantees to non-nuclear weapons states that detonate a nuclear explosion. The Glenn Amendment would also cut off U.S. Export-Import Bank support for India and require the U.S. Government to block American bank loans as well as exports of dual-use technology. We would also be required to oppose World Bank and other IFI loans to India. The implications of these sanctions for India's economic reforms are significant.[64]

This evidence reveals that the United States' primary policy approach emphasized the role of threatening negative inducements, without simultaneous rewards, to alter New Delhi's nuclear behavior. In Congressional testimony that included a question and answer session, the then-Ambassador to India was specifically asked whether the administration was considering offering India inducements to not test additional nuclear devices. The Ambassador's response was, "we do not believe presenting the issue to India as negotiable is practical or desirable. Our focus is to make PM Rao aware of the full costs and bilateral, regional, and international implications of a nuclear test, and to leave it to him to draw the right conclusion."[65] Declassified State Department memos from 1995 (on the eve of Operation Shakti) reveal discussions emphasizing how the U.S., in conjunction with the broader international community, would have a difficult time deterring India and Pakistan from further going down the nuclear path. Robert Rochlin, senior scientist at the Arms Control and Disarmament Agency, in a

1995 memo to a senior State Department official as they contemplated actions in South Asia, stated,

> U.S. leverage alone is probably insufficient to head off this gloomy scenario. It is possible, however, that strong, concerted intervention by all the major states could deter India and Pakistan from embarking on this dangerous course. It would require vigorous U.S. leadership to mobilize the worldwide effort required to persuade India and Pakistan that their long-term national security interests can be best served by joining, rather than obstructing, the global movement toward nuclear disarmament. To succeed, the major states would need to give the effort top priority in their dealings with South Asia. Moreover, the chances of success will be greater to the extent that the nuclear-weapons states demonstrate significant progress of their own toward global nuclear disarmament.[66]

This document reveals that the U.S. was at least somewhat aware that their current nonproliferation strategy was unlikely to prevent India (and perhaps Pakistan) from acquiring nuclear weapons without a marked change in tactics. Even though the U.S. government was beginning to explore nonproliferation policies that de-emphasized unilaterally punishing proliferators and instead focused on multilateral efforts to provide incentives in line with India and Pakistan's national interests, these were not cohesive and compelling enough to persuade the Indians to reverse their nuclear course.

Concluding Remarks

By examining the Indian proliferation case in the context of a strategic interaction between New Delhi and Washington, we are able to gain better insight into how the United States had the opportunity to discourage proliferation at various points of India's nuclear development but failed to do so. Through this analysis, an interesting picture of these dynamics emerges. First, it reveals some interesting implications about the conditions or factors that might best contribute to a proliferator's decision to reverse its nuclear course. Competing preferences for maintaining India as an erstwhile ally, while simultaneously attempting to garner more support against the Soviets through Pakistan, left the United States without a coherent and convincing counterproliferation strategy. This revealed that the United States is not always able to seriously and credibly counter nuclear proliferation by providing a sufficient and necessary basket of inducements—a behavior that proliferators are able to observe. India ultimately built nuclear weapons because the U.S. was unable to offer the necessary inducements (rewards and punishments) at optimal times during the proliferation process.[67]

Further, in addition to providing a detailed account of a particular case among the universe of proliferators, an in-depth case-study analysis provides the opportunity to delve into mechanisms at play and make better inferences about causality. Specifically, I am able to demonstrate with declassified memos and archival data how the United States sought to apply pressure to compel India to reverse its nuclear program and how New Delhi reacted to these actions. This case reiterates an important conclusion: if the U.S. does not approach proliferators with the correct strategy (i.e., using positive and negative inducements), not all proliferation attempts can be countered.

Almost ten years after successful proliferation, the United States' halfhearted stance against Indian proliferation was overturned with the 123 Agreement or U.S.-India Civil Nuclear Agreement that once again allowed India access to nuclear materials and the opportunity to carry out trade with the Nuclear Suppliers Group (NSG), the only de facto nuclear weapons state to be granted such an exemption by the NSG. By agreeing to separate India's civilian and military nuclear facilities, and to place all its civilian nuclear facilities under the International Atomic Energy Agency (IAEA) safeguards, the U.S. and India decided to pursue full nuclear cooperation that allowed India to purchase nuclear fuel and technology from the United States. This new agreement provided an instrumental advantage to India over other non-NPT signatory nuclear weapons states and helped to reset the relationship between India and the United States after a decade of tense relations. In accord with the new agreement, the Indians have made significant strides toward safeguarding their arsenal and taking measures to ensure the safety and security of their nuclear facilities—a key demand issued by the international community in the wake of India's sudden nuclearization. While there is no indication that India has any plans to reduce or dismantle its nuclear weapons program, New Delhi has made an important concession to the international community, and especially the U.S., by agreeing to place its civilian nuclear program under IAEA safeguards in exchange for technical assistance.

The Indian case provides an important foundation with which to examine the recent agreement to end, at least for the time-being, Iran's decades-long nuclear program. In many ways, the United States' approach to the Iranian nuclear program suffered similar pitfalls: competing policy preferences that took priority over stopping Iran's nuclear pursuit, and initially, a lack of willingness to employ military force to stop Iran's nuclear ambitions. Despite these initial missteps, the United States eventually was successful in countering Iran's nuclear program. How did this occur? The next chapter employs similar primary-source and original interview data to answer this question.

Iran: Adversaries and Nuclear Reversal

Introduction

I introduced in Chapter 5 the first of three in-depth case studies of counterproliferation failures and successes that serve to illustrate four core categories of proliferation derived in Chapter 2. In the analysis that follows, I examine another critical counterproliferation case: Iran. An adversarial state which the U.S. was willing to stop with military force, Iran was ultimately persuaded to stop its nuclear weapons program through a negotiation strategy that included positive and negative inducements. Further, the U.S. leveraged a window of opportunity with the election of a relatively moderate leader, President Hassan Rouhani. Below, I examine the trajectory of the Iranian nuclear program, the numerous attempts to stop its successful proliferation, and the agreement that eventually stopped Iran's nuclear progress. I conclude with an assessment of the implementation and compliance of the Iran Deal to date, and how evolving geopolitics may endanger its lasting success.

The summer of 2015 saw the transition of the Iranian nuclear program—from pursuing the acquisition of nuclear weapons to definitively delaying further progress. Some have lauded the tough stance of the United States, specifically President Barack Obama and Secretary of State John Kerry, for motivating Iran to return to the negotiation table after decades of previous failed attempts and for ensuring this landmark deal's success despite significant opposition in the U.S. Congress. In a speech marking the success of the agreement, President Obama stated, "today, because America negotiated from a position of strength and principle, we have stopped the spread of nuclear weapons in this region. Because of this deal, the international community will be able to verify that the Islamic Republic of Iran will not develop a nuclear weapon."[1]

Others have criticized that the accomplishment of the Joint Comprehensive Plan of Action (JCPOA) reached in July 2015 was the result of President Obama's

Delaying Doomsday, Rupal N. Mehta. Oxford University Press (2020). © Oxford University Press.
DOI: 10.1093/oso/9780190077976.001.0001

insistence on the use of a softer, diplomatic approach, rather than the use of other more coercive levers, in curbing Iran's nuclear weapons program. Senator Tom Cotton (R-AR) reiterated the need for a "credible threat of military force" such that the Iranians will abandon "their nuclear-weapons capabilities"—a move that the former Secretary of Defense Robert Gates has stated could "prove catastrophic, haunting us for generations."[2] Senator Cotton also suggested, in an unprecedented open letter to the leaders of the Islamic Republic of Iran, that the subsequent president of the United States would renege on any agreement made by the Obama administration (a decision ultimately made by President Donald Trump in June 2018).[3] Other critics, including Israeli Prime Minister Benjamin Netanyahu, suggested that in addition to leaving Iran with the infrastructure and capacity to "break out" and acquire nuclear weapons in a short time frame, the agreement had increased the risk of conflict and hostility in the already-tense region. A senior Israeli official stated, in response to the news that President Obama had secured enough votes to uphold his veto of the Republican-backed resolution to reject the agreement, "Prime Minister Netanyahu has a responsibility to speak out about the grave dangers the Iran deal presents to Israel, the region and the world, and he will continue to do so."[4]

For observers of the Iranian nuclear program, this process, and the outcome it led to, can be seen in a variety of lights: "expected," "cautiously optimistic," "unlikely to remain peaceful in the long-term," "in line with Iranian political preferences."[5] Regardless of the ultimate fate of the Iranian nuclear program and whether it will ever escalate to a military-scale nuclear weapons program in the future, or if the domestic desire for nuclear weapons is somehow satiated by fundamental changes in Iran's relationship with the international community, and the United States in particular, important questions remain about how the international community arrived at this position. Specifically, under what conditions did the Iranian government choose to forego the option to pursue nuclear weapons, at least for the next decade? Why was the JCPOA, more so than any other previous attempt at negotiations, successful in having the Iranians agree to halt their nuclear weapons program despite years of economic sanctions and failed diplomatic overtures from the international community?

My theory of nuclear reversal provides answers to these critical questions. By examining the history of the Iranian nuclear program and forays into negotiations with members of the international community, the rationale for why the JCPOA was finally successful in curbing further development becomes clearer. If my theory is correct, Tehran, even though it had previously been resistant to reversing its nuclear ambitions when targeted with economic sanctions, should have been more likely to agree to an agreement when offered rewards, especially if it is concerned about a credible threat of a military strike or escalatory punishment. If the null hypothesis is correct, and international pressure plays no distinct role in altering domestic nuclear decision-making, we should expect to see no impact from external incentives (especially given Ayatollah Ruhollah Khomeini's long-standing role in crafting Iranian foreign policy).

Yet, when we take a detailed survey of Iran's strategic interactions over time with the international community, we find strong empirical support for my theoretical argument. In a path that is remarkably consistent with my theory and the implications laid out earlier, the tandem offer of rewards (i.e., lifting of the oil embargo and diplomatic reengagement) in conjunction with further economic punishment, and even the threat of war, if the program were to continue, provides critical clues as to the success of the JCPOA in 2015. The evidence provided by this critical case is even more salient in debates on counterproliferation policy and nuclear reversal as Iran has previously been viewed as intransigent and immovable on the nuclear front—by Iranians and non-Iranians alike. Indeed, this case provides significant support for a related hypothesis that reveals the particularly important role that new leaders, especially during periods of leadership change, can play to motivate nuclear reversal when they are offered appropriate inducements to do so.

This chapter provides an in-depth overview of the Iranian nuclear program since its inception in the 1970s. In addition to describing the technical evolution of the program and the development of dual-use technology that revealed to external observers the deliberate use of hedging at best and a clandestine ambition to produce nuclear weapons at worst, I discuss the evolving political dynamic between Tehran and Washington, as well as the broader international community. This chapter also describes the various, mostly unsuccessful, negotiation attempts that were made prior to the conclusion of the JCPOA. This analysis furthers our understanding of why the international community, with the U.S. at the helm, was unable to deter India from acquiring nuclear weapons but had better luck with the Iranians.

Lastly, in addition to primary- and secondary-source evidence of the Iranian nuclear program, the chapter introduces original data collected through extensive interviews with American, Iranian, and international officials on the Iranian nuclear program, the path that ultimately led to the establishment of the JCPOA, and the likelihood of success moving forward. These interviews provide a previously unseen glimpse into how diplomats, intelligence and policy analysts from a variety of states, and officials at international institutions such as the International Atomic Energy Agency view counterproliferation policy writ large. They provide unique insights into the Iran case in particular, and whether the continued success of the JCPOA may set an important precedent for nuclear reversal in the future.

Atoms for Power: The Creation of the Iranian Nuclear Power Program

As with other early proliferators, Iran's nuclear timeline began with the 1957 signing of a bilateral civilian nuclear cooperation agreement with the United States, as part of the Atoms for Peace program that ultimately went into force in 1959. In early years of the nuclear program, Iran sought and received the support of the United States, as well as other nuclear states such as France, West Germany, Great Britain, Italy, Canada, and Belgium. Aside from purchasing research reactors from these suppliers, Iranian scientists received technical training and advise integral to the early phases of the program.[6] Remarkably, the Iranians received similar technical and personnel support, and even inspiration, from the Indians in the early days. Despite tense relations after the 1971 Bangladeshi Liberation War and the fact that Iran often viewed India as an adversary, both saw each other as regional powers that desired a minimum nuclear capability to establish their status in the international system.[7]

The quest for assistance and materials was driven in part by Iran's decision to balance other regional nuclear aspirants, namely Iraq and Egypt, and the conventional military dominance of Saudi Arabia. Concerns over regional hegemony and power among these adversaries likely prompted Iran to pursue a latent nuclear capacity that could serve as a stepping stone to nuclear weapons if necessary.[8] From all accounts, this was an ambitious project. Iran wanted to build 10–20 nuclear power reactors and produce more than 20,000 MW of nuclear power within thirty years. Over the next two decades, Tehran became increasingly interested in obtaining additional nuclear technology and materials, integral to the nuclear fuel cycle.[9]

After a short halt in proliferation activities in the mid-1970s, Iran reinitiated its nuclear power pursuit and enlisted international support to continue building the Bushehr reactors. Soon after, the Iranians began construction of a light-water nuclear reactor, a dual-use reactor that was less proliferation-resistant than other choices in the Bushehr complex. Simultaneously, the Iranians began to reach out to nuclear suppliers, such as the United States, to acquire a latent nuclear capability, uranium enrichment and plutonium reprocessing technologies (ENR). According to National Security Council documents, while the United States was initially willing to supply Iran with these technologies (but ultimately decided against it), the Iranians also became interested in developing an indigenous enrichment facility.[10]

These actions led the international community to question Iran's true motives for its nuclear pursuit. Thus far, Iran had argued that its pursuit of nuclear reactors and a uranium enrichment capability was exclusively for nuclear power purposes.[11] Shah Mohammed Reza Pahlavi stated, "the present world is confronted with a problem of some countries possessing nuclear weapons and some not. We are among those who do not possess nuclear weapons, so the friendship of a country such as the United States with its arsenal of nuclear weapons . . . is absolutely vital."[12] However, given that Iran was rich with oil and natural gas reserves, Tehran's decision to heavily invest in nuclear power was initially perplexing. As a result of international concerns, Tehran took steps to signal its benign intentions for maintaining a latent nuclear capacity. Iran signed and ratified the NPT in 1970 and started a draft resolution to the United Nations General Assembly a few years later that called for the creation of a nuclear-free zone in the Middle East. Despite these actions, the international community remained unconvinced by Iran's declaration of peaceful nuclear intentions. According to a Special National Intelligence Estimate drafted in August 1974, after Iran's call for a nuclear-free zone in the region, the U.S. Department of State expressed "uncertainty over" Iran's "long-term objectives despite its NPT status."[13]

This dynamic of development and doubt persisted throughout the Cold War. Fueled by the Iran-Iraq War and concerns about Israel's burgeoning nuclear capability, Tehran restarted its nuclear program after a brief pause during the 1979 revolution.[14] The Iranian government defended its aim to expand its nuclear power capacity to meet growing energy demands, substitute nuclear power for oil and gas consumption, and eventually export fossil fuels. This was not a new rationale. The previous regime had discussed the potential political and economic benefits of pursuing nuclear energy. Throughout the late 1970s, the head of the Atomic Energy Organization of Iran referenced these positive externalities for its bold pursuit of nuclear energy and dual-use technology.[15]

In an effort to refocus on nuclear ambitions, Tehran began longer-term economic planning. This included a five-year development plan that specified reinstating Iran's nuclear program, specifically with assistance from the Indians, Chinese, and even Soviet partners. The program took a significant leap forward when, in 1989, the USSR signed a nuclear cooperation agreement. This later expanded in 1992 with further arrangements with the Russian Federation codifying nuclear energy cooperation and assistance for the Bushehr nuclear power plant.[16] It was during this time that the IAEA also began to question why Iran had opted to revamp its nuclear program.

With these developments and heightened nuclear latent capacity, Iran's status as a nuclear state grew murky. What had been designated and condoned by the U.S. as a nuclear energy program increasingly had the potential to produce nuclear weapons if and when Tehran, and Ayatollah Ruhollah Khomeini, chose to. According to a 1985 National Intelligence Council report, the United States considered Iran a potential "proliferation threat" as their interest in developing nuclear latency—specifically the construction of facilities that could produce higher-purity fissile material necessary for nuclear weapons.[17] Despite this progress and concern over the future of the Iranian nuclear program, the report concluded that Iran was unlikely to succeed in acquiring a nuclear weapons capability for at least a decade.

Nuclear Turning Point

International concerns were heightened when Iranian scientists located and procured over 5,000 metric tons of uranium ore, one of the largest deposits in the Middle East.[18] After unsuccessfully attempting to mine and mill these deposits indigenously, Tehran sought external assistance from the Russians and the Chinese. Iran also approached the Argentinians for assistance on a uranium mill and a fuel fabrication plant, but President Carlos Menem blocked Argentina's Applied Research Institute from providing such aid because of proliferation concerns.[19] In 1996, however, China opted to withdraw from its agreement to construct an enrichment facility in Iran due to pressure from the United States. Indeed, Iran's subsequent decision to pursue building the enrichment facility on its own marked a turning point in Iran's relationship with the international community.

Within the next decade, Iran had begun construction of its first indigenously designed light-water reactor at Darkhovin and gas-centrifuge-based uranium enrichment facilities.[20] These centrifuges produced both low-enrichment uranium (which can be used in nuclear power reactors) and highly-enriched uranium (HEU) that is used as fissile material for nuclear weapons. Lastly, Iran had recently taken steps to construct a heavy-water reactor at Arak,[21] and to design and build component parts for nuclear submarines. The heavy-water reactor provoked significant concern as the spent fuel from the reactor contains plutonium that is well suited for use in nuclear weapons after reprocessing (a capability that Iran never successfully possessed).

These developments and the incorporation of dual-use technologies that were unequivocally useful for the production of nuclear weapons marked another significant turning point in the international community's perception of Iran's nuclear intentions. By 2002, Iran's pursuit of dual-use technologies (and its arbitrary and inconsistent cooperation with the IAEA) raised concerns that Tehran may indeed be pursuing a nuclear weapons program.[22] These concerns and ensuing heated debates over Iranian nuclear intentions were magnified when an Iranian exile group, National Council of Resistance on Iran (NCRI), revealed that Iran had built nuclear facilities at Natanz and Arak that they had failed to report to the IAEA.[23] Parties to the NPT are obligated to establish a safeguards agreement with the IAEA, and non-nuclear-weapons states, such as Iran, must allow for agency inspectors to monitor suspected nuclear facilities and materials to ensure that they are not being used for military purposes. Prior to the statement by the NCRI regarding undisclosed facilities, the IAEA had already expressed concerns that Tehran had withheld relevant information about the full extent of its nuclear programs. Yet, IAEA intelligence of the program did not find Iran to be in violation of the agreement.[24] An interview with a former IAEA official in the Director General's Office at the time, confirms that the IAEA remained concerned about Iranian nuclear intentions, especially considering the political developments in the region. The war in Iraq and the removal of Saddam Hussein may have served as an additional impetus for Iran to refocus its efforts on acquiring a nuclear deterrent.[25] To the Iranians, the U.S. invasion of Iraq in 2003 highlighted the very concerning threat of regime change, especially for states that had started nuclear weapons programs but had not acquired nuclear weapons. The Iraq War may have prompted Iran to hasten its pace to attain regional hegemony and provide for its own security to prevent U.S. intervention. The IAEA's concerns centered on recent Iranian behavior: an ambiguous nuclear doctrine, consideration to withdraw from the NPT, attempts to address nuclear weapons viability without testing, and assessments of infrastructure survivability (i.e., placing nuclear installations and facilities deeper underground and further apart).[26] It was during this time that the IAEA Board of Governors adopted its first resolution that would require Tehran to suspend its covert enrichment activities, and to establish and increase cooperation with the IAEA investigation into its suspected weapons program. This announcement and the tacit confirmation that Iran was engaging in nuclear weapons activity, in violation of the NPT, sparked the first of many strategic negotiations between Iran and the international community.

An examination of the technical developments of the Iranian nuclear program ostensibly provided signposts to the IAEA that Tehran had moved from a civilian nuclear program to something beyond. This stood in contrast to statements from Iranian leaders and the most significant political authority in the country, the Supreme Leader Ayatollah Ruhollah Khomeini. Until his death in 1989, Ayatollah Khomeini insisted that Iran was not interested in pursuing weapons of mass destruction, even in light of the Iran-Iraq War earlier that decade. According to Mohsen Rafighdoost, who served as minister of the Islamic Revolutionary Guard Corps (IRGC), the Ayatollah had specifically rejected calls to acquire nuclear weapons and closed the door on a domestic program.[27] According to those close to the Supreme Leader, this clear decision to not pursue nuclear weapons was driven in part by his extreme aversion to both chemical and nuclear weapons in the aftermath of the use of chemical weapons by Iraqi soldiers on Iranian troops and civilians, ultimately killing more than twenty thousand

Iranians. Indeed, according to Rafighdoost, the Supreme Leader had told him twice that Iran would not acquire WMD as they were forbidden by Islam and that the IRGC should focus instead on defensive weapons.[28]

By most accounts, international observers were not persuaded by these overtures. The distrust of Iranian nuclear intentions came from three primary corners of the policy-making community: the Bush administration; policy analysts' look at both technical and political intelligence, and statements coming from Tehran; and international inspectors and observers of the Iranian nuclear program. First, the most memorable and vehement statement on an ongoing nuclear weapons program in Iran came during President George W. Bush's 2002 State of the Union address that declared Iran to be a member of an "Axis of Evil." In the speech, President Bush argued that Iran "aggressively pursues these weapons and exports terror, while an unelected few repress the Iranian people."[29] In the aftermath of the September 11, 2001 attacks and in gearing-up for the war in Iraq and the "Global War on Terror," the Bush administration remained unconvinced that Tehran's intentions were benign when it came to the pursuit of nuclear weapons. And perhaps more importantly from the U.S. perspective, the Bush Administration was concerned that Tehran was supplying conventional and nuclear technology or weapons to non-state actors engaging in politically motivated violence. To the U.S. government, Ayatollah Ali Khamenei's 2004 renewed declaration, fatwa, against nuclear weapons was merely seen as propaganda. Members of the Iranian government did not help their case with public declarations such as the one by the Press Secretary for the Iranian Embassy in Azerbaijan that stated, "Tehran has never and will never try to acquire nuclear weapons from other countries as Iran itself is capable of solving this problem relying on its own resources if the need should arise."[30]

Further, these concerns were shared by domestic and international policy analysts looking at the intelligence about the Iranian nuclear program. Conversations with members of the U.S. policy community who were frequently privy to discussions within the Bush administration illuminate a deep skepticism about why the evidence available about Iran's nuclear program was not clear evidence of a *weapons* program.[31] In late 2002, the CIA issued a report that suggested that Iran "remains one of the most active countries seeking to acquire [weapons of mass destruction and advanced conventional weapons] technology from abroad. . . . In doing so, Tehran is attempting to develop a domestic capability to produce various types of weapons—chemical, biological, nuclear—and their delivery systems."[32] In one interview, an American policy analyst and academic who had previously served in the Clinton Administration and was, during the time of the Iranian nuclear revelation, involved in the creation of a strategic dossier on Iran, noted the strategic calculation Iran made to publicly declare at this time its secret nuclear program and accept inspections. This was not to persuade the international community of its benign intent, but purely to avoid the fate of Saddam Hussein and Iraq.[33] This approach, approved by Ayatollah Ali Khamenei despite a multi-decades-long interest in nuclear weapons, was meant to ensure that Iran would not suffer regime change or war like its regional adversary. And this strategy, according to this expert's perspective, was "simply a calculation about the risk of pursuing their nuclear weapons activities."[34]

Third, doubts about the full extent of Iranian nuclear activity were expressed in internal meetings and public statements from the IAEA. Both at this time and subsequently, the IAEA expressed concerns that Tehran's willingness to allow inspectors may still be limited to only certain facilities. By 2001, the IAEA had found no evidence (in contrast to the CIA reporting) that Iran was using its nuclear technology (i.e., nuclear reactors) for military purposes with suspected assistance from Russia.[35] Yet, in my recent conversations, former IAEA officials, including those in the Department of Safeguards and in the Director General's Office, indicated there were concerns even at that time that Iran had not been fully forthcoming about the entirety of its nuclear materials and installations.[36] In recent public testimony in front of the House Committee on Financial Services Task Force to Investigate Terrorism Financing, former Deputy Director General of the IAEA, Olli Heinonen, confirmed this sentiment by commenting on the need for an exhaustive assessment of Iranian nuclear facilities in 2001. He argued that "a complete declaration of all Iran's nuclear activities, including past ones—for example, the status of equipment and materials from dismantled installations"—would be important to set a credible baseline for monitoring and verification.[37]

Evidence of these previously undisclosed installations was made public in December 2002 when CNN published photos of two additional nuclear facilities in Iran: (1) Natanz, a possible uranium enrichment facility located 100 miles south of Tehran; and (2) Arak, a possible underground heavy-water production facility located about 150 miles south of Tehran.[38] Tehran responded with a statement by Foreign Minister Kamal Kharrazi rejecting these allegations, stating, "the Islamic Republic of Iran's activities in this field are totally transparent, clear, and peaceful and there is no secret and obscure point on the launch of these (plants) in the future. . . . [B]asically there is no possibility of concealing such centers."[39] Former IAEA Director General Mohamed El Baradei later stated that he himself learned of these facilities six months ago, three months prior to when the Iranians officially notified him. He said, "the Iranians told me we could not visit the sites as planned this week because then-President Mohammad Khatami would be out of the country and 'they need some time to prepare.'"[40] These newly declared Arak and Natanz facilities confirmed increasing U.S. and international concerns about Tehran's "across-the-board pursuit of weapons of mass destruction and missile capabilities."[41]

The announcement of these facilities and the ensuing debate over the full extent of Iran's nuclear program launched the next key phase in nuclear negotiations. Within the next few years, Iran would sign the Additional Protocol (AP) allowing for further IAEA inspections, court a prospective nuclear agreement with the European Community, and face the beginning of the Bush administration's reliance on negative inducements (i.e., Pentagon plans to use covert action to destabilize the Iranian clergy and third-party sanctions on China and North Korea for their supply of weapons technology to Iran). By the mid-2000s, Iran appeared to be making significant progress toward nuclear weapons, and the international community finally began its efforts to persuade Iran away from the bomb.

Initial Attempts at Negotiation: The EU-3 Agreement

The next few years saw heightened tensions between Iran and much of the international community.[42] While Europe focused its rhetoric on seeking to compel Iran to abide by the NPT, the United States took a slightly different approach aimed at democracy promotion and the destabilization of the Iranian religious authority. Yet, importantly, at this time, the United States continued to reject the consideration of the use of military force as an option. In May 2003, then-Secretary of State Colin Powell stated, "we are concerned about what Iran is doing (with its nuclear program) . . . We will work with the international community to persuade Iran they should not move in this direction. . . . But it's not a matter for the armed forces of the United States at the moment."[43]

This statement reflected the United States' conflicted approach to the Iranian nuclear question at the time. Despite its fervent opposition to an Iranian bomb, the Bush administration was bogged down with an election campaign, the wars in Iraq and Afghanistan, and the war on terrorism, in general. At its core, there did not appear to be a clear counterproliferation strategy except one that relied on preventing Iran from continuing to build up its program until there was a change of regime—an improbable and unwise plan under the best of circumstances. Additionally, the Bush administration tied its policy (and plan for success) in Iraq to Iran. The U.S. wanted Iranian assistance with Al-Qaeda suspects in its custody and to offset Tehran's efforts to undermine the U.S. goals in Iraq. Under these conditions, the U.S. leadership in countering the spread of nuclear weapons in Iran was limited, even more so by the fact that there was no consideration of the threat of military force to condition the interactions with Tehran.

Unsurprisingly, other states began to look for ways of negotiating with the Iranians to curb their nuclear development. For the previous decade, Europe and Japan had been deterred from taking any action on the Iranian question (despite their history with Iran on nuclear cooperation) by the prospect of a lack of American support for an agreement with Iran. Yet, the conclusions from the IAEA about the extent of Iranian nuclear development, that it was not purely civilian, appeared to prompt a shift in their thinking. To demonstrate their evolving thinking, the European Union began to exert its influence by conditioning future trade agreements and a general economic relationship on whether Tehran agreed to sign the Additional Protocol (AP). According to the IAEA, "the AP not a stand-alone agreement, but rather a protocol to a safeguards agreement that provides additional tools for verification. In particular, it significantly increases the IAEA's ability to verify the peaceful use of all nuclear material in States with comprehensive safeguards agreements."[44] Similarly, the Japanese government pegged discussions about its involvement in Iran's oil industry on the signing of the AP. These attempts to influence nuclear decision-making in Iran exemplified a renewed effort by the international community at counter-proliferation. By Fall 2003, England, France, and Germany (the EU-3) put forward an agreement to incentivize Iran to suspend its enrichment activities, with IAEA verification, and implement the AP. With these measures in place, the IAEA would be able to inspect Iran's program and confirm that it did not have any clandestine nuclear sites.[45] And finally, the Iranians and EU-3 signed the Paris Agreement which successfully suspended Iran's military nuclear activity, in exchange for some level of political and economic benefits—though not completely in line with Iranian expectations with what it should receive for foregoing nuclear weapons development.

While Tehran agreed to curb much of its work on nuclear weapons at this time, its nuclear program continued to some extent afterward. Ultimately, the suspension in centrifuge activity lasted for three years until Iran restarted its gas centrifuge program and resumed activity at Isfahan, a uranium-conversion facility. By 2006, Iran stopped complying with the AP and refused to address concerns by the IAEA about its efforts at weaponization and the production of warheads for delivery systems.[46]

These concerning developments in Iran's nuclear trajectory prompted the U.S. to rejoin diplomatic efforts to alter Iranian nuclear decision-making. Unfortunately, these efforts were to little avail. Instead of stopping Iran from continuing its nuclear development, the international community discovered a secret enrichment site near Qom, a site that Tehran ultimately agreed to place under IAEA safeguards. But to a certain extent, the damage was done. With this discovery, the UN Security Council announced four additional rounds of economic sanctions against Iran between 2006 and 2010 for failing to stop its enrichment activity and for failing to adhere to IAEA guidelines as indicated by the Paris Agreement.[47] These sanctions, used in isolation, were aimed at actors associated with Iranian nuclear program, including financial and trade entities suspected of supporting the program. Despite these expanded sanctions, Iran persisted in its enrichment program. It continued to install more centrifuges at Natanz, and ramped up production at Natanz and Fordo. By and large, by the beginning of 2010, efforts at negotiating nuclear reversal had stalled and Iran remained committed to acquisition of nuclear weapons.

How can we understand these developments and the failure to persuade Iran to abandon its nuclear program? My theory would suggest that there are three primary reasons why this attempt at counterproliferation was not successful. First, both the Paris Agreement (which had limited success in getting Iran to sign the agreement and adhere to it initially), and the 2006 expansion of economic sanctions did not credibly employ a strategy of rewards and sanctions in tandem that was sufficient to compensate for what the Iranians were foregoing. The Europeans were offering general economic relief (including a trade agreement) if the Iranians suspended their nuclear enrichment. However, given Iran's security concerns, search for prestige, and belief that they were permitted civilian nuclear development under the NPT, these were not sufficient rewards. Both the Supreme Leader Ali Khamenei and Iranian President Mohammad Khatami argued that the international community's response was meant to stymie Iran's progress as a regional and world power. In 2004, during the EU-3 negotiations, Foreign Minister Kamal Kharrazi told European officials that Iran would not produce nuclear bombs, so long as its right to enrich uranium—ostensibly for nuclear power production—was recognized. According to the Associated Press, Kharrazi stated, "the time has come for Europe to take a step forward and suggest that our legitimate right for complete use of nuclear energy is recognized [in return for] assurances that our program will not be diverted toward weapons."[48] During the negotiations, Iran provided a list of compensatory rewards it was seeking in exchange for foregoing a nuclear deterrent, including "access to advanced dual-use nuclear technology, removal of restrictions on Iranian nuclear sales, agreement to sell conventional weapons to Iran, assurances regarding the Europeans' commitment to Iran, and support for a nuclear-free Middle East."[49] Yet, European discussions on reversing Iran's nuclear progress included none of these incentives.

Second, the initial attempt at negotiations with the Europeans did not involve the United States. Despite the progress of these talks, there was no guarantee that the U.S. would credibly agree to cooperate. It was not clear to either the Europeans or the Iranians that the U.S. would suspend its sanctions or agree to diplomatic reengagement, for example, removing Iran from the "Axis of Evil" if they stopped their nuclear pursuit. Indeed, in my own conversations with

Iranian and French diplomats, it became increasingly clear that an agreement that did not include the United States would be unlikely to persuade the Iranians to negotiate a nuclear deal.[50] After evidence surfaced that Tehran had continued its nuclear progress, including enrichment activities, despite signing the Paris Agreement, the U.S. only intervened to implement additional sanctions. While the U.S. and Great Britain favored immediate and severe sanctions, they ultimately conceded to low-level sanctions that would persuade Russia and China to join.[51] If the U.S. had been involved in these negotiations from the outset, the offer of rewards and punishments may have been deemed more credible to the Iranians and may have persuaded Tehran to abide by any agreement reached—knowing that it had the full support of the most powerful member of the non-proliferation regime. Yet, some argue that credibility posed a significant obstacle to any agreement. At this stage in U.S.-Iranian relations, it is likely that Iran would not have believed that the Bush Administration would follow through on a nuclear agreement, given the policies that Washington pursued at that time. Potential offers from the U.S. in the mid-2000s, therefore, might have been easily dismissed by Tehran as non-credible.

Lastly, and most importantly, these talks were not conducted in the shadow of military force. The U.S. made it clear during this time that military force was not on the table and indeed, their involvement in any negotiations was limited. Further, the Europeans were not keen to condition their talks on military force—a fact that was known to the Iranians. A senior nuclear negotiator for the Iranian Supreme National Security Council, Hossein Mousavian, stated, "as a result of the negotiations [between the EU-3 and Iran], not only Iran's nuclear capabilities were preserved, and we were spared a military attack, but we were also able to complete our nuclear capabilities because of the atmosphere it created."[52] There was little concern in Tehran that potential non-adherence to the Paris Agreement would result in escalatory punishment, such as a military attack on Iranian nuclear facilities. According to Iranian diplomats, Tehran preferred to face economic sanctions than give in, as there was not likely to be additional punishment for doing so. In 2005, Iranian Defense Minister Ali Shamkhani stated, "Tehran would rather face sanctions than back down on its nuclear program and submit to humiliation."[53] The lack of a credible military threat may have been one reason why the Iranians opted to continue their nuclear activities, in contravention to the EU-3 agreement.

Based on these three factors, it is not difficult to see why the early attempts at Iranian nuclear reversal by the European Union were unsuccessful. Despite this lack of progress, the Iranian response to the imposition of sanctions from 2006 to 2010, as well as its specific list of demands proposed during the EU-3 talks, revealed important information about Iranian intentions and preferences. Continuing sanctions were an important negotiating tool that allowed the

U.S. to assess that Iran was more committed to its nuclear pursuit than previously anticipated, and importantly, determine what strategy of inducements may work to incentivize nuclear reversal when the next opportunity arose. The following section describes the next potential window of opportunity.

After the reelection of President Obama in 2012 and the election of President Rouhani in 2013, the international community, with the United States at the helm this time, approached Iran with a tailored set of policy levers aimed at providing sufficient incentives to motivate changes in its nuclear decision-making. After two years of intense negotiations, the U.S. and its European partners were ultimately successful in countering and stopping nuclear weapons proliferation in Iran. Why was this attempt successful?

Road to the Joint Comprehensive Plan of Action (JCPOA)

"There can no longer be any reasonable doubt that Iran's ambition is to obtain nuclear weapons capability."[54] By 2008, this sentiment rang true for much of the international community grappling with the potential for a new addition to the nuclear club. The U.S. concern went further, "that Iran is actively pursuing the weapons, not just the capability."[55] President Obama's election in 2008 saw a renewed interest in the United States to talk to the Iranians about their nuclear program. In an interview with Al-Arabiyya, President Obama stated, "the U.S. will extend the hand of diplomacy to Iran if its leaders 'unclench their fist.' It is very important for us to make sure we are using all the tools of U.S. power, including diplomacy, in our relationship with Iran."[56] Susan Rice, then-Ambassador to the United Nations, qualified this statement by articulating that Tehran needed to suspend its uranium enrichment, in line with UN Security Council Resolution 1803, before talks would commence.[57]

However, for the majority of President Mahmoud Ahmadinejad's tenure through mid-2013, Iran maintained its hawkish, hardliner position and refused to discuss the nuclear program, resulting in a stalemate between the Iranians and the international community. Despite some instances of cooperation between Tehran and the IAEA, Iran failed to halt its nuclear development and remained in violation of the safeguards agreement and other international obligations. President Ahmadinejad repeatedly stated that while Iran may be willing to discuss some issues with the U.S. or other members of the international community, the question of nuclear technology or capability was not up to debate. He stated, "we are in favor of talks but we will not negotiate with anyone about our right to nuclear technology . . . they said that if Iran suspends its activities, they will hold talks with us. But they don't know that the Iranian nation is in favor of negotiations but will not negotiate over its rights at all . . . Iran will not retreat one iota."[58] While President Ahmadinejad was not averse to discussing the nuclear issue, he made it clear that he valued keeping open the nuclear weapons option and any agreement must allow Iran to retain a nuclear capability. The election of President Obama reaffirmed Iran's general interest in talks when President Ahmadinejad announced in 2009, "our nation is ready to hold talks based on mutual respect and in a fair atmosphere," but that the talks could only be held with the Ayatollah's blessings.[59]

For the next few years, efforts to negotiate the program stalled with increasing tensions, additional sanctions, and Iran's accelerated work on the Natanz and Fordo plants. By 2010, most analysts and observers estimated that Iran was six to twelve months away from being able to produce a sufficient quantity of weapons-grade uranium for a nuclear weapon.[60] Within the next year, the IAEA expressed further concern that in addition to ramping up its centrifuge production, Iran was also working on building a missile delivery system—a claim that Iran rejected as being invented for political purposes. In 2012, President Obama responded to this progress by signing and ratifying the Iran Threat Reduction and Syria Human Rights Act that sought to expand sanctions against Iran through a ban on Iranian shipping services that may have been used for proliferation.[61] The European Union similarly imposed a set of sanctions on Iran's oil industry that effectively restricted its ability to export oil and natural gas.

It is important to note three key developments that occurred during the period 2010–2012. First, the U.S. and the European Union were continuing to accelerate the imposition of economic sanctions. These sanctions included financial and oil sector restrictions and embargoes, as a means of delaying further development of Iran's nuclear program, without offering any compensatory benefits or rewards. In my own interviews, an Iranian diplomat expressed his surprise at this tactic. These sanctions did little to impact Iran's technological capacity to build centrifuges to produce weapons-grade uranium or to develop missile delivery systems.[62] These sanctions further frustrated hardliners in the Iranian government, including President Ahmadinejad, and entrenched their position on retaining a nuclear capacity in spite of international pressure. Second, public rhetoric notwithstanding, the U.S. and Iran began to hold backchannel discussions about the possibility of holding nuclear talks in the future. Within months of President Obama's election in 2008, U.S. officials were surprised by an offer from an Omani liaison, Salem ben Nasser al-Ismaily, to broker talks on the Iran nuclear question. President Obama had already attempted to begin clandestine talks by sending a secret letter to Ayatollah Ali Khamenei, but the overture had been rejected. Al-Ismaily, on the other hand, "assured [Dennis] Ross he could bring the Iranians to the table" and that Oman would be "an ideal venue for secret negotiations."[63] Al-Ismaily was able to deliver on both promises.

The United States began talks with the Iranians, which were ultimately unsuccessful but led to the beginning of the JCPOA negotiations at a later date. Third, and relatedly, the international community began talking in earnest about a joint U.S.-Israeli strike on Iranian nuclear facilities. This was likely the first time that the United States, and some of its allies, had openly discussed the likelihood of using military force to stop Iran's nuclear development. This development marked an important turning point in the United States' counterproliferation approach to the Iranian nuclear program and had a significant impact on future negotiation attempts.

This era also saw other significant changes in the international community's reaction to the Iranian nuclear program. First, the United States went to great lengths to prevent Israel, who was on the verge of attacking Iran, from doing so. Washington was able to effectively persuade Tel Aviv that the U.S. was better equipped and, importantly, *willing* to strike suspected Iranian nuclear facilities if necessary.[64] Relatedly, the United States was in the process of building a new weapon—the Massive Ordinance Penetrator—that was specifically designed to destroy the underground facility at Qom.[65] This capability prompted a significant debate within U.S. policy-making communities about whether the United States should actually attack the Iranian facilities or pursue other strategic approaches. By 2012, President Obama had ostensibly acknowledged that the use of military force could serve as a game-ending move, if efforts at diplomacy failed. During a speech at the American Israel Public Affairs Committee (AIPAC), he stated,

> We all prefer to resolve this issue diplomatically. Having said that, Iran's leaders should have no doubt about the resolve of the United States— just as they should not doubt Israel's sovereign right to make its own decisions about what is required to meet its security needs. I have said that when it comes to preventing Iran from obtaining a nuclear weapon, I will take no options off the table, and I mean what I say.[66]

Indeed, the year 2013 seemed to mark the perfect storm of conditions to negotiate Iran's nuclear reversal. After nearly a decade of non-engagement, aside from contributing to multilateral economic sanctions, the U.S. was once again willing to take on a leadership role in counterproliferation. Through sanctions, a desire to restart negotiations, and the consideration of military force as a possible policy tool, the U.S. demonstrated its commitment to working on this issue. These efforts came to fruition once it found a more flexible and credible partner, something that the June 2013 election of President Hassan Rouhani made possible.

Recall from my theoretical framework that the ability of the United States to persuade leaders to reverse their nuclear weapons programs may be especially effective during periods of leadership change. According to this logic, new leaders may be particularly susceptible to challenges to their tenure if they decide to abandon the nuclear efforts, especially a long-running pursuit endorsed by predecessors. The opportunity to receive positive inducements, while being threatened with negative inducements and the real potential for military attacks, allows new leaders to save face, withstand domestic pressures, and ultimately change nuclear policy. This argument can be examined in the context of the Iranian nuclear program and the election of President Rouhani. Indeed, the successful initiation of nuclear talks after Rouhani's election provides a clear illustration of this causal logic.

Despite his prior experience as a tough negotiator on the Iranian nuclear program under Ahmadinejad, Rouhani was not the Ayatollah's preferred successor and his win in 2013 surprised domestic and international analysts. While the Supreme Authority was focused on the consolidation of control after the 2009 Green/Velvet Revolution, the Iranian populace preferred Rouhani's platform that emphasized resolving Iran's domestic economic downturn as a result of the previous decades' sanctions, including a damaging oil embargo. In his inaugural address, President Rouhani, stated that "elevating Iran's position based on national interest and lifting of the oppressive sanctions," was his policy priority in the upcoming term.[67] President Rouhani went on to state in his first press conference that he was open to talks with the U.S., stating, "we are determined and ready to enter serious and substantive negotiations with the other side and if they are prepared like us, then I am confident that the concerns of both sides will be removed through negotiations within a period which will not be very long."[68] He went on to discuss the previous "mostly stick" approach to the nuclear issue by stating, "sanctions and threats have always cast a shadow over negotiations, and we should move toward the resolution of old grievances in an atmosphere of calm and peace."[69]

Political analysts in Iran believed that President Rouhani's approach demonstrated an evolving understanding of how best to engage the U.S. and other members of the international community. Iranian political analyst Ali Alizadeh, for example, stated, "he showed awareness of the west's impatience with mere rhetoric around negotiations and suspicion that Iran is attending talks merely to buy time, by promising fast and substantive talks and not wasting time."[70] American analysts, such as Karim Sadjadpour, argued that his election represented "the best hope for detente with Iran."[71] President Rouhani's approach to negotiations on the nuclear weapons issue since his arrival in office in June 2013 illustrates the power of a new leader clearly. In addition to using his transition to power to credibly demonstrate an openness to discuss the nuclear issue, Rouhani also emphasized the need for the inclusion of positive inducements to effectively persuade Iran to reexamine its commitment to the nuclear option. In a historic phone call in the Summer of 2013 that broke a decades-long freeze of relations between Iran and the United States, Presidents Obama and Rouhani agreed to negotiate and potentially reach a deal over Iran's uranium-enrichment program.[72] President Obama stated about the call, "the very fact that this was the first communication between an American and Iranian president since 1979 underscores the deep mistrust between our countries . . . But it also indicates the prospect of moving beyond that difficult history."[73]

Rouhani capitalized on his political "mandate" to move forward with the progress made during the Oman negotiations. Within a few months, Iran and the P5+1 (permanent members of the United Nations Security Council and Germany) held the first round of talks for what would eventually be termed the Joint Plan of Action (JPOA). While not comprehensive, this agreement established the Framework of Cooperation (FOC) that would bind both parties to act "with respect to verification activities to be undertaken by the IAEA to resolve all present and past issues."[74] In addition to codifying the IAEA verification, the FOC also ensured continued negotiations and discussion of the nuclear issue until a final agreement could be reached.

And, in April 2015, after nearly two years of intense and complex discussions and bargaining, the P5+1 and Iran came to an agreement that would constrain Iran's nuclear weapons intentions and pursuit in exchange for a variety of political and economic benefits, including the revocation of economic sanctions in place. The finalized agreement, the Joint Comprehensive Plan of Action (JCPOA), reflected the first, successful, substantive move toward reaching an agreement that would stop Iran's potential development of a nuclear weapon and allow IAEA inspections.[75] The JCPOA required that Iran reduce the number of its operational centrifuges at the Natanz enrichment plant from 19,000 to 5,060 until 2025. Further, the Fordo plant would primarily be used for research and development, would not enrich uranium for a total of fifteen years, and maintain only 1,044 operational centrifuges. Iran agreed to ratify the Additional Protocol, to abide by a comprehensive safeguards agreement, and to accept an expansive inspection regime that would give the IAEA unequaled and unprecedented access to Iranian nuclear facilities. Also, the JCPOA established a supply channel that allows Iran to acquire the necessary materials to operate its civilian nuclear facilities, from international suppliers like the Nuclear Suppliers Group (NSG). Finally, and most importantly for Iran, the JCPOA provided Iran with key rewards. These included the lifting of the oil embargo, sanctions relief, and the gradual resumption of diplomatic ties with the United States and other states in the international community.[76]

Success in Iran:
The Conditions Underlying the JCPOA

At first glance, it is somewhat surprising that the international community and Iran managed to achieve an agreement on the nuclear question after more than two years of intense negotiations. The primary obstacle to the agreement seemed to stem from significant domestic opposition in *both* Iran and the United States, as well as from some key interlocutors such as Israel and Saudi Arabia. In the United States, key opposition to the agreement came from GOP members in Congress as well as Republican lobbyists and donors. For example, while Senator Ted Cruz (R-TX) argued that with the agreement, "the Obama administration will become the leading financier of terrorism against America in the world," mega-donors, such as Sheldon Adelson, who opposed the agreement, contributed more than $13 million to advocacy groups to lobby against the deal.[77] These concerns were shared broadly by some allies of the United States as well. The then-Israeli ambassador to the United States frequently attacked the proposed agreement publicly and lobbied members of Congress to oppose the deal, while Prime Minister Netanyahu himself stated, "Israel is not bound by this deal with Iran because Iran continues to seek our destruction. We will always defend ourselves."[78] Similarly, while Saudi Arabia ultimately accepted the agreement, it expressed its concerns about Iran's sincerity in upholding the agreement given its history as a long-term adversary of the majority Sunni Arab states in the region.[79]

Further, some of the discord and challenges to the agreement came from certain hardliner circles in Iran itself. The anti-agreement coalition included former President Ahmadinejad, former nuclear negotiator Saeed Jallili, various conservative clerics, and commanders of the Revolutionary Guard. Indeed, President Rouhani and Foreign Minister Javad Zarif, the primary negotiators of the agreement, had to spend much of the review period (the eighty-day period before signing the agreement) defending the deal against hawks in the Iranian government. Ultimately, the agreement overwhelmingly passed in the Iranian Parliament with more than 160 votes in favor of the agreement. In October 2015, EU High Representative Francesca Mogherini and Foreign Minister Zarif announced "Adoption Day" to signify the implementation of the JCPOA for all sides.[80]

These obstacles reveal the complex nature of Iran's nuclear reversal and raise the question: why was the JCPOA, more so than prior attempts, ultimately successful? My theory of nuclear reversal provides a useful framework with which to examine the negotiations behind the Iran agreement. My interviews with Iranian, American, and other diplomats involved in the nuclear negotiations provide critical evidence to support this logic. Specifically, I argue that there are three primary reasons why the JCPOA achieved its objective in inducing nuclear reversal in Iran: (1) the Obama Administration's "dual track" policy of pressure and engagement; (2) a credible threat of military force if negotiations broke down and the Iranians persisted in their nuclear effort; and (3) the opportunity afforded by the introduction of a new leader, President Rouhani, as a relative moderate within in the Iranian government.

First, the JPOA and the outline of the subsequent JCPOA included significant rewards: the highest two priorities for the Iranians: (a) economic assistance (including but not limited to sanctions relief and the lifting of the oil embargo);[81] and (b) retention of some nuclear capacity as allowed by the Nonproliferation Treaty. It was ultimately the strategy that incorporated key compensatory benefits for foregoing the nuclear weapons option (at least until 2025) that finally persuaded the Iranians to agree to the deal. To American and European analysts privy to the negotiations themselves, there is no doubt that the international community could not have arrived at this agreement without coercion.[82] Rather, these diplomats argue, the crucial motivation for agreeing to serious discussions with American and European leaders was the fact that finally these agreements were based on conditions that were amenable to the Iranians—key benefits such as centrifuge reductions, not elimination.[83] This evidence provides important qualitative support for the finding from Chapter 3 that the retention of nuclear latency can serve as a useful counterproliferation inducement.

Moreover, the sanctions imposed during the prior decades served as a mechanism and shed light on Iran's ambition to continue to develop a nuclear program given its belief that it had the inherent right to do so. Perhaps more importantly, Iran received what it believed were the appropriate rewards in exchange for giving up this right. Indeed, conversations with Iranian diplomats reveal a different and interesting implication of the sanctions regime. While they concur that the sanctions were useful in providing a domestic rationale for considering the possibility of a dialog with the West, these diplomats argue that the sanctions themselves did little damage to the nuclear program or hardliner perspective on their right to acquire and develop a civilian nuclear program.[84] This feedback supports my theory. Used alone, the sanctions entrenched anti-deal factions in Iran and may have prolonged nuclear development. On the other hand, the deal was likely able to get broad support from international leaders, domestic constituencies, and analysts and observers worldwide because it allowed a formal mechanism (i.e., snap-back of international sanctions) for punishment *if* Iran ever violated the agreement.

The conclusion of the agreement and its continued success two years later provide significant support for my theory. The joint use of rewards and sanctions can motivate nuclear reversal in even the most persistent of nuclear proliferators.

The "dual track" policy of pressure and engagement was instrumental in motivating Iran to come to the negotiating table and conclude the JCPOA. More broadly, it marks a critical advancement in the United States' approach to nuclear reversal. Despite earlier failures (such as India), the process underlying the Iran nuclear deal reveals that U.S. counterproliferation policy has improved over time. And this analysis provides systematic social scientific support for the general efficacy of this rewards and punishments approach.

Second, and relatedly, the success of this agreement was contingent on the credible consideration of the use of military force if the Iranians continued to reject negotiations on the nuclear question or clearly pursued a weapons program. Statements by American government officials such as Secretary of State Hillary Clinton, Secretary of State John Kerry who famously stated that "all options are on the table . . . President Obama doesn't bluff," as well as President Obama himself who contended that, "I continue to keep all options on the table . . . The United States obviously has significant capabilities," were effective in conveying to the Iranians that the U.S. was serious in its threats of military force.[85] These public declarations of the availability of a military force option resounded in Iran. The Iranian Revolutionary Guard responded to these statements with their own warning, by claiming, "Mr. Obama, do not make a mistake: we too have all our options on the table. Before you get deeper in the region's quagmire, go back home!"[86] Iranian military further reacted by staging military drills in the Strait of Hormuz after threats of military force by both the Americans and the Israelis.

Indeed, there is perhaps no stronger evidence of the United States' willingness to keep all options on the table, including "acts of war," than the use of the Stuxnet computer worm, the world's first digital offensive weapon. First deployed in 2009, the computer code, now generally acknowledged to have been built by the American and Israeli intelligence services despite their denials, targeted Iranian nuclear facilities such as Natanz in an effort to sabotage centrifuge operations. Estimates by the Institute for Science and International Security suggest that by January 2010, Stuxnet had destroyed up to 1,000 centrifuges (or 10%) of the Natanz capacity. A report released later that year stated,

> If its goal was to quickly destroy all the centrifuges in the FEP [Fuel Enrichment Plant], Stuxnet failed. But if the goal was to destroy a more limited number of centrifuges and set back Iran's progress in operating the FEP, while making detection difficult, it may have succeeded, at least temporarily.[87]

While the report also assumed that the Iranians would detect the cyberattack and replace the destroyed centrifuges, to some extent, the damage was already done. Iranian nuclear facilities had been accessed and infiltrated, nuclear development had been temporarily halted and, most importantly, the willingness of the United States to employ novel weapons to counter the spread of nuclear weapons was demonstrated. While effective in this limited context, the use of the Stuxnet worm was certainly indicative of the United States' willingness to think outside the box of known military strategies and perhaps a harbinger of things to come if the Iranians persisted in their nuclear attempt at the time or were to violate the JCPOA moving forward.[88]

Lastly, Iran's nuclear reversal shortly after the election of President Rouhani provides significant support for the extension of my theory that highlights the advantages of externally incentivizing nuclear reversal during periods of leadership transition. Since the end of the Ahmadinejad administration and the election of President Rouhani, the P5+1 and Iran (with Rouhani and Foreign Minister Javad Zarif at the helm) had worked continuously to find a resolution of the Iranian nuclear weapons program despite various political roadblocks. Likely, the United States and its European allies saw this transition as an opportune time to broach the nuclear issue with Iran. Upon his election, President Rouhani revealed Iran's new preference for nuclear reversal which culminated in the JCPOA. He stated during the eventual signing of the JCPOA, "this is a new page in history. It didn't happen when we reached the deal in Vienna on July 14; it happened on the fourth of August 2013, when the Iranians elected me as their president."[89] The initial success of the JCPOA reinforced the historical evidence. New leaders, like President Rouhani, have the opportunity to reveal their nations' preference to shift course and reengage the international community upon nuclear abandonment. Their willingness to ignore the biases of their predecessors and end long-running nuclear programs is based in part on the domestic political dividends they are likely to reap with successful negotiations. Without adequate rewards, new leaders are not afforded the necessary political cover to reverse their nuclear pursuits. The JCPOA provided President Rouhani, a moderate in Iranian politics, key economic and political benefits that had not been sufficiently and credibly offered to previous Iranian leaders, and helped ensure his reelection in 2017.

To further support this logic, I conducted interviews with diplomats participating in the negotiations to assess what specific role leadership transition played in the success of the JCPOA. It was readily apparent to most American and European diplomats, as well as former officials at the IAEA, that the elections of Obama in 2012 and Rouhani in 2013 were among the core reasons that an agreement could be reached. While examining the decisions underlying U.S. counterproliferation policy historically is outside the scope of this project and is the subject of future research, it is important to consider whether the deal would have been possible with another U.S. president, especially a Republican president. The post-2016 political rhetoric suggests that reaching an agreement of this kind today would be highly unlikely. Indeed, President Trump's withdrawal from the JCPOA in June 2018 provides support for this perspective.

Western observers highlight the important role that Rouhani (and his negotiators Foreign Minister Zarif and Ali Akbar Salehi) played in these talks. Rouhani's election came as a turning point both domestically, as more of the Iranian public became disillusioned with a nuclear program that came at such high costs, and internationally, as available off-ramps to the nuclear course were becoming rare. Rouhani, especially after the intransigent Ahmadinejad, was seen as the best possible partner for negotiations and identifying the right combination of inducements was deemed a requisite strategy for approaching negotiations with this new leader.

However, my discussion with an Iranian interlocutor reveals a slightly different take on why the agreement occurred in 2015. He downplayed the specific role that Rouhani played, given the Supreme Leader's ultimate authority in all foreign policy matters including the nuclear program. Instead, the Iranian diplomat suggested that the success of the JCPOA stemmed from the reasoned and thoughtful approach taken by President Obama, compared to his predecessors, in these talks. This historic agreement sets a useful precedent for the international community if and when it faces future proliferation attempts and indicates the need to exploit natural changes in leadership, potentially on both sides, to incentivize changes in nuclear decision-making.

When considering all of these factors in the context of my theory of nuclear reversal, it is not difficult to see why the agreement was ultimately successful in reversing Iran's nuclear course in 2015. Indeed, these factors may also play a significant role in ensuring Iran's compliance with the agreement in the future. The final section discusses the future of the agreement and how structural changes in the United States and the international community may impact its success.

The Future of the JCPOA and U.S.-Iran Relations

To date, the agreement has been largely successful in stopping further nuclear development in Iran. Further, it has ensured that the time to breakout—the amount of time needed to acquire nuclear weapons once a leader decides to do so—is lengthened. In January 2016, the Director General of the IAEA declared that Iran was in compliance with the JCPOA obligations.[90] Given the narrow goals of the agreement, we can take some comfort that the P5+1 would also remain on track for their compliance obligations. There are three facets of the deal to consider as we look to the future of the JCPOA, and the future of Iranian relations with the international community more broadly.

First, it may be useful to examine how one of the rewards from the JCPOA—Iran's retention of a nuclear latent capacity—affects both regional and international dynamics. In my own research on the causes and consequences of nuclear latency, we find that latency, in general, yields a mixed bag of effects and often provides more burdens than true benefits.[91] These analyses reveal that, on average, latency emboldens and invites risk-acceptance rather than yielding deterrence or other positive benefits for states that possess it.[92] In particular, this finding would mean that while Iran's retention of operational enrichment capabilities makes it no less likely to be the target of a militarized dispute, especially by the United States or regional adversaries, it could entice Iran to engage in riskier behavior or even incite neighboring states to seek to develop their own civilian (or military) nuclear programs. In facing a conventionally superior state, such as some of Iran's proximate and distant adversaries, nuclear latency is not likely to change the balance of power, the likelihood of victory, or the costs of conflict (as operational nuclear weapons do). Thus, Iran may be no better off, and likely worse off, because of the latent nuclear capacity the JCPOA allowed. Indeed, while it is impossible to prove the counterfactual, it may even be the case that Iran might have been better off never having gone down the nuclear path in the first place.

Second, and relatedly, it is important to consider the impact of the JCPOA on other issues of international security involving the U.S. and Iran. Though obviously outside the scope of the agreement, there are renewed concerns about how this agreement would impact Israeli-Iranian relations, proxy conflicts in Syria and Yemen in the fight against the Islamic State, and regional tensions with Gulf states such as Saudi Arabia. As analyst Bruce Reidel stated in 2016, "one unintended but very important consequence of the Iran nuclear deal has been to aggravate and intensify Saudi Arabia's concerns about Iran's regional goals and intentions. This fueling of Saudi fears has in turn fanned sectarian tensions in the region to unprecedented levels."[93] While Tel Aviv and Riyadh are less worried about a nuclear Iran, at least for the next ten years, they are concerned that the JCPOA has politically and economically benefited Iran. These benefits will assist Iran in its ambitions to become a regional hegemon and continue to sponsor and support terrorist organizations in Lebanon, Palestine, and elsewhere.[94] In response, the Saudis and other Gulf states have sought to reset the balance through their own agreements with the United States, through conventional arms deals and enhanced military aerial assistance in the dispute in Yemen.[95] In analyzing these metrics on security issues peripheral to the JCPOA, it is no surprise that the agreement has heightened, rather than eased, tensions in some quarters.

Lastly, it is useful to assess the nuclear deal with regard to domestic politics in Iran, the United States, and European members. As the reelection of President Rouhani in May 2017, and his public statements since suggest, Iran is committed to complying with the agreement and allowing IAEA inspectors to assess their nuclear progress.[96] As American policy analyst Vali Nasr, stated,

> Many American observers assumed the election would be a refer-endum on the nuclear deal, and that Rouhani would coast to victory. But, for the most part, that was not the case. Unlike in the U.S. presidential campaign, none of the Iranian candidates threatened to rip up the deal. Even the most hardline candidate said that there was no going back on its terms.[97]

The Iranian elections certainly came at a pivotal moment in Iranian foreign relations. While crises abound in the region and fresh tensions arise with long-time rival Saudi Arabia, Iranian leadership and the public are focused on reaping the benefits promised in the Iran deal. These include sanctions relief, profits from the lifted oil embargo (muted by the falling global crude oil price), and the resumption of trade and economic relations with the international community. Opponents capitalized on slowing economic growth as a result of the deal, but Rouhani emphasized fundamental reforms. He announced he would challenge the ruling establishment to press for better relations with the United States, and ideally, seek the removal of the additional U.S. sanctions placed on Iran's missile program and its ties to regional instability and terrorism.[98] This evidence, along with my interviews with Iranian diplomats, suggests that Iran largely remains firmly committed to complying with the deal and even tackling some of the peripheral issue areas not covered under the nuclear deal to improve its political and economic standing in the international community.

Similarly, there appears little doubt that the European members of the P5+1 agreement hope to stand by their obligations in the agreement. After Rouhani's reelection in May 2017, newly elected French President Emmanuel Macron congratulated Rouhani and reiterated his support of the nuclear agreement and his hope that the French government will continue to advance its economic, cultural, and scientific relationship with Iran.[99] And while expressing concern about Iran's other "illegal proliferation-sensitive procurement activities," namely its missile-related activity, Germany as well as former United Nations Secretary General Ban Ki-Moon have expressed their desire to uphold the deal and address potential violations constructively.[100] In my own conversations with IAEA officials as well as members of the European and Latin American diplomatic missions involved in these discussions, the sentiment is consistent. While certainly not the best deal that could have been reached, there is great hope that the Iranians and the European parties to the agreement will not violate the terms in the next decade. What then are the factors or conditions most likely to lead to the ultimate success or failure of the JCPOA?

Implications for Counterproliferation:
Conditions for Success and Failure

The greatest threat to the Iran agreement may indeed come from certain quarters of the U.S. political establishment. Some politicians, including President Donald Trump, have been critical of the agreement from the start and remain committed to decertifying the current deal and negotiating a new, and better, deal for the United States.[101] It is not clear what he means and how he proposes to accomplish it. In particular, it is necessary to consider the fate and survival of the Iran agreement in the Trump administration. The election of President Trump has raised key questions about whether the U.S. will continue its role as a nonproliferation regime leader and will maintain its commitment to preventing the spread of nuclear weapons to other states in the international community. Throughout his campaign, Donald Trump demonstrated a dangerous, blasé attitude toward nuclear matters suggesting that nuclear proliferation was "going to happen anyway," and that "If Japan had that nuclear threat, I'm not sure that would be a bad thing for us."[102] President Trump's apparent encouragement of nuclear weapons proliferation to allies such as Japan, South Korea, and even Saudi Arabia is at odds with his desire to renegotiate the nuclear deal with Iran that would certainly raise the likelihood of nuclear proliferation in Iran (especially if a new deal could not be concluded).[103] This new geopolitical era raises a set of concerns about the future of the Iran Deal, despite buy-in from other partners, and about U.S. leadership in counterproliferation more generally. I lay out these concerns in what follows.

Though the Trump Administration had grudgingly recertified the nuclear agreement with Iran twice in 2018, it renewed its adversarial approach to Iran by imposing additional sanctions and flaming tensions between Iran and its Gulf adversaries such as Saudi Arabia. In June 2018, after months of temperamental exchanges with European allies and Iran itself, President Trump officially withdrew from the JCPOA. At the time, President Trump stated, "it is clear to me that we cannot prevent an Iranian nuclear bomb under the decaying and rotten structure of the current agreement. The Iran deal is defective at its core. If we do nothing we know exactly what will happen."[104] The Trump Administration opted to withdraw from the agreement, despite uniform compliance across the partners, and reinstated economic sanctions on Iran. In 2019, the Trump Administration further destabilized the situation by imposing new sanctions and issuing threats of force (even deploying an aircraft carrier strike group and B-52 bombers to the region) in a display of American resolve.[105] Perhaps unsurprisingly, President Rouhani responded by indicating that Iran would withdraw from some of its commitments and appealing for new negotiations, or "diplomacy with a new language and a new logic."[106] The future of the Iran deal remains increasingly uncertain.

These developments are problematic for three reasons. First, according to my theory, this approach is the wrong way to manage nuclear abandonment or reversal for this type of state. If we consider the core categories of proliferation as laid out in my theoretical framework, Iran clearly fits into the category of a U.S. adversary for whom there is a credible threat of preventive military force. For these states, the most effective way to incentivize nuclear reversal is through a combination of positive and negative inducements that provide sufficient pressure and incentives to abandon their nuclear programs. A punishment-only approach may further antagonize Iran into continuing to develop other facets of its military, including a ballistic missile program (that is outside the purview of the JCPOA).[107] Second, at this time, Iran has not engaged in behavior that would warrant the suspension or abandonment of the nuclear agreement. Thus, observers and analysts have generally been suspect of the motivation behind the Trump Administration's unilateral decision to withdraw from the agreement despite evidence from allies and third parties, like the IAEA, that the deal has successfully arrested Iran's nuclear development. Third, and finally, this strategy may provide political incentives for leaders, including President Rouhani or his successor, to want to *restart* their nuclear weapons program. As the Iranians have indicated, economic sanctions have done little to restrain their technical development, and the imposition of new sanctions may serve as political fodder for renewed opposition in Iran, including that of Ayatollah Ali Khamenei, to adhering to the JCPOA.[108] This supports an interesting statistical finding from Chapter 3: used on their own, sanctions may further harden the determination or augment the nuclear capability of proliferators.

Second, it remains unclear how the United States will manage future proliferation challenges in a geopolitical environment where U.S. credibility worldwide, especially among allies, is at an all-time low.[109] This foreign policy decision to unilaterally withdraw from JCPOA has raised serious concerns over U.S. credibility, regional objectives, and adherence to international norms. In conversations with European policy officials, in response to recent U.S. behavior, the international community has begun to more openly question the trustworthiness and credibility of the United States as a leader or partner. While exacerbated by United States' position on the Iran nuclear deal, these concerns surround other decisions as well. For example, it has prompted severe doubts about the United States' desire, and ability, to remain a leader in counterproliferation or nonproliferation under President Trump.[110] While potentially just rhetoric,[111] an "America First" foreign policy, may encourage an increase in the number of states, and potentially non-state actors, with access to nuclear weapons, technology, and latent capability. These developments will undoubtedly exacerbate a new era of uncertainty, arms racing, and other forms of destabilization in the international system.

Finally, the current situation in Iran raises an important question about the role of preventive war. At this time and based on the intelligence and evidence available, Iran has successfully transitioned from a nuclear weapons aspirant (a state engaged in nuclear weapons activity) to a nuclear latent state (a state that has retained nuclear technology for a civilian nuclear program).[112] Incentivizing nuclear latency reversal or encouraging states to retain a latent capacity without progressing (or re-starting in Iran's case) a nuclear weapons program requires a different toolkit.[113] At this juncture on the nuclear pathway, threats of preventive war may yield a less desired outcome than when countering nuclear weapons activity. Indeed, in my own research on countering nuclear latency, threats of military force or preventive war have the opposite effect and may increase the likelihood that the Iranians restart their nuclear development. Qualitatively, challenges to security or threats of military action may indeed prompt states, such as Iran, to reconsider their nuclear weapons reversal. And given the retention of a latent capacity, a decision to start a weapons pursuit anew could have disastrous consequences on international peace and security. Thus, while maintaining the shadow of military force is an integral part of countering nuclear *weapons* program, current and future U.S. policy toward Iran must entail a nuanced and diplomatic approach.

North Korea:

The Remaining Challenge

Introduction

North Korea's nuclear program remains the most significant challenge to the nonproliferation regime currently. It is also one of the greatest threats to international security that we face today. Pyongyang's tradition of antagonistic behavior on the Korean peninsula and the recent rise in belligerence toward the United States are increasingly troubling, especially in light of its continued nuclear and missile testing, including that of an ICBM believed capable of reaching the continental United States. Despite continued efforts by the U.S. and other key members of the international community to negotiate with Pyongyang, North Korea remains committed to its nuclear program.

Unlike many other proliferators, North Korea's commitment to nuclear weapons is abundantly clear. As recently as 2013, a top North Korean decision-making body issued a statement, calling its nuclear weapons "the nation's life" and stated they will not be traded even for "billions of dollars."[1] North Korea's persistence in the development of nuclear weapons as a deterrent against foreign aggressors and as a means to revise the status quo in its favor has become increasingly clear over the past two decades and has significantly shaped the interactions between the North Koreans and the international community. Further, North Korea has taken clear steps to demonstrate its continued advancement in nuclear capability: the past half-decade has seen not only a half dozen increasingly advanced underground nuclear tests but a significant increase in the number of tests of new missile technology, including recent tests of a new ICBM capability.

Yet, despite the growing tensions in the region, ramped-up nuclear development under Kim Jong-un, and aggressive rhetoric aimed at the United States, there remains a significant debate about how the United States should approach the North Koreans—including a serious consideration of military force.[2] A preemptive military strike may prompt a retaliatory military response against

Delaying Doomsday, Rupal N. Mehta. Oxford University Press (2020). © Oxford University Press.
DOI: 10.1093/oso/9780190077976.001.0001

U.S. interests, its allies, and other states in the region, all of which would be a prohibitively high cost to pay. Thus, discussions of a preventive military strike against North Korea are generally seen as non-credible.

Under these conditions, where the United States maintains a low resolve to use force against an adversary, my theory of nuclear reversal would predict that the U.S. would face a significant challenge in motivating a North Korean denuclearization. A revisionist, pariah state with markedly divergent preferences from those of the U.S., and for whom the possibility of a military attack is miniscule—the options are exceedingly limited. Indeed, the past half century has revealed exactly this difficulty: the Democratic People's Republic of Korea (DPRK) has hardly moved from its nuclear intentions despite myriad interventions. The following discussion outlines its nuclear trajectory and concludes with some implications for policymakers attempting to manage an intractable North Korean threat.

North Korea's Transition from Nuclear Explorer to Possessor

North Korea's nuclear ambitions began in the aftermath of the Korean War and growing tension in the newly divided Korean peninsula. By 1959, Pyongyang had signed a nuclear cooperation agreement with the Soviets, wherein for the next thirty years Moscow agreed to supply the North Koreans with the necessary training and technology for basic nuclear development. This agreement resembled others of the era: the Soviets (and the U.S. with the Atoms for Peace program) supplied client states and allies with basic nuclear technology and training.[3] Though not specifically designed to assist in developing nuclear weapons, the Soviet-DPRK agreement initiated a series of scientific exchanges (including the construction of the Yongbyon Nuclear Research Center) and provided basic technologies required to separate plutonium.[4] When they became operational in 1965, the Yongbyon facilities comprised a small research reactor, IRT-2000, that could conduct basic nuclear-related research, and a radiochemical laboratory that could produce small quantities of radioisotopes, both of which gave the North Koreans the ability to experiment with plutonium.[5] Though the Yongbyon complex was placed under IAEA inspection in 1977, these types of facilities were not subject to intrusive scrutiny.[6]

Throughout the next decade, North Korea ramped up its nuclear ambitions by launching a national program aimed at building several industrial-scale facilities that could produce significant amounts of plutonium for the country's nuclear power industries and weapons production. The North Koreans built three gas-cooled natural-uranium-fueled reactors, and factories to process and refine uranium ore for fuel fabrication, and a radiochemical laboratory/reprocessing plant (with a second plant in construction) that could extract plutonium from the spent reactor fuel. This indigenous dual-mode approach to pursuing a nuclear weapons program was made easier from already-public reactor designs and easy access to significant quantities of raw materials, such as natural uranium ore.[7] At this stage, the North Koreans had acquired most of the components of the nuclear fuel cycle needed to build an operational nuclear weapons program.

However, when North Korea acceded to the Nonproliferation Treaty in December 1985, all its nuclear facilities and materials were placed under international inspection. It appeared as though the immediate danger had subsided. In its initial negotiation effort, the United States attempted a strategy of combinative rewards and sanctions. First, in exchange for allowing inspections of all of their nuclear facilities, the North Koreans demanded that the United States withdraw all of its naval and land-based tactical nuclear weapons deployed in South Korea (nearly 100 warheads). Further, they demanded that South Korea agree to a Declaration on the Denuclearization of the Korean Peninsula under which Seoul promised not to "produce, possess, store, deploy, or use nuclear weapons."[8] In December 1991, the U.S. and South Korea acceded to these demands, and DPRK and South Korea signed the Joint Declaration, agreeing to non-nuclearization and mutual inspections for verification. Yet, troubling signs began to emerge when Pyongyang waited to sign this agreement until 1992 though it had only eighteen months under the treaty to negotiate a comprehensive safeguard agreement with the IAEA.[9] In response to the delay and the ensuing concerns about North Korea's commitment to the Joint Declaration, the United States began to impose targeted sanctions on specific North Korean corporations for their missile proliferation activities.[10] It is important to note that at this first significant attempt to reverse DPRK's nuclear course, there was virtually no serious consideration of military force.[11]

Indeed, concerns about North Korea's adherence to the agreement soon came to fruition. After six official inspection missions in the early 1990s, the North Koreans denied inspectors access to potential nuclear waste storage facilities and threatened to withdraw from the NPT. The early inspections, however, revealed discrepancies between Pyongyang's initial declarations to the IAEA and the analyzed samples collected onsite. These inspections, coupled with satellite imagery, indicated that the North Koreans had produced much more plutonium (between two and four kg) than authorized or disclosed.[12] By this time, the U.S. assessed that the North Koreans had potentially produced enough plutonium for one to two nuclear devices, about 8–12 kg of separated plutonium, that they had concealed throughout IAEA inspections.[13] And in 1993, after repeated refusals for greater access (including an IAEA request for a "special inspection" of two alleged waste sites), Pyongyang withdrew from the NPT. Thus began the 1993–1994 nuclear crisis that culminated in one of the most significant efforts to reverse North Korea's nuclear program.

In October 1994, the Clinton Administration and North Korea signed the Agreed Framework—the first serious attempt to counter North Korea's nuclear progress. The deal included various provisions, such as the freezing and replacement of North Korea's indigenous nuclear power plant with more proliferation-resistant light-water reactor plants, the normalization of diplomatic relations between the two states, and formal assurances from the U.S. that it would not threaten or use nuclear weapons against the North Koreans. To verify the freeze on plutonium production facilities, the IAEA placed seals on the key access points and installed monitoring devices, and DPRK allowed a team of resident inspectors at Yongbyon, who were authorized to conduct surprise inspections on short notice.[14] Pyongyang also agreed to a series of additional containment and surveillance measures to confirm the freeze on production but resisted others that could possibly reveal the extent of progress made before the arrested development.

In return for complying with these limited counterproliferation demands, Pyongyang was offered several political and economic rewards. These included food and economic assistance, as well as continued discussions with the Americans on signing the Agreed Framework. During this time, the Clinton Administration also sent Former President Jimmy Carter as an envoy to help negotiate a deal between the U.S. and North Korea regarding implementation of further restrictions, points of access, and inspections.[15] As part of the effort to keep North Korea in the NPT, the U.S. issued negative security assurances (agreeing not to use force including the use of nuclear weapons against North Korea) and assured non-interference in DPRK internal affairs. As such, the 1994 Agreed Framework represented a significant concession to North Korean demands. Given the DPRK's fear of regime survival due to a preemptive strike, the United States' assurance to not threaten to attack the North Koreans, even in defense of their allies in the region, was important to Pyongyang. This agreement, with a focus on benefits desired by the North Koreans, was a critical shift in how the international community, and especially the United States, approached negotiating with North Korea. Yet, rather than motivate Kim Jong-il to abandon its nuclear effort, the Agreed Framework seemed to reveal a growing concern about the North Korean program. Pyongyang was willing to endure sanctions, and even the withdrawal of food and economic aid guaranteed in the agreement, to maintain a nuclear capability, even if there was no reason to fear that the United States (or any other member of the international community) would use military force to permanently end its effort.

North Korea's proliferation attempt did not end with the signing of the Agreed Framework as hoped. To the extent that Pyongyang sought to maintain a nuclear hedge to protect itself, the regime had strong incentives to pursue alternative avenues of proliferation that would allow it to comply with international nonproliferation demands, while clandestinely preserving its nuclear ambitions. Although neither has publicly acknowledged their cooperation, it is generally known that the North Koreans provided Pakistan with functional missiles and missile production technology in exchange for sensitive nuclear assistance, such as gas centrifuge technology. This allowed the DPRK to produce weapons-grade fissile material.[16]

By 1996, the Agreed Framework had fallen apart and the United States began re-imposing a series of sanctions on North Korea for Pyongyang's transfer of missile technology and components to AQ Khan's Research Laboratory in Pakistan. The United States, in conjunction with South Korea and Japan, also continued diplomatic negotiations with North Korea to encourage the termination of its missile program in exchange for relief from economic sanctions. This strategy resulted in some temporary successes. For example, Pyongyang agreed to a moratorium on testing any long-range missiles for the duration of the bilateral talks with the U.S. in exchange for a partial lifting of economic sanctions.[17] In addition, in response to the historic North-South summit to be held in 2000 regarding the question of reunification of the Korean Peninsula, the U.S. temporarily relaxed sanctions, allowing a wider range of trade in commercial and consumer goods, easing restrictions on investments, and removing prohibitions on direct financial transactions. By 1999, North Korean policy coordinator, former Secretary of Defense William Perry recommended "a new, comprehensive and integrated approach to . . . negotiations with the DPRK, which would involve a coordinated reduction in isolation by the U.S. and its allies in a 'step-by-step and reciprocal fashion.' "[18]

However, these advances were short-lived, despite continued efforts at diplomacy by the U.S. and other members of the international community. By 2000, U.S. intelligence had discovered Pyongyang's suspected attempts to acquire nuclear technology and materials, such as high-strength aluminum tubes, for a centrifuge program. Less than two years later, the U.S. concluded that the North Koreans had reneged on their commitment to curb proliferation. They had initiated a secret production-scale centrifuge facility to produce enough weapons-grade uranium for two or more nuclear weapons per year when fully operational.[19] This revelation resulted in the collapse of the Agreed Framework in late 2002. North Korea disabled the IAEA monitoring equipment at its reactor and reprocessing facility, restarted plutonium production, and expelled inspectors from Yongbyon.[20] In January 2003, the IAEA Board of Governors adopted a resolution that condemned Pyongyang's decision to restart its reactor and resume its nuclear activities. Less than five days later, the North Koreans withdrew from the NPT, ostensibly confirming that they had fully re-embarked on their nuclear ambitions and were determined to maintain their nuclear deterrent.[21]

North Korea's decision to renege on its commitments signified an important turning point in the interactions between Pyongyang and Washington. With this move, the North Koreans revealed their commitment to remain a nuclear weapons state as neither the prior use of economic sanctions nor the recent offer of rewards would persuade them to abandon their nuclear program, especially since they did not believe that the United States would resort to escalatory punishment or a military attack. After years of ineffective economic sanctions and seemingly reasonable offers of political and economic benefits, North Korea revealed they had little intention of ever abandoning their nuclear program. The collapse of the Agreed Framework and North Korea's continued commitment to its nuclear program reaffirmed a critical implication for the study of nuclear reversal: not all counterproliferation attempts are successful.

Aftermath of the Agreed Framework: 2000–2016

The withdrawal of the DPRK from the NPT was unprecedented and produced a new set of challenges. Following this withdrawal, indications that Pyongyang may lift its moratorium on long-range missile testing prompted a series of attempts at multilateral negotiations, to no avail. For example, in 2003, North Korea proposed an agreement whereby the U.S. would conclude a non-aggression treaty that included the following terms: (1) normalized bilateral diplomatic relations; (2) non-interference in North Korean economic affairs; (3) completion of the nuclear reactors promised under the Agreed Framework; and (4) increased food aid. These benefits were to be provided in exchange for the dismantlement of the "nuclear facility," the termination of missile-testing, and restrictions on the export of missile technology to other state and non-state entities.[22] Throughout these negotiations, the North Korean delegation, however, continued to threaten to test nuclear weapons and demonstrate that they have the capability to deliver them. This tactic was seemingly meant to coerce the U.S. to abide by North Korean demands. Unsurprisingly, the U.S. did not agree to acquiesce to these demands. In the aftermath, the U.S.-North Korean relations stagnated and little progress was made in broader efforts to counter the vertical and horizontal proliferation in North Korea. Rather, verbal hostilities, interspersed with occasional multilateral talks and several new rounds of sanctions, continued for more than a decade.

The George W. Bush Administration oversaw the introduction of the short-lived Six-Party Talks that included both South and North Koreas, Japan, China, Russia, and the United States. Following little direct interaction with North Korea after 2009, Kim Jong-il's death in December 2011 raised serious concerns and uncertainty about North Korea's nuclear future while raising some level of optimism with the arrival of new leader. North Korea's behavior following Kim Jong-il's death was remarkably consistent with my theoretical expectation regarding leadership change. After the death of the Supreme Leader, Pyongyang agreed to stop nuclear testing, uranium enrichment, and even long-range missile testing in exchange for foreign assistance, namely food aid from the United States.[23] This moment may have been a good opportunity to significantly influence North Korea's nuclear trajectory.

However, a rocket launch in April 2012 signified that North Korea, now led by Kim Jong-un, had remained resolved to maintain the nuclear option. He thus rendered the agreement to suspend uranium enrichment, nuclear tests, and long-range missile tests void. In a statement rejecting the United Nations' rebuke of the test, the North Korean Foreign Ministry stated that the DPRK is, "no longer bound by the deal, we have thus become able to take necessary retaliatory measures . . . The U.S. will be held wholly accountable for all the ensuing consequences."[24] Soon after, the United States suspended its food aid (nearly 240,000 tons) and its assurances to not have "hostile intent" against the North Koreans.

One key implication emerged from this incident with North Korea. Analysts assessing North Korea's nuclear development became increasingly convinced that sanctions, on their own, had little impact on Pyongyang's nuclear program. In particular, observers noted the similarity in rocket vehicle design to a known Chinese vehicle. However, the recent 2009 Security Council Resolution had banned any state from supplying North Korea with "any arms or related materiel, or providing financial transactions, technical training, services or assistance to such arms."[25] Analysts suggested that the Chinese may have violated this resolution by providing a new missile launching vehicle that was seen during a military parade in Pyongyang. One analyst at Jane's Defense Weekly highlighted the similarities in designs and stated that the appearance of this Chinese vehicle "in North Korea's missile program would require approval from the highest levels of the Chinese government and the People's Liberation Army."[26]

By the beginning of 2013, the UN Security Council passed a unanimous resolution to strengthen existing sanctions (by expanding the scope of materials covered) and to add financial sanctions (including the blocking of large cash transfers, and targeting specific individuals and entities for asset freezes).[27] On their own, the evidence suggests that these sanctions were relatively ineffective.[28] In addition to having a limited impact on North Korea's nuclear capability, the sanctions imposed by the United States and the United Nations seem to have had similarly small impact on North Korea's economy. For example, evidence from Hufbauer et al. estimated the projected cost of sanctions to be approximately 1.2% of North Korea's GNP in a given year.[29] In years when the international community imposed sanctions, China provided compensatory economic and military assistance, and food aid to offset those sanctions.[30] With this approach to negotiation that relied on negative inducements (rendered moot by the Chinese partially bypassing them), and without simultaneous positive inducements, North Korea acted in accord with my theoretical expectations. Rather than forego a nuclear deterrent, North Korea withstood the cost of economic sanctions and redoubled efforts for its nuclear program, as there was little fear of escalatory punishment for continuing. And without an offer of rewards, even those that had been offered (and often refused) before, there was little reason for Kim Jong-un to consider a suspension of nuclear activities.

By April 2013, Pyongyang had restarted all of its nuclear facilities at Yongbyon and renewed its uranium enrichment program. Further, new evidence revealed that North Korea may also have the ability to reprocess plutonium at its graphite-moderated reactor.[31] Recent satellite imagery had revealed an uptick in uranium and plutonium production capabilities suggesting that North Korea was focused on continuing to build up its arsenal of nuclear warheads.[32] Tensions between the North Koreans, their immediate neighbors, and the broader international community intensified as Kim Jong-un continued to conduct missile and nuclear tests in contravention of United Nations Security Council resolutions aimed to deter these tests. These actions were accompanied by increasingly bellicose rhetoric out of Pyongyang that suggested imminent aggression against Seoul, U.S. military bases in the Pacific, and the Western coast of the United States. Yet President Obama, throughout his 2012 presidential campaign and in his inaugural address, indicated a desire to engage with "rogue" governments. Despite North Korea's recent belligerence, the Obama Administration maintained a policy of "strategic patience," waiting for North Korea to come back to the bargaining table.[33]

Fire and Fury: 2016 to Present

The election of President Donald Trump saw an evolution in U.S. foreign policy across a wide range of issue areas, including how to manage the growing threat from North Korea. The North Koreans soon reached two major milestones in their nuclear development: (1) the successful testing of their first intercontinental ballistic missile in July 2017; and (2) a purported and suspected successful test of a hydrogen bomb in September 2017.[34] Ostensibly, the threat that the

North Koreans now posed extended beyond the region and if their capabilities were confirmed, they potentially had the ability to reach and threaten the United States.

The response from the Trump Administration was markedly different from previous administrations. While other presidents certainly admonished the North Korean leader, they generally did so in a reasoned, deliberate, and cautious manner. President Trump took a different approach. First, the Trump Administration decided to impose "secondary sanctions" or "301 sanctions" on North Korea in an effort to stop their further nuclear development.[35] In an address to the United Nations General Assembly in September 2017, Trump stated, "if it [the U.S.] is forced to defend itself and its allies, we will have no choice but to totally destroy North Korea." Referring to Kim Jong-un as "rocket man," Trump said the North Korean leader was "on a suicide mission for himself and for his regime."[36] What ensued was an alarming war of words between the two leaders. Kim quickly replied by warning that Trump "would 'pay dearly' for threatening to destroy North Korea." He also said Trump's comments "have convinced me, rather than frightening or stopping me, that the path I chose is correct and that it is the one I have to follow to the last."[37]

Within a few months of President Trump's inauguration, it seemed that the latent crisis that had been brewing between the United States and North Korea for decades may erupt into a full-blown war. The following few months saw increasingly alarming and provocative language from both Washington and Pyongyang, continued missile testing, and considerations of military plans for ground action in North Korea.[38] Perhaps concerned that a major crisis was looming, South Korean President Moon Jae-in began to reach out to North Korea to suggest joint cooperation during the 2018 Winter Olympics. This détente prompted officials from North Korea to reveal that Pyongyang was willing to begin talks with the United States.

By March 2018, Kim Jong-un had extended an invitation to President Trump to discuss the North Korean nuclear program. Soon after President Trump's surprise on-the-spot acceptance to meet Kim, CIA Director Michael Pompeo conducted a secret trip to North Korea. It was the first such high-level meeting since Secretary of State Madeleine Albright's visit in 2000. After this trip, North Korea announced that it would suspend nuclear and missile testing, and it had purportedly closed the site where missile testing had occurred.[39] Washington and Pyongyang soon began to discuss plans for a summit to discuss DPRK's nuclear program. After weeks of back-and-forth about whether the summit would go on (especially after National Security Adviser John Bolton's remarks comparing North Korea to Libya), Donald Trump and Kim Jong-un finally met on June 12 in Singapore. During the meeting, both leaders signed a document that provided guarantees to North Korea in exchange for their commitment to denuclearize the Korean Peninsula (while short on specifics), and the meeting was hailed as a success. President Trump stated, "we're very proud of what took place today. I think our whole relationship with North Korea and the Korean Peninsula is going to be a very much different situation than it has in the past."[40]

Observers to the summit recognized that while the Trump Administration lauded it as a success, the meeting with Kim Jong-un came with significant costs to the United States and its allies, while almost entirely benefitting the North Korean regime.[41] First, the North Koreans received international recognition and normalization, a summit with and words of praise from a sitting U.S. president, a capitulation on a long-standing demand from the North Koreans. In exchange for a more managed nuclear weapons program—potentially, retention of their nuclear infrastructure in exchange for inspections/access—North Korea may receive foreign assistance and security assurance from the United States. Further, they demanded, and received, a commitment for decreased U.S. involvement with South Korea (i.e., canceling planned U.S.-ROK military exercises).

Second, these developments were a significant loss for South Korea as well, given its sixty-years-plus relationship with the United States. As a result of the recent discussions with North Korea, the U.S. has started the process of distancing itself from its obligations to the ROK, namely joint military exercises. Relatedly, the summit has had political repercussions for the United States. The U.S., already suffering a loss of reputation with allies in the region, and broader international community, invited further criticism about its appeasement to North Korea.[42] The administration had ostensibly normalized the North Korean regime (despite its rampant human rights violations and historical belligerence to states in the international community). President Trump even praised the North Korean leader in recent weeks.[43] Such overtures, coupled with shifting alliance dynamics, began to worry other U.S. allies in the international system who had already started to question U.S. credibility and Trump's seemingly erratic policy in the region.[44]

In the months that followed, President Trump and Kim Jong-un met for a second summit in Hanoi, Vietnam. Despite the White House's optimism in the lead-up to the summit, the leaders hastily walked away without an agreement in place—effectively resulting in yet another failure.[45] Within months, North Korea resumed testing of three missile systems, including an unidentified Short-Range Ballistic Missile (SRBM) and two multiple rocket launchers (MRL).[46] At this time, the situation with North Korea remains as uncertain as ever. Aside from President Trump's own assertions about the success of the two summits and a vague signed statement, there is little to show.[47] Furthermore, there is little doubt (and in fact growing certainty) that North Korea remains committed to its nuclear program and that denuclearization in the Korean peninsula is a distant prospect, at best.[48]

Understanding Counterproliferation Failure to Date

How can we explain why the United States has continually been unsuccessful in working to reverse North Korean nuclear pursuit? To answer this question, I focus primarily on the three most recent U.S. administrations (Clinton, Bush, and Obama), who have engaged Pyongyang on this issue.

Consider first the Clinton Administration's approach to North Korea during the 1990s. Though the Agreed Framework was drafted to provide North Korea with political, economic, and technical rewards, it did so without maintaining the sanctions in place until the North Koreans halted their nuclear progress (at which times the sanctions would be lifted). Further, there was no credible background threat that the United States would use military force if the North Koreans continued their nuclear pursuit. In accord with my theoretical framework, this strategy of rewards without any punishment (especially a credible threat to employ military force if necessary), is not likely to motivate adversaries like North Korea to reverse their nuclear weapons programs. This failure in counterproliferation strategy was compounded by the United States' decision to renege on the Agreed Framework (i.e., a failure to lift sanctions or deliver rewards as promised).[49] My theory assumes that actors are credible in their commitments and will follow through if proliferators abandon their nuclear efforts. The United States' failure to uphold the Agreement Framework (though ineffective), all but ensured that it would be unsuccessful.[50]

The Bush Administration's approach was similarly unsuccessful but for different reasons. After confronting North Korea for secretly building nuclear weapons and violating prior agreements, President Bush chose a different tactic which relied primarily on punishment. In public declarations, including the infamous "Axis of Evil" speech, the Bush administration approached a willful North Korea with a fresh round of economic sanctions aimed at delaying or stopping further progress. North Korea's response to this punishments-only strategy was to withdraw from the NPT in 2003 after announcing DPRK's new nuclear status. When the United States later sought to return to the negotiating table, North Korea used food assistance and other political concessions from the United States to bargain for a short suspension in weapons-building (which was later violated). Within three years, the North Koreans had successfully tested a nuclear device and had sold nuclear weapons technology to Syria.[51]

Lessons from this era of nuclear negotiations again reveal the importance of a dual approach. The initial sticks-only strategy provided little in terms of incentives for Kim Jong-il to abandon a nuclear program, especially one that was favored by his military cadre. Only after North Koreans demonstrated their commitment to nuclear weapons (by leaving the NPT, among other acts), did the U.S. acquiesce and offer rewards with no parallel punishment strategy. According to observers, North Korea then "successfully gamed the United States. As the Bush administration waited for the country to collapse under the weight of sanctions, Mr. Kim successfully developed a nuclear weapon, shifting the stakes of all future courses of action."[52] Kim Jong-il ended up reaping significant concessions without altering his decision-making on the nuclear program.

President Obama did not follow either of his predecessors in defining his approach to North Korea. Perhaps alarmed by the failures of both the Clinton and Bush Administrations in their carrot-only, and stick-only approaches, respectively, President Obama chose neither. Despite a series of nuclear tests early during President Obama's first term, the administration chose the policy of "strategic patience" that included neither positive nor negative inducements but rather a plan to wait out the rogue state.[53] Without pressure from and engagement with the United States, the North Koreans proceeded to build up their weapons program and engage in other hostile actions on the international stage. And despite President Obama's assertions that the U.S. "will not hesitate to use our military might," these vague threats of force were not joined by offers of rewards or sanctions to incentivize the DPRK to avoid preemptive military attack.[54] As discussed previously, it is not clear the extent to which the international community, let alone the North Koreans, saw these threats as credible enough to actually motivate a change in DPRK's nuclear trajectory. Without any of the necessary pieces of counterproliferation strategy in play, Kim Jong-un significantly ramped up the DPRK's nuclear and missile programs.

Negotiating in the Shadow of Force: A Dangerous Future

What began with an emphasis on policy that was "the best option" has now turned into a sanguine, resigned assessment that "there are no options—good or otherwise."[55] That may indeed reflect the current state of affairs between Pyongyang and Washington, but there is no more important time to consider short-term stopgap and de-escalatory tactics as well as long-term strategies aimed at security and stability on the Korean peninsula. I conclude with three recommendations for policymakers seeking to manage the North Korean problem, given that, for the time being, successful (and peaceful) nuclear reversal seems unlikely.

First, the option to credibly threaten military force must be "on the table." While a *preventive* attack on North Korea is extremely unlikely, it must be made clear to North Korea that the United States will not hesitate to respond to either conventional or nuclear aggression against the homeland or our allies and interests abroad.[56] This is, to some degree, the status quo. According to North Korea expert Dae-Sook Suh, "the reason for the North Korean nuclear weapons program is based on its need to survive. It is not to improve its power position vis-a-vis South Korea or to use nuclear blackmail in its international relations. It is not the purpose of the North Korean nuclear weapons program to engage in nuclear arms trade . . . North Korea thinks it needs such weapons for its survival."[57] Analysis of the North Korean case provides additional evidence to suggest that Pyongyang deeply fears a military strike by the Americans and is primarily focused on existential deterrence to ensure the survival of the regime. North Korea scholar Bruce Cummings states, regarding President Reagan's decision to sell F-16s to South Korea which was seen as a direct threat to DPRK in the 1980s, "this scenario truly horrified the North Koreans, and during the remaining Reagan years they shouted themselves hoarse in opposition to U.S. policy."[58]

The United States must work to assure the North Koreans, the South Koreans, and the Chinese that it will not initiate a conflict with the DPRK and endanger its allies in East Asia. However, it must also demonstrate its resolve to respond in such a way that it would be willing to end Kim Jong-un's regime if they were to strike first—a strategy that emphasizes deterrence by punishment.[59] As stated by a former American diplomat, "this means that even if we can't prevent North Korea from gaining the ability to hit us or our allies, we can deter it from actually doing so, and thus have time to pursue, by means more effective than sanctions and less dangerous than war, our ultimate goal of a reunified Korea that threatens no one."[60]

Second, a future policy approach toward North Korea must include both sanctions (or other punishments) *and* rewards. Targeted economic sanctions, especially if channeled through Chinese companies that work with the North Korean military, and cyber intervention that affect "left of launch" capabilities are useful in causing pauses and disruptions (which may now be the best option).[61] However, evidence from the historical record, and the North Korean case in particular, demonstrates the necessity for a parallel path of rewards, such as economic trade with or financial assistance from the Chinese and other partners. If the acceptance of a nuclear North Korea and the paring down of the U.S. presence in the region are prerequisites for any formal accord, an agreement may be impossible. Negotiating an ad-hoc "carrots and sticks" approach that does not demand these conditions as a starting point in exchange for shorter-term suspensions or inspections may be more credible and durable.

Further, this combinative approach may alleviate concerns that the United States is focused solely on regime change. By de-emphasizing isolation and encouraging economic opportunities for North Korea, it may be possible to garner more support from the Chinese who remain primarily concerned about a North Korean state collapse on their border. As stated by retired U.S. Admiral Mike Mullen in 2016, "The stakes are huge . . . Instability generated on the peninsula could cascade into China."[62] This strategy of positive and negative policy levers may help elicit more partners to help manage the North Korean threat, especially if the United States maintains its desire to retire from its role as a global leader in counterproliferation. For the Chinese, South Koreans, and the Japanese, a strategy that seeks to influence nuclear decision-making and a slowing down in nuclear development may be more preferable than a return to policies that exacerbate instability.[63]

Finally, this strategy entails identifying acceptable stop-gap measures in search of a longer-term solution. It will require engaging the Chinese more on the North Korean issue while alleviating their concerns about the externalities of the regime's collapse. It will require American restraint and de-escalatory rhetoric to ensure that Kim Jong-un does not seek to employ short-range nuclear capabilities against a conventional invasion, and stage long-range ICBM capabilities to deter American nuclear retaliation. Lastly, it may entail learning to live with a nuclear North Korea, imbued with "strategic patience," while assuring the world of the strength of our deterrent and our resolve to respond if deterrence fails.

Lessons Learned: Nuclear Reversal, International Relations, and Future Challenges

Introduction

This book has broadly addressed the utility of external policy levers to influence nuclear decision-making in states, namely to reverse or refrain from the pursuit of nuclear weapons. It has analyzed two key questions: Given the benefits associated with nuclear weapons, why are states willing to give them up? And, if the United States and the broader international community are able to influence nuclear reversal, what types of tools are most effective in doing so?

I have argued that nuclear reversal is most likely when the United States offers inducements that include sufficient face-saving incentives for political leaders to reap the benefits of a negotiated end to their costly nuclear pursuit *and* threatens/imposes sanctions or other escalatory punishment if the proliferator persists. These tools used in tandem can persuade even the most committed proliferators to stop their nuclear pursuits. To most effectively bargain, the U.S. exploits existing relationship with proliferators and demonstrates a willingness to expend significant effort to counterproliferation. My research revealed that while the U.S. is particularly effective in persuading allies to abandon their nuclear programs, this compellent strategy also works for non-allies and even its adversaries. Further, leadership transitions in proliferating states can provide unique, short-term windows of opportunity to encourage a nuclear reversal. Operating in the background of these strategic interactions is the willingness of the United States to credibly threaten the use of military force—a game-ending move that can permanently end a nascent nuclear program. Statistical tests and several qualitative analyses of the historical record, based on original archival and interview evidence, lend critical support to my theory of nuclear reversal.

Delaying Doomsday, Rupal N. Mehta. Oxford University Press (2020). © Oxford University Press.
DOI: 10.1093/oso/9780190077976.001.0001

Through this analysis, I have also been able to discount some of the alternative explanations for nuclear reversal. A punishment-only strategy that includes either economic sanctions or military force solely is not likely to have the expected or desired outcome. Domestic political factors such as waning interest from leaders or other bureaucratic hurdles matter less in explaining why states are willing to stop their costly nuclear pursuits. Lastly, the removal of security concerns, enduring rivalries, or other motivating factors for the initial proliferation decision, may not be sufficient to influence nuclear decision-making.

The arguments articulated and evidence presented in this book not only challenge some of the conventional wisdom about nuclear proliferation and nuclear reversal, but they also highlight the advances in U.S. policy that encourages pressure and engagement. There is evidence to suggest that U.S. counterproliferation policy has evolved and improved over time and this book provides systematic social scientific support for the general efficacy of *both* carrots and sticks to alter nuclear decision-making. This last chapter concludes by delving into important implications for key issues in international relations regarding tools of statecraft, nuclear latency, the utility of military threats, multilateral bargaining, and how to contend with current and future proliferation threats to the international community.

The Politics of Statecraft: Rewards on Tough Cases

Scholars have long suggested that actors can provide external incentives to impact decision-making. Despite this contention, there has been little direct evidence to suggest how exactly states are persuaded and what causal effects these tools may have. Further, there appears to have been some degree of confusion or conflation about how positive and negative tools actually interact to produce the desired effect: could one persuade with either tool or were they mere opposites in their impact? For example, Robert Dahl stated, "the existence of both negative and positive coercion is sometimes a source of confusion in political analysis, since writers often either confound the two or ignore positive coercion."[1]

This book provides an answer to this debate in international relations and establishes the strong utility of employing rewards and sanctions together. While the debate has centered thus far on distinguishing the competing effects of negative versus positive tools, my study reveals the need for a combinative approach to their use. Sanctions are necessary to hasten negotiations and deter the action in question while rewards must be employed to provide a compellent political benefit to proliferators for forgoing or stopping their actions. While adopting this strategy in international relations is critical, extension of this logic to other issue arenas may become potentially transformative. It could prove to be an effective approach to coerce other negative behavior in the international system, including the development and potential use of other forms of weapons of mass destruction, dispute resolution, or even domestic political behavior.

My research reveals that an approach of sanctions and rewards may be more effective in persuading even the toughest proliferators to reverse their nuclear course. This conclusion may seem reasonable for the majority of cases in the historical record—states that acquire a nuclear capability as a means to achieve status or prestige, or simply because they have the technological background to do so easily. Offering rewards to these proliferators, even if they are not core allies of the U.S., seems politically feasible and effective. And again, when considering extensions to other issue areas in international relations, the offer of positive and negative inducements to compel a change in trade or dispute behavior among friendly states may be similarly attractive.

In this book, I argue that this same approach must be extended to states that are not allied with the U.S. or other major powers and who may have significantly divergent preferences to those of the international system. While coercion might seem like an appropriate and politically desirable strategy for rogue states or committed proliferators, this tactic clearly has not been sufficient to motivate actual changes in decision-making. Sanctions alone cannot do what is necessary. I demonstrate that a simultaneous offer of rewards is necessary to persuade these hardline states to give up their nuclear weapons programs or compel other changes in their decision-making. No doubt this may be politically challenging for the U.S. or other members of the international community that must defend decisions to "reward" pariah or rogue states for what is seen as bad behavior.

My research also reveals that, at least in the nuclear context, policymakers have often made the decision to employ a combinative rewards-and-punishments strategy despite the political costs of doing so, and often in contrast to the policy rhetoric and academic scholarship recommending a different approach. Policymakers truly interested in nonproliferation and in countering the spread of nuclear weapons among nuclear-capable states must continue to make this calculation, perhaps in defiance of recommendations from other domestic and foreign political leaders. The controversy surrounding the Iran deal highlights this decision-making process. The Obama Administration concluded that stopping Iran's nuclear development through a pressure and engagement approach (despite protestations from American politicians and foreign leaders) was more important than continuing the historical punishments-based strategy that did little but strengthen Iran's commitment to its nuclear program. Rewards, even for adversaries, must be on the negotiating table for nuclear reversal to succeed.

Bargaining Value of Military Force and the Importance of Credibility

Underlying these strategic interactions and the success of rewards and punishments to incentivize a change in nuclear decision-making is the shadow of military force. Thus far, military force has been used to permanently stop nuclear weapons programs, as in Iraq and Syria, by destroying suspected nuclear facilities and infrastructure. Yet, this book reveals the importance of the threat of military force as an effective bargaining tool that can shape future negotiations with proliferators. The success of a rewards-and-punishments strategy is conditional on the ability of the United States or other states in the international community to credibly signal that they will follow through on the use of force if proliferators do not accept the inducements being offered. Accordingly, the United States' position on the use of force with regard to a particular proliferator can have a dramatic impact on the strategic interaction between the two actors and the ultimate outcome. If the use of force is a politically viable tool and policymakers can credibly signal their threat to use force, it may shape how a proliferator responds to the offer of inducements and may stop even the most committed of proliferators.

This is, no doubt, a controversial finding that demands more in-depth analysis within the policy community and among nuclear decision-makers. There are at least two important considerations. First, it is important to assess how reasonable it is for the United States to threaten a military strike (and perhaps increase the likelihood of conflict with a potential nuclear weapons state) in order to shift the bargaining dynamic between the two states. While my research suggests that this strategy is effective, especially against states that truly desire nuclear weapons, it is important to examine its long-term consequences, especially if it becomes necessary to follow through on the threat to use force. For example, counterproliferators are more likely and able to credibly threaten the use of military force against states with whom they have divergent preferences, or states that are revisionist and hoping to use their new-found nuclear status to alter the status quo in their favor. For these states, threats of military force from the United States or one of its proxies are particularly salient and may raise the specter of confrontation and conflict. Counterproliferation objectives where consideration of the use of force translates into preventive military attacks or worse, that is, full-scale military operations akin to war, may result in disastrous consequences. One need only look to the Second Gulf War to examine how decisions to use military force to stop the proliferation of weapons of mass destruction (the Bush Administration's stated objective in initiating the war in Iraq) can go awry. This long-running war reveals another complex cost-benefit calculation that trades off successfully countering proliferation with an increased likelihood of military dispute.

Second, it is critical to consider the importance of credibility. In strategic interactions, states are compelled to change course because they believe the U.S. (or other designated members of the international community) will actually follow through on their commitments *and* their threat to escalate to the use of force if they persist in their current behavior. Issuing redlines for action or openly declaring "all options are on the table" for deterrent and compellent purposes requires that your opponent believe in the threat being issued. In the nuclear realm, proliferators must believe that the U.S. will impose both rewards and sanctions to stop their nuclear pursuit. The U.S. must similarly believe that the proliferator will stop its nuclear program before it delivers the benefits promised and suspends punishments imposed or threatened. Reputation matters, especially in such a high-stakes environment.[2] And as counterproliferators do actually differ in their consideration of military force,[3] only those that are truly willing to issue an order to strike a suspected nuclear facility or engage in another form of military attack should signal as much.

Naturally, this yields important implications not just for the proliferation case in question but for other states observing this dynamic to assess the resolve of the U.S. to credibly commit to a strategy and follow through on it—negotiations or escalatory punishment alike. In my interviews with Iranian and European diplomats regarding the Iran nuclear deal, each referenced their concerns regarding the U.S. credibility after previous negotiation failures, notably the Agreed Framework with North Korea during the mid-1990s. While also recognizing North Korea's own violations of the agreement, they stressed the importance of the United States' credibility in its declarations of the consideration of force and its commitment to the agreement itself. Similarly, the rest of the international community observed the United States' lack of credibility in its recent policy toward Iran for implications for dealing with North Korea and other proliferators. Indeed, many believe that the U.S. withdrawal from the JCPOA sets an important precedent for counterproliferation negotiation in the twenty-first century. And given the current political landscape, the rise in bombastic leaders both at home and abroad, and the increase in potential crises across the international system, there can be no better time to reiterate the importance of reputation, trustworthiness, and integrity in such strategic interactions.

Nuclear Latency

This book highlights the importance of a baseline level of nuclear technology as an effective counterproliferation inducement. Allowed within the confines of the nonproliferation regime and codified as part of the NPT, there is little doubt that states are interested in acquiring a certain level of nuclear capability. The acquisition of uranium enrichment and perhaps plutonium reprocessing technology can be used not only for civilian purposes but for reasons of prestige and status, among others. In my collaborative research on the determinants of nuclear latency, we find that a state's nuclear reversal is likely to increase the desire for acquiring nuclear latency.[4] Indeed, this desire makes sense given that previous scholarship has argued that states retain latency partially to mitigate the price for publicly renouncing the weapons option or giving up the nuclear pursuit entirely.[5] If states that reverse their weapons programs or renounce the bomb option seek to retain high levels of latent capabilities, it may indicate that incentives for hedging may be driving the states to maintain such nuclear infrastructure. However, nuclear reversal agreements that codify international inspections and enforce monitoring may provide the best hope for assuring that states do not restart down the nuclear weapons path.

This logic suggests a somewhat counterintuitive possibility for counterproliferation policy. States interested in curbing nuclear weapons proliferation may be able to dangle the carrot of the pursuit or possession of nuclear latency to a proliferator. This incentive may serve as a substitute for a weapons pursuit in the first place or as an attractive off-ramp for dismantling the weapons capability. Seen in this light, latency may suit the needs of both sides in a nuclear bargain. The nuclear aspirant retains some of its advanced nuclear infrastructure as opposed to having to dismantle it entirely, and the nonproliferation community manages to limit the spread of nuclear weapons. While certainly not without its own set of concerns,[6] nuclear latency may represent an ideal compromise between the nuclear haves and haves-not, and even curb the appetite of states on the cusp of seeking sensitive nuclear assistance and other dual-use technology.[7] It is necessary to examine the strategic consequences of this underappreciated and underexplored policy option in relation to proliferators that may populate the twenty-first-century nuclear landscape. And if the pursuit of nuclear latency represents the next wave of proliferation as the evidence is beginning to suggest,[8] the nonproliferation regime must decide if this is the "least bad" of the options available in dealing with new proliferation challenges.

Multilateral Bargaining

In this book, I focus on the unique role that the United States plays in nonproliferation and counterproliferation. Since 1945 and the introduction of nuclear weapons to the international system, the United States has carried the mantle of preventing the spread of nuclear weapons beyond the original nuclear club.

Fairly consistently over time, consecutive U.S. presidents have committed to and lauded curbing nuclear weapons proliferation. This trend was particularly evident during President Barack Obama's recent administration that saw a renewed commitment to nuclear arms reduction, and even the noble aspiration of a world without nuclear weapons, all of which were signaled clearly in his 2009 Prague Speech. In addition to working to reduce the U.S. nuclear arsenal, the Obama administration also took a firm stance toward robust monitoring and against nuclear treaty violations, such as the Russian Federation's purported violation of the Intermediate Nuclear Force (INF) Treaty, and Iranian violations of a series of UN Security Council Resolutions and its Nonproliferation Treaty membership obligations.[9] Indeed, during the previous decade, U.S. leadership in nonproliferation was steadfast and unambiguous.

The 2016 election of President Donald Trump in the United States has raised questions about whether the U.S. will continue its role as a nonproliferation leader and maintain its commitment to preventing the spread of nuclear weapons to other states in the international community. To date, President Trump has demonstrated a dangerous attitude toward nuclear matters suggesting that nuclear proliferation was "going to happen anyway" and that it may actually serve U.S. national security interests to see more countries procure nuclear weapons capabilities, to ease the burden on the U.S. conventional and nuclear forces. President Trump's apparent encouragement of nuclear weapons proliferation to allies such as Japan, South Korea, and even Saudi Arabia raises questions about the U.S. desire, and ability, to remain a nonproliferation leader under President Trump.[10]

With these changing tides in global leadership, China, Germany, and France are stepping up to the challenge in a variety of arenas, including climate change, nuclear energy, trade, and potentially nonproliferation. As stated by Vikram Singh, a former top Pentagon official for Asian affairs, "if the biggest country in the world is saying, 'It's the law of the jungle, every man for themselves, you're with me or you're against me,' you're going to see a lot of people following that advice. This is a completely seismic shift in how America is behaving on the world stage."[11] This change opens up new opportunities for other states, including Russia, China, Germany, and France to play more important roles in international relations. Each seems eager to do so in light of the United States' apparent retirement from its global leadership role.

In the context of nuclear proliferation *and* reversal, this evolution in U.S. policy also raises implications about the need for renewed attempts at multilateral bargaining, with a different set of world leaders taking a front and center role in nuclear negotiations.[12] For example, North Korea analysts, in addition to members of the Trump administration as well as President Trump himself, have looked to the People's Republic of China to assist in examining the set of policy options available in managing the accelerated nuclear development and testing in DPRK. To date, the Chinese have oscillated between generally unhelpful to actively obstructionist. They often present inherent challenges in counterproliferation by circumventing sanctions or provide alternative means of foreign assistance to DPRK. China's objectives for stability and peace on the Korean Peninsula is long-standing. As argued by regional analysts,

> Chinese Mao Zedong consistently, albeit unsuccessfully, opposed Stalin and Kim Il-sung's plan to launch the Korean War in 1950. Moreover, when Kim Il-sung, after witnessing the communists' victory in the Vietnam War, visited Beijing in 1975 to request aid for a second attempt to unify Korea by force, Mao rejected this plan for a second Korean War. This is not to say that China is humanitarian and philanthropic, nor does it mean the "blood brothers alliance" between China and North Korea is obsolete. Instead, it means that China opposes war or instability on the peninsula regardless of the instigator. That is why, even under strong criticism from the international community for its lenient implementation of economic sanctions on North Korea, Beijing cannot simply let the dictatorial regime in Pyongyang collapse. China firmly believes, as the PLA report put it, that "the security problem of the Korean peninsula itself is inseparable from China's national security."[13]

Heightened tensions between North Korea and the U.S. may soon spill over into China. Beijing is actively boosting forces on its border with North Korea in the event of a military conflict, however unlikely and undesirable this may be. The Chinese remain cautious about any aggressive action against Pyongyang, including joint U.S.-South Korean military exercises and the deployment of the anti-ballistic missile system, THAAD, aiming instead to increase stability on the peninsula through arbitration. It may then become necessary to open up a larger role for the Chinese if there is to be a resolution to the North Korean problem. Discussing areas of common interest, and often contention, such as trade, exclusive economic zones (E.E.Z.), and even the U.S. presence in the region, may help facilitate a more focused discussion about Pyongyang, the future of the Korean Peninsula, and what China can do as an erstwhile ally of the DPRK. Panda and Narang lamented after Pyongyang's 2017 ICBM test, "there are thus no good options at the moment for addressing the North Korean threat, only bad ones and catastrophic ones."[14] Yet, it is still necessary to consider diplomatic solutions, however politically unpopular and improbable they may seem, that seek to reduce the likelihood of heightened aggression and the prospect of war, even as we may be resigned to the prospect of successful North Korean proliferation.[15]

Concluding Remarks

Nuclear weapons bestow significant advantages to their possessors. They may ensure survival in otherwise unstable regions, they deter foreign aggression at their borders, and they may allow leaders to revise the status quo in their favor. Yet, for as long as states have sought nuclear weapons, the international community has endeavored to dissuade their acquisition and compel their abandonment. Though scholars long ago began to unpack the complex motivations behind nuclear pursuit, we are just now starting to understand the decision-making that underlies the opposite process. It is not just change in domestic politics or the lessening of security threats from neighboring foes; the international community too can change the politics of nuclear reversal. While there is no doubt that the current global strategic environment may make nuclear weapons more desirable and more attainable, we are also armed with the knowledge to prevent the future that President Kennedy so bleakly envisioned almost sixty years ago.

NOTES

Chapter 1

1. Beschloss 1991.
2. Sagan and Waltz 2003.
3. Woods, Palkki, and Stout 2010, 262–263.
4. U.S. Government Printing Office 1975.
5. Lake and Powell 1999, 4.
6. Asal and Beardsley 2007; Sechser and Fuhrmann 2017.
7. Brodie 1946, 1959; Kissinger 1957; Schelling 1960, 1966; Quester 1973; Sagan and Waltz 1995; Bueno de Mesquita and Riker 1982; Shultz 1984; Jervis 1989; Mearsheimer 1990, 1993; Feaver 1993; Sagan 1993, 1996/97; Thayer 1994; Jo and Gartzke 2007; Betts 1977a, 1977b; Waltz 1979, 1990; Russett 1988; Huth and Russett 1994; Organski and Kugler 1980; Kugler 1984; Solingen 1994, 2007; Singh and Way 2004; Gartzke and Kroenig 2009; Potter and Mukhatzhanova 2010; Monteiro and Debs 2014; Debs and Monteiro 2016.
8. Bleek and Lorber 2014; Fuhrmann 2009; Jo and Gartzke 2007; Kroenig 2009; Rauchhaus 2009; Sagan 2010; Narang 2013; Weeks and Way 2014; Fuhrmann and Sechser 2014; Sechser and Fuhrmann 2017.
9. Debs and Monteiro 2016; Miller 2018; Cone 2018; Mattiacci and Jones 2016.
10. Shultz 1984; Hymans 2001, 2006; Levite 2002/2003; Solingen 2007; Müller and Schmidt 2008; Reiss 1995; Walsh 2000; Reardon 2010; Rublee 2009; Debs and Monteiro 2016; Mattiacci and Jones 2016.
11. This argument was reiterated during a recent conversation with a Brazilian diplomat (Vienna, 2018).
12. Sagan 1993, 1996/97; Thayer 1994; Jo and Gartzke 2007; Betts 1977b; Russett 1988; Huth and Russett 1994; Organski and Kugler 1989; Kugler 1984; Solingen 1994, 2007; Cohen 1998; Singh and Way 2004; Gartzke and Kroenig 2009; Monteiro and Debs 2014; Debs and Monteiro 2016.
13. Sagan 1996/1997.
14. Rublee 2009; Kroenig 2010; Fuhrmann 2012; Brown and Kaplow 2014; Gibbons 2017.
15. Fuhrmann 2012; Kroenig 2010; Mehta and Whitlark 2016, 2017.
16. Kroenig 2012.
17. Kahl 2012.
18. Forland 1997.
19. Meyer 1984; Singh and Way 2004; Hymans 2006; Jo and Gartzke 2007; Montgomery and Sagan 2009.
20. Levite 2002/2003; Mueller and Schmidt 2008; Narang 2014, 2015; Mehta and Whitlark 2016. I do not consider cases where states "slow" their nuclear programs as nuclear reversal. I expand on these coding rules in Chapter 3.

21. Narang and Mehta 2019.
22. These states are not included in subsequent analyses as they did not choose to pursue nuclear weapons, but rather, inherited them after the collapse of the USSR.
23. Past studies have looked at the role of positive and negative incentives in various outcomes of interest: conflict resolution, state repression, adhering to treaty or international legal obligations. See Haaas and O'Sullivan 2000; Cowhey 1993; Leeds 1999; Drury 1998; Litwak 2007; Pape 1997; Solingen 1994, 2012; Crumm 1995; Pevehouse 2002; Cone and Mehta 2020.
24. Schelling 1966; Pape 1996; Art and Cronin 2003; Hirschman 1945; Keohane and Nye 1997; Baldwin 1971, 1985; Reardon 2010.
25. Schelling 1960, 1966
26. Schelling 1960, 1966; George 1991, 1994; Jervis 1976, 1983; Fearon 1994; Davis 2000.
27. Baldwin 1971, 1985, 2000; Nincic 2010.
28. Edelman, Ross, and Takeyh 2015.
29. Miller and Narang 2018; Mehta and Spaniel 2019.
30. Perkovich 2002; Sagan 2009.
31. Debs and Monteiro 2016.
32. For a detailed discussion of the coding rules, see Chapter 3.

Chapter 2

1. Debs and Monteiro 2016; Miller 2018; Spaniel 2019; Cone 2019.
2. I use the terms "nuclear reversal," "counterproliferation," and "abandonment" interchangeably. They generally refer to the political decision-making process of beginning and ending the pursuit of nuclear weapons. For clarity, I adopt the definition put forward by Ariel Levite: "the phenomenon in which states embark on a path leading to nuclear weapons acquisition but subsequently reverse course, though not necessarily abandoning altogether their nuclear ambitions . . . including a governmental decision to slow or stop altogether an officially sanctioned nuclear weapons program" (Levite 2002/2003, 61). However, I diverge on one key point: I do not consider cases where states simply "slow" their nuclear progress as this may not result in nuclear reversal.
3. Fuhrmann and Kreps 2010; Whitlark 2017.
4. Sagan 1996/1997; Meyer 1984; Jo and Gartzke 2007; Singh and Way 2004.
5. Monteiro and Debs 2014; Kroenig 2009a, 2009b, 2010; Miller 2014, 2018; Gerzhoy 2015; Debs and Monteiro 2016.
6. Campbell et al. 2004; Paul 2000. More recently, see Monteiro and Debs 2014; Levite 2002/2003; Miller 2014; Gerzhoy 2015; Fuhrmann and Kreps 2010; Debs and Monteiro 2016.
7. Sagan 1996/1997; Hymans 2006; Levite 2002/2003; Reiss 1995; Halperin 1974; Solingen 2007; Solingen et al. 2012; Müller and Schmidt 2008; Rublee 2009.
8. Foran and Spector 1997; Thayer 1994; Sagan and Waltz 2003; Sagan 1996/1997; Reiss 1995; Levite 2002/2003; Müller and Schmidt 2008. T. V. Paul 2000 is among the first to highlight the logical inconsistencies in the neorealist argument about proliferation by noting the negative security externalities of proliferation: developing weapons program could trigger a reaction that may actually make the proliferating state less secure. Anticipating this would make a threatened state less likely to want to pursue nuclear weapons.
9. Jo and Gartzke 2007; Singh and Way 2004. Recent quantitative work on nuclear proliferation (Gartzke and Kroenig 2009), have emphasized the need to examine supply-side or opportunity variables in analyses of the determinants of nuclear proliferation.
10. Hymans 2006; Solingen 2007; Müller and Schmidt 2008.
11. Hymans 2006; Müller and Schmidt 2008.
12. Solingen 1994, 2007.
13. Liberman 2001.
14. Kroenig 2009b, 2010; Debs and Monteiro 2016; Miller 2014; Gerzhoy 2015; Coe and Vaynman 2015; Bas and Coe 2016; Fuhrmann and Kreps 2010; Whitlark 2017; Mattiacci and Jones 2016; Cone 2019.
15. Fuhrmann and Kreps 2010; Whitlark 2017.

16. Bas and Coe 2016.
17. Debs and Monteiro 2016.
18. Debs and Monteiro 2016, 38–39.
19. Gerzhoy 2015; Miller 2014, 2017; Lanoszka 2018; Debs and Monteiro 2016.
20. Coe and Vaynman 2015.
21. Gerzhoy 2015; Lanoszka 2018.
22. Campbell et al. 2004; Braun and Chyba 2004; Sagan 1996/1997; Solingen 2007; and Levite 2002/2003. Important exceptions include Verdier 2008; Cone 2019; and Spaniel 2019.
23. Miller 2014.
24. Based on interviews with Iranian, American, French, and Argentine consular officers, a variety of perspectives emerge about the role of sanctions in nuclear negotiations. The Iranians, for example, deny the effectiveness of economic sanctions but still began the negotiations by asking for sanctions to be lifted. American policymakers, on the other hand, suggest that economic sanctions were entirely responsible for bringing Iran to the negotiating table. And Argentinian and French policymakers suggest that there is likely truth to both perspectives and that effective counterproliferation requires the use of both carrots and sticks. These divergent perspectives suggest that more attention, both theoretically and empirically, must be paid to this conventional wisdom to determine the conditions in which it holds.
25. Baldwin 1971; Galtung 1967; Pape 1997; Morgan and Schwebach 2002; Drezner 1999; Brooks 2002; Hossein et al. 2003; Lacy and Niou 2004.
26. Debs and Monteiro 2016.
27. In this analysis, I focus less on the other side of the story, such as how domestic politics, including new leaders in the U.S. impact the likelihood of nuclear reversal agreements. Future work will examine this side of the equation: what factors determine which approach the U.S. chooses when negotiating nuclear deals?
28. Kroenig 2010; Fuhrmann 2012; Gibbons 2017; Brown and Kaplow 2014.
29. Sagan 1996/1997.
30. Mehta and Whitlark 2017, 2016; Fuhrmann and Tkach 2015.
31. Fuhrmann and Kreps 2010; Whitlark 2017.
32. Renshon 2006; Monteiro and Debs 2014; Whitlark 2017.
33. It is important to note that this rationale primarily applies to the U.S. as the primary actor in threatening military force. It could be the case that in other military alliances, some threats to use military force against allies may be seen as credible. For example, some argue that the Soviets could have credibly threatened to attack nuclear facilities in many of the countries with whom it was allied (e.g., Hungary and Czechoslovakia). In future work that examines the role of the USSR in counterproliferation behavior, it would be interesting to see whether these conditions hold for military alliances in which the United States is not the patron state.
34. Fuhrmann and Kreps 2010; Frantz and Collins 2007; Corera 2006.
35. LBJL 1963; Chang 1990; Whitlark 2017.
36. Verdier 2008.
37. Early 2015.
38. Early 2015; Hufbauer et al. 2007.
39. Some analysts and scholars would suggest stopping or impeding potential proliferators by simply imposing sanctions in an effort to either slow their development or punish state elites. This strategy does not incorporate rewards but suggests that the eventual lifting of sanctions would be seen by proliferators to be rewards. While technically a future benefit, I argue that this is an insufficient strategy for a wide variety of proliferators. Sanctions are not always eased or lifted effectively and completely, and may stay in effect despite their formal lifting by Executive Order or Congressional legislation in the United States. Proliferators are aware of the difficulties in sanctions easing (especially with regard to getting banks or other actors in the financial sector to act accordingly) and may not be satisfied with just this as a "reward." Instead, I argue that nuclear reversal requires using both sanctions and rewards simultaneously at the outset. Here the rewards include offers of military, political, or economic assistance, while maintaining negative pressure through sanctions. While sanctions could be lifted in the future, this is unlikely to be considered a sufficient reward to actually change nuclear

decision-making, especially if leaders in proliferating states do not believe that they will be in office to recoup these rewards.

40. Many of the most formal, and often the most employed, models of conflict suggest that "uncertainty exists over the distribution of military power or the costs of war and not over the resolve of individual leaders" (Wolford 2007). It follows then that if uncertainty is derived from capabilities, there are unlikely to be significant differences among leaders—successive leaders do not vary in their resolve over conflict behavior. Concerns over this misspecification or biased estimate that rely solely on state-level data prompted the incorporation of leader-specific dynamics, resulting in a host of different implications for the role of states in conflict behavior, reputation, and interstate relations more broadly. Perhaps it could be the case that leaders vary in their resolve, the value they place in certain domestic and international policies, and ultimately in their decisions to maintain or deviate from their predecessors' choices. With this granularity and the incorporation of relevant factors like time in office, reputation, relationship to the prior leader, and political position (incumbent, first- or second-term leader), recent scholarship has been able to differentiate between leaders in the level of their resolve and to identify the origin (and outcome) of their policy differences. See George 1969; Wolford 2007; Fearon 1995; Filson and Werner 2002; Morrow 1989; Powell 1999, 2003; Slantchev 2003; Chiozza and Goemans 2003, 2004; Gaubatz 1991; Gelpi and Grieco 2001; Guisinger and Smith 2002; McGillivray and Smith 2006; Press 2005; Sartori 2005; Schelling 1966; Horowitz, McDermott, and Stam 2005; Horowitz and Stam 2015; Fey and Ramsey 2006; Smith and Stam 2004; Goldgeier 1994; Clark and Nordstrom 2005.

41. In democratic and quasi-democratic states, nuclear decision-making often includes additional actors and veto players in the military, legislature, and the other government bureaucracies that are integral to both proliferation and counterproliferation policy; this may occur even in more autocratic regimes (e.g., Pakistan's nuclear program). See Hymans 2006; Solingen 2007; Müller and Schmidt 2008; Liberman 2001.

42. Wolford 2007; Fearon 1995; Filson and Werner 2002; Morrow 1989; Powell 1999, 2003; Slantchev 2003; Croco 2011.

43. There are obvious exceptions where the emergence of a new leader is completely outside the purview of a broader citizen constituency. Even if not elected or chosen by natural turnover as in liberal democracies, leaders of autocratic or semi-authoritarian states may still be able to signal new preferences for or against nuclear weapons.

44. Chiozza and Goemans 2004; Fearon 1995; Schultz 2005.

45. Fey and Ramsay 2006; Smith and Stam 2004; Goldgeier 1994; Clark and Nordstrom 2005.

46. Malici and Walker 2016.

47. Hayes and Moon 2011.

48. It is also important to consider these dynamics with a neutral proliferator—neither a friend nor a foe. First, however, is it feasible to employ the same logic to examine allies (e.g., South Korea) and neutral states (e.g., India)? In many respects the Indian and South Korean cases are quite different—the U.S. was able to wield its leverage as a patron through the parameters of an alliance to incentivize South Korea to alter its decision-making, while such an avenue was infeasible with India. However, it is important to consider which part of the dynamic is affected by the proliferator's implicit or explicit neutrality. Certainly, in many cases, the U.S. is able to negotiate and bargain almost as effectively with neutral states as with friends, and both types of states are likely to be similarly receptive to these offers. Second, a state's neutrality may be the result of historical context, not necessarily because of any differences or divergences in policy preferences. Both friends (like the UK) and neutral states (like Switzerland) could have similarly convergent preferences on a variety of policy issues that influence their nuclear decision-making because they are not seeking to upset the U.S.-led world order/status quo. Lastly, the U.S. is likely to have had some interactions with neutral states in the past. If the U.S. is using its relationship with the proliferator as an informational heuristic for the progress and intent of the nuclear program, even neutral states may respond as favorably as an ally.

In other instances, neutral or non-allied proliferators are likely to view threats of force as credible and indicative of U.S. resolve to stop their weapons attempt. Likewise, there may be little affinity or good standing between the two states to encourage a rewards-based avenue as seen more often with allies. However, one key difference between both allies and adversaries on the one hand, and neutral states, on the other, is that some of the rewards traditionally used to incentivize nuclear reversal may be undesirable and ineffective. Neutral states are unlikely to be swayed by offers of nuclear umbrellas or defense pacts, because this is orthogonal to their status in the international system. There may even be concerns at offers of military assistance. Instead, the U.S. may have to rely on a more nuanced set of positive and negative tools, with which to compel counterproliferation in these instances. Here, we can consider the Indonesian or Egyptian experience where the U.S. attempted to negotiate a nuclear reversal. While neither state is an ally or a foe of the United States in the traditional sense, both responded to offers of foreign assistance (specifically military aid) as incentives to reverse their nuclear programs.

49. The sequencing of inducements is likely to be proliferator/proliferator-type specific. For example, in the South Korean case, the U.S. first threatened to weaken its security commitment to the ROK when Park Chung-hee seemed interested in acquiring nuclear weapons. This led South Korea to rethink its policy. The U.S. then offered to reaffirm its defense pact in exchange for South Korea's nuclear reversal. To motivate a change in nuclear decision-making, the counterproliferator will generally look at its existing relationship with the proliferator to assess in which order to use available tools. Though these tools can be offered simultaneously or in quick succession, it is important to note that for successful counterproliferation, a negotiation strategy must ultimately employ both positive and negative inducements to compel changes in nuclear decision-making.

50. Albright and Gay 1998; Hersman and Peters 2006.
51. Hersman and Peters 2006.
52. Hersman and Peters 2006.
53. Braut-Hegghammer 2016.
54. Gartzke and Jo 2009.
55. Volpe 2017.
56. The literature has resulted in mixed findings about whether nuclear cooperation (such as sensitive nuclear assistance and the Atoms for Peace program from the 1950s) contributed to proliferation. See Kroenig 2010, Fuhrmann 2012.
57. Braut-Hegghammer 2016.
58. Fearon 1995; Monteiro and Debs 2014; Debs and Monteiro 2016.
59. Debs and Monteiro 2016.
60. Harvey and Mitton 2016; Pew 2017.
61. Gavin 2004, 2015.
62. Kroenig 2010.
63. Sagan 1996/1997.
64. Nuclear Threat Initiative 2006.
65. Harvey and Mitton 2016; Renshon et al. 2018; Kertzer 2016; Mehta 2017.
66. This conclusion is based on interviews with policymakers in the United States and consular officers from Iran and the United States.

Overview

1. Achen and Snidal 1989; Achen 2004; Geddes 1990; King, Keohane, and Verba 1994; Debs and Monteiro 2016.
2. George and Bennett 2005, 5.
3. George and Bennett 2005, 19.
4. Debs and Monteiro 2016; Sechser and Fuhrmann 2017; Kroenig 2010; Fuhrmann 2012; Miller 2018.
5. Miller 2014; Gerzhoy 2015; Fuhrmann 2012; Debs and Monteiro 2016.
6. Sagan 1996/1997; Jo and Gartzke 2007; Debs and Monteiro 2016; Bell and Miller 2015.
7. In addition to Bleek's original data (Bleek 2017), I consider the case of Spain (Blanc and Roberts 2008; Mueller and Schmidt 2008). Spain first began its foray into nuclear weapons activity when it built its first research reactor in 1959. Within the next decade, Spain went on to develop the capability for weapons-grade plutonium and declined to sign the NPT. In 1971, the Spanish government initiated a feasibility study of nuclear weapons development that concluded that Spain required plutonium reprocessing technology for nuclear pursuit.

These technical and political investments in nuclear weapons pursuit place Spain among the list of states that pursued nuclear weapons activity but eventually renounced it.

8. Fuhrmann 2012; Kroenig 2010.
9. Gartzke, Kaplow, and Mehta 2014, 2019.
10. These subjects granted my request to speak with them for off-the-record, background information. While I have extensive records and notes of these conversations, I can only generally reference them (without any attributing information) in these analyses.
11. In related work, I am collecting new data on nuclear reversal involving other major world powers, beyond just the United States. See Berkemeier et al. 2018.

Chapter 3

1. Nincic 2010; Stein 2013; Fuhrmann and Kreps 2010. It is important to note that there are important limitations to these data. The Fuhrmann and Kreps dataset includes all cases where a state at least considered attacking an adversary's nuclear facilities. This is not a strong measure of credibility for two primary reasons. First, preventive war is not seen as credible in some of the cases contained in their dataset. Second, the data may exclude some cases where preventive attack threats were credible, but not employed. It is plausible, for example, that the U.S. or Israel would have bombed nuclear sites in Libya if its nuclear program advanced to a stage similar to Iran's in the early 2000s. Relatedly, measures of actual attacks against nuclear programs look different from threats of military force. This could be seen as a test of whether preventive strikes against nuclear facilities work by actually delaying the technical pathways to proliferation. My theory focuses on how threats of military force are background to the use of inducements to actually stop nuclear weapons pursuit. Though there are some problems with and limitations of these data, I still choose to use this dataset, as it is still the most comprehensive data source on threat (and actual use) of force in the preventive war context. Thorough and systematic data on this issue is likely to remain sparse given both selection effects (i.e., some threats are only made known if they fail), and the relative scarcity of both threats and preventive war in the nonproliferation space.

   However, I consider two other sources of data. First, Sechser's Militarized Compellent Threat dataset includes variables such as threats of military force (I narrow the scope to threats regarding policy) and whether force was actually used (Sechser 2011). Second, I consider a variable from the Correlates of War project, a five-year-running-averaged measure of militarized threat environment to assess whether the proliferator experienced threats of force/actual force from either the counterproliferator or other members of the international community. This is not a clean measure of military threats or the use of force, but it does reflect the dispute environment the proliferator may be facing if it were to continue its nuclear weapons program. Using all three measures (though I only include the Militarized Interstate Dispute (MID) results in Appendix 3.1), I find similar effects. Future work would be aimed at improving these variables to establish clearer, less ambiguous measures of when international threats to use military force are useful in the background of decisions to stop nuclear weapons programs.

2. Nonetheless, in some model specifications, clearly identified, I include the credible threat of military force as an additional independent variable to assess the effect of this form of coercion independently on nuclear reversal, without previous or simultaneous imposition of economic sanctions.
3. Miller 2014; Gavin 2012, 2015.
4. Fuhrmann 2012; Kroenig 2010; Fuhrmann and Tkach 2015; Mehta and Whitlark 2017.
5. Hypothesis 1: External inducements (rewards and sanctions) increase the likelihood of nuclear reversal, given a credible threat of military force.
6. Tables A3.1–A3.6 present preliminary bivariate analyses of some of the alternative explanations from the literature. While without covariates these analyses are not conclusive, they do suggest that many of the factors typically associated with nuclear reversal are limited in their explanatory scope.
7. Steinhauer 2015.
8. One important exception is Clary 2019.
9. Sabet 2016.

10. Ibid.
11. Staw 1997.
12. Goemans, Gleditsch, and Chiozza 2004.
13. This variable measures the affinity or the relationship and similarity of policy preferences between states.
14. Debs and Monteiro 2016; Nephew 2017.
15. Harvey and Mitton 2016; Mehta 2017; Narang and Mehta 2019.
16. USAID 2007.
17. USAID 2007.
18. In the robustness section, I consider alternative operationalizations of these variables to include in my analysis. To avoid collinearity in a given model, I include only one operationalization of each construct at a time. The models included in the robustness check evaluate whether other operationalizations result in the same general types of effects. I find similar results in these robustness checks.
19. Fuhrmann and Tkach 2015.
20. In all model specifications, sensitive nuclear assistance is collinear with the likelihood of nuclear reversal. See Fuhrmann 2012 and Kroenig 2010.
21. Bapat and Morgan 2009; Hufbauer et al. 2007.
22. Clifton et.al. 2014.
23. Miller 2014, 2018.
24. Schelling 1960.
25. Fuhrmann and Kreps 2010, 814. However, as a robustness check, I also include an alternative operationalization, Militarized Interstate Disputes (MIDs), discussed later in Appendix 3.1, Gochman and Maoz 1984.
26. Jo and Gartzke 2007; Jones et al. 1996.
27. Marshall, Gurr, and Jaggers 2010.
28. Jones et al. 1996.
29. Signorino and Ritter 2001.
30. Ghosn et al. 2004.
31. Goertz et al. 2016.
32. Ghosn et al. 2004.
33. This is an unfortunately common concern in observational analyses where the "treatment" is not randomly applied. To best accommodate for these selection effects, I include a battery of covariates traditionally found in the literature.
34. The existing literature (Fuhrmann 2012; Kroenig 2010) identifies this form of assistance as an important step along the nuclear pathway. By offering sensitive nuclear assistance under an NCA as an inducement, the United States may be able to compensate the proliferator for its loss of nuclear technology. Yet, the results show that nuclear assistance is frequently collinear with reversal. This result is important and interesting, and supports my theoretical expectations but given its collinearity, it does provide enough variation about the nature of the nuclear program upon retention. Thus, to supplement this variable measuring nuclear cooperation agreements, I include data on retaining a latent nuclear capacity (Fuhrmann and Tkach 2015).
35. In this one model specification, I consider the threat or use of military force as an explanatory variable, not a conditional variable as used elsewhere in my theoretical framework.
36. Sagan and Waltz 2003.
37. Goemans et al. 2009.
38. Jo and Gartzke 2007; Gartzke and Jo 2009; Bell and Miller 2015.
39. Beck et al. 1998.
40. Goemans et al. 2009.
41. Wolford 2007; Fey and Ramsey 2006; Smith and Stam 2004; Goldgeier 1994; Clark and Nordstrom 2005.
42. When modeled separately, positive inducements have a positive and significant impact on nuclear reversal while negative inducements are negatively and significantly associated with nuclear reversal.
43. Fuhrmann 2012; Kroenig 2012; Mehta and Whitlark 2017.

44. Nuclear umbrellas impose both monetary costs on patron states, as well as create political and military tradeoffs. See Narang and Mehta 2019 and Sechser and Fuhrmann 2017.
45. Braut-Hegghammer 2006, 2008, 2016.
46. Leeds et al. 2002.
47. Leeds et al. 2002.
48. Singh and Way 2004.
49. Hufbauer et al. 2007.
50. Ghosn et al. 2004. I thank an anonymous reviewer for suggesting an alternative approach to this analysis.

Chapter 4

1. Bowen 2006.
2. Shen and Xia 2012
3. Bowen 2006.
4. Bowen 2010; Braut-Hegghammer 2008.
5. Bowen 2006.
6. Office of the Secretary of Defense 1996; Sinai 1997.
7. Ibid.
8. Bowen 2006.
9. Bowen 2006; Braut-Hegghammer 2008; Blakely 2010.
10. Sinai 1997; Spector 1995.
11. Bowen 2006; Braut-Hegghammer 2008.
12. Ibid.
13. Bowen 2006; Braut-Hegghammer 2008; Blakely 2010.
14. Braut-Hegghammer 2008.
15. Ibid.
16. Squassoni and Feickert 2004.
17. Ibid.
18. Ibid.
19. Braut-Hegghammer 2016.
20. Squassoni and Feickert 2004.
21. Ibid.
22. Bowen 2006; Braut-Hegghammer 2008, 2016; Blakely 2010.
23. Braut-Hegghammer 2008, 2016; Bowen 2006.
24. MacLeod 2006.
25. Federation of American Scientists 2006; Nuclear Threats Initiative 2013.
26. Burr and Richelson 2000.
27. Ibid.
28. O'Neill 1992.
29. Federation of American Scientists 2006; Nuclear Threats Initiative 2013.
30. Shen and Xia 2012.
31. Ibid.
32. Burr and Richelson 2000.
33. Ibid.
34. Ibid.; Director of Central Intelligence 1963.
35. Burr and Richelson 2000.
36. Shen and Xia 2012; Federation of American Scientists 2006.
37. Burr and Richelson 2000; Director of Central Intelligence, 1963.
38. Federation of American Scientists 2006; Nuclear Threats Initiative 2013.
39. Burr and Richelson 2000.
40. Ibid.
41. Ibid
42. Ibid.
43. Ibid.
44. Ibid.

45. Ibid.
46. Ibid.
47. Ibid.
48. Ibid.
49. Ibid.
50. Ibid.
51. Ibid.
52. Ibid.
53. Narang and Mehta 2019; Burr and Richelson 2000.

Chapter 5

1. Given the nature of these discussions, the subjects were reticent to be interviewed on record. Instead, I am able to generally reference, without specific citations, on background from these interviews.
2. Sagan 1996/1997; Jo and Gartzke 2007; Singh and Way 2004.
3. Sagan 1996/1997; Tellis et al. 2001.
4. Chellaney 1991.
5. Ibid.
6. Blanc and Roberts 2008.
7. Ibid.
8. Arms Control Association 2003
9. Fuhrmann 2012.
10. Arms Control Association 2003.
11. Ibid.
12. Ibid.
13. Fuhrmann 2012.
14. IAEA Atoms for Peace Speech 1953.
15. There is an ongoing debate about the impact of nuclear assistance and the supply of nuclear technology on proliferation. See Kroenig 2010 and Fuhrmann 2012.
16. Gavin 2004.
17. Perkovich 1999; Blanc and Roberts 2008.
18. Sagan 2009; Narang 2009; Abraham 2010.
19. Perkovich 1999; Blanc and Roberts 2008.
20. Jaipal 1977.
21. United Nations Office of Disarmament Affairs 1970; Arms Control Association 2003.
22. Fuhrmann 2012; Kroenig 2009.
23. Jaipal 1977.
24. Ibid.
25. Bhutto 1974; Nuclear Threat Initiative 2001, 2010.
26. Hoodbhoy 2011; Khan 1974.
27. Burr 2011.
28. Ibid.
29. Ibid.
30. India Today 1978; American Presidency Project 1978.
31. Ibid.
32. Perkovich 2002.
33. Ibid.
34. Noorani 2001.
35. Nuclear Weapons Archive 2001.
36. Ibid.
37. Nuclear Threat Initiative 2013.
38. Federation of American Scientists 2013.
39. Perkovich 2002; Sagan 2009.
40. Carey 2011.
41. United Nations Security Council Resolution 1172.

42. Incidentally, both countries agreed in their reactions to Resolution 1172, deeming it coercive and unhelpful.
43. Morrow and Carriere 1999.
44. Only France and Russia refrained from sanctioning the Indians after their nuclear tests.
45. Morrow and Carriere 1999.
46. Ibid.
47. Ibid.
48. Kapur 2007.
49. Gartzke, Kaplow, and Mehta 2014.
50. Bajpai 2009; Morrow and Carriere 1999.
51. This situation was made more difficult given that the Chinese were also allying with Pakistan and providing them with arms during Indo-Pakistan wars in the 1970s and 1980s.
52. Bajpai 2009; Perkovich 2002.
53. Burr 2005.
54. Ibid.
55. Perkovich 2002.
56. Ibid.
57. Ibid.
58. Bajpai 2009.
59. Sagan 1996/1997; O'Neill 2006.
60. Bajpai 2009; Narang 2009.
61. Bajpai 2009.
62. Ibid.
63. U.S. Department of State 2009a.
64. Ibid.
65. U.S. Department of State 2009b.
66. Ibid.
67. This analysis focuses on the role of the United States in counterproliferation, especially with regards to threatening military force to stop weapons programs (the trade-off in this theoretical and empirical design are discussed more fully in Chapters 2 and 3) but does not assess whether other states, such as regional adversaries or other rivals, are effectively able to threaten military force to compel nuclear reversal. This raises an important question in the context of the Indian nuclear program. While U.S. threats to bomb Indian nuclear facilities may have lacked credibility, could Pakistan have made this same threat believable? While regional actors do play an important role in encouraging proliferation, my theory suggests that these dynamics are not as salient to nuclear reversal decision-making as influence by the United States or potentially other major world powers. I argue this for two reasons. First, proliferators are primarily focused on responding to influence by major world powers, such as the U.S. or the USSR/Russia. My theory suggests that external influence or incentives by these actors are the most likely to actually alter decision-making. And though regional actors play an important role in understanding the process by which states may initiate nuclear programs, these dynamics are likely to be less relevant in nuclear *reversal*. Second, and relatedly, in specifically considering the Indian case, threats by the Pakistanis (or even the Chinese) to bomb Indian nuclear infrastructure would likely have encouraged India to hasten and ramp up its nuclear development, given the impact of these security threats in their decision to pursue nuclear weapons in the first place. In principle, threats from regional adversaries may have different, perhaps even a negative impact on nuclear reversal decisions.

Chapter 6

1. U.S. News and World Report 2015.
2. Beinart 2015.
3. Landler 2018.
4. Greenberg 2015.
5. These descriptions are based on interviews with Iranian and U.S. negotiators, and analysts involved in JCPOA, February–April 2017.

6. Fuhrmann 2012.
7. Quillen 2002.
8. Mehta and Whitlark 2016, 2017; Quillen 2002.
9. Quillen 2002.
10. Kerr 2019; U.S. Department of State 1975.
11. Kerr 2019.
12. Islam 2013.
13. U.S. Department of State 1975.
14. Central Intelligence Agency 1988.
15. U.S. Department of State 1975.
16. Kerr 2019.
17. Mehta and Whitlark 2016, 2017.
18. Kerr 2019; Schaffer 2003; Blanc and Roberts 2008.
19. Kerr 2019; Schaffer 2003; Interview with an Argentine diplomat and former IAEA official from the Director General's Office, February 2017.
20. Kerr 2019; Schaffer 2003; Arms Control Association 2013.
21. Kerr 2019.
22. Kerr 2019; Schaffer 2003.
23. Ibid.
24. Kerr 2019.
25. Interviews with former IAEA officials from the Director General's Office, February and March 2017.
26. Interviews with former IAEA officials from the Director General's Office, February and March 2017; Bowen and Brewer 2011.
27. Porter 2012.
28. Ibid.
29. White House Presidential Address 2002.
30. Nuclear Threat Initiative 2011.
31. Interview with an American analyst and policy advisor, April 2017.
32. Nuclear Threat Initiative 2011; Gedda 2002.
33. Interview with an American analyst and policy advisor, April 2017.
34. Ibid.
35. Nuclear Threat Initiative 2011.
36. Interview with former IAEA official from the Director General's Office, April 2017.
37. Heinonen 2014.
38. Nuclear Threat Initiative 2011.
39. Nuclear Threat Initiative 2011; Iran Press Service 2002.
40. Nuclear Threat Initiative 2011.
41. Ibid.
42. Iran's cooperative relationship with Russia is a notable exception. During this time, President Vladimir Putin agreed to maintain Russia's nuclear cooperation with Iran, conditional on Iranian adherence to IAEA regulations.
43. Thatcher 2003.
44. IAEA 2014.
45. Nuclear Threat Initiative 2011.
46. Ibid.
47. Ibid.
48. Sorkin 2005.
49. Nuclear Threat Initiative 2011.
50. In part, this reiterates the necessity of the United States as the primary actor in nuclear negotiations. It also suggests that other states are interested in engaging in counterproliferation, alongside the United States. This conclusion is based on conversations with Iranian consular officials and French defense policy officials, February 2017 and June 2018.
51. Mufson and Wright 2007.
52. Nuclear Threat Initiative 2011.
53. Associated Press 2005.

54. Fitzpatrick 2006, 5.
55. Ibid.
56. Melham 2015.
57. Nuclear Threat Initiative 2011.
58. Reuters 2007.
59. Sanger 2009.
60. Albright and Stricker 2010.
61. Nuclear Threat Initiative 2011.
62. Interview with Iranian diplomat and consular officer, February 2017.
63. Ignatius 2016.
64. Kroenig 2014.
65. Kroenig 2014; Edelman et al. 2015.
66. Politico 2012.
67. Nuclear Threat Initiative 2011; Rezaian and Warrick 2013.
68. The Guardian 2013.
69. Ibid.
70. Ibid.
71. Nuclear Threat Initiative 2011.
72. Wilson and Lynch 2013.
73. Ibid.
74. Nuclear Threat Initiative 2011; IAEA Press Release 2013.
75. Samore 2015.
76. Ibid.
77. Baker 2015; Ho 2015.
78. Reuters 2015.
79. Cooper 2015.
80. Reuters 2015.
81. The Iran Deal raises an important question about whether sanctions relief (i.e., the removal of a punishment) constitutes a reward. While discussed in a theoretical context in Chapter 2, this question emerges most clearly when considering the provisions of the JCPOA signed in 2015. This important point has no clear consensus in the academic community—either theoretically or empirically. Some argue that the lifting of a cost can be seen as a delayed perk while others argue that actors may require actual, new benefits to compensate for the loss incurred by sanctions (Baldwin 1971; Schelling 1960). To date, the lifting of sanctions is not necessarily seen in the same light as the extension of assistance or other carrots. Indeed, even in the context of the Iran deal, the Iranians required additional benefits, beyond just the removal of sanctions (such as the SWIFT sanctions) and the lifting of the oil embargo. While sanctions were seen as unprovoked punishments, their removal was not seen as sufficient. To agree to reverse its nuclear weapons progress, Iran required access to frozen assets and the global financial system for trade, and retention of a civilian nuclear program.
82. Interviews with IAEA officials and analysts from the United States and Europe, February-April 2017.
83. Interview with Iranian diplomat and consular officer, February 2017.
84. Ibid.
85. Nuclear Threat Initiative 2011.
86. RT 2013.
87. Albright et al. 2010.
88. Lindsay 2013; Long 2015.
89. Erdbrink and Gladstone 2015.
90. IAEA Director's General Report 2018.
91. Mehta and Whitlark 2016, 2017.
92. Fuhrmann 2018.
93. Riedel 2016.
94. Ibid.
95. Whitlark and Mehta 2019.

96. Foreign Minister Javad Zarif reiterated Iran's unequivocal commitment to the JCPOA in a Charlie Rose interview on PBS in July 2017.
97. Nasr 2017.
98. Ibid.
99. Reuters 2017.
100. Fassihi 2016.
101. Miller 2018.
102. Gerzhoy and Miller 2016; Mehta 2016.
103. Whitlark and Mehta 2019.
104. Liptak and Gaouette 2018.
105. Sanger et al. 2019.
106. Ibid.
107. Taleblu and Goldberg 2018.
108. Serjoie 2018.
109. Pew 2017.
110. Interview with current and former French defense and foreign affairs officials, June 2018.
111. It is important to note that formal U.S. defense policy, especially nuclear policy, is declared in the Nuclear Posture Review (NPR). The Trump Administration's NPR, including its commitment to working with allies in limiting the spread of nuclear weapons, is generally consistent with previous NPRs and related defense policy documents.
112. IAEA Director's General Report 2018.
113. Berkemeier et al. 2018.

Chapter 7

1. Associated Press 2013.
2. As discussed in Chapter 2, there are several reasons why the United States may not choose to issue a threat against a proliferator even if it would prefer that the state not acquire nuclear weapons. For example, it is not particularly credible that the United States would employ military force against some proliferators for fear of retaliation against itself, its allies, and other states in the region. This is certainly part of the debate with using force against North Korea. The U.S. has historically been reticent to take actions against North Korea to avoid endangering South Korea, Japan, or other states in the region. However, there is evidence that the United States has at least considered the use of military force to manage the North Korean crisis. For example, there is some evidence that President Clinton considered a military strike on a North Korean nuclear facility, Yongbyon, during the 1990s and more recently, President Trump contemplated a "bloody nose strike," among other provocative actions that could have resulted in conflict between the United States and North Korea (Boghani 2018). While there is contention about whether these considerations would have resulted in military action, it is important to note that generally, threats to attack North Korea have historically been seen to be non-credible, given our commitments to South Korea and Japan.
3. Nitikin 2013; Fuhrmann 2012.
4. Nitikin 2013; Niksch 2009; Hecker 2010; Arms Control Association 2019.
5. Ibid.
6. Niksch 2009; Arms Control Association 2019.
7. Nitikin 2013; Niksch 2009.
8. Ibid.
9. Arms Control Association 2019; Niksch 2009.
10. Arms Control Association 2019; Nitikin 2013; Niksch 2009.
11. The Fuhrmann and Kreps (2010) dataset does suggest that the U.S. first considered using military force against North Korea in 1994 when the North Koreans left the NPT in 1993. This would suggest that the withdrawal from the NPT, as well as a CIA assessment that North Korea had secretly developed one or two nuclear weapons illegally, likely prompted a discussion of military force to counter the program. It is unlikely that in 1991 during the signing of the Joint Declaration between North and South Koreas, the U.S. had a serious contemplation of military force against North Korea.

12. Nitikin 2013.
13. Ibid.
14. Niksch 2009; Nitikin 2013.
15. Niksch 2009.
16. Kroenig 2010.
17. Nitikin 2013; Niksch 2009.
18. Arms Control Association 2019.
19. Nitikin 2013.
20. Without inspections it is obviously difficult to ascertain the exact status of plutonium production and the extent to which DPRK restarted its nuclear weapons pursuit.
21. Arms Control Association 2010.
22. Niksch 2009; Arms Control Association 2019.
23. Arms Control Association 2019.
24. BBC News 2012.
25. Sang-Hun 2012.
26. Ibid.
27. Nitikin 2013; Arms Control Association 2019.
28. Nanto and Maynin 2010; Haggard 2012.
29. Hufbauer et al. 2007.
30. Hufbauer et al. 2007; Nanto and Maynin 2010; Haggard 2012.
31. Arms Control Association 2019.
32. Broad 2017.
33. Kim 2015.
34. Boghani 2018. It has not been confirmed whether the September nuclear test was indeed a thermonuclear device (hydrogen bomb), but it was recorded as North Korea's most powerful yet at an estimated yield of 250 kilotons.
35. White House 2017. The implementation of these sanctions raises a question about the efficacy of traditional sanctions in stopping or reversing nuclear development. For example, many sanctions experts argue that these "secondary sanctions" and "301 designations," on North Korea are powerful weapons that, over time, are starting to have a real effect on nuclear proliferation (Nephew 2017; Harrell and Zarate 2018). If this is the case, does this suggest that the earlier findings indicating the negative correlation between economic sanctions and nuclear reversal are historical artifact? This could be the case, but given their relatively recent implementation, it will take time to ascertain. However, there is some reason to think that secondary sanctions, when used on their own, will be similarly ineffective. First, they are aimed at punishing any state that engages in trade with the proliferator. For the most part, this has a huge impact on the trading partner, but not necessarily on the proliferator in question. And relatedly, these trading partners (especially in the case of the partners of North Korea and Iran), are either allies of the United States or conduct significant trade with the U.S. The imposition of these punishments is also likely to have a significant negative effect on the U.S. economy and its relationship with these trading partners, without a discernable impact on the proliferator's economy. As one Chinese official stated, "It is obviously improper to use one issue as a tool to exercise pressure on the other" (Korte 2017). And in accord with my theoretical framework, without parallel rewards, proliferators may still not be motivated to engage in nuclear reversal—the June 12, 2018 Singapore Summit between Trump and Kim serves as a useful example.
36. Boghani 2018.
37. Ibid.
38. Ibid.
39. Reports indicate that the North Koreans are expanding other nuclear and missile testing facilities. See Neuman 2018.
40. Boghani 2018.
41. Rapp-Hooper 2018.
42. Pew 2017.
43. Forgey 2018.
44. Based on conversations with European and Latin American policy officials, June 2018.

45. Terry 2019.
46. Ward 2019.
47. Gearan and Hudson 2018.
48. Neuman 2018.
49. My theory, as discussed previously, requires and assumes credibility of commitment on both sides.
50. Mehta and Spaniel 2019.
51. Goldman 2017.
52. Ibid.
53. Ibid.
54. Ibid.
55. Ibid.
56. Sagan 2017.
57. Cha 2002.
58. Ibid.
59. Sagan 2017.
60. Malinowski 2017.
61. Malinowski 2017; Panda and Narang 2017.
62. Griffiths and Wang 2017.
63. It is important to note that the objective for United States and South Korea, among others in the international system, is denuclearization. While recent evidence suggests that this presents an up-hill battle, it is potentially possible that a future agreement could address this primary requisite.

Chapter 8

1. Baldwin 1971.
2. Harvey and Mitton 2016; Renshon et al. 2017; Kertzer 2016; Mehta 2017.
3. Saunders 2011; Whitlark 2017.
4. Mehta and Whitlark 2016, 2017; Fuhrmann and Tkach 2015.
5. Levite 2003; Mehta and Whitlark 2017.
6. Mehta and Whitlark 2016, 2017.
7. Fuhrmann 2012; Kroenig 2012; Gibbons 2017.
8. Mehta and Whitlark 2017, 2019.
9. Pifer 2018.
10. Mehta 2016
11. Shinkman 2017.
12. Berkemeier et al. 2018.
13. Daekwon 2017.
14. Panda and Narang 2017.
15. Ibid.

WORKS CITED

Abraham, Itty. 2010. "'Who's Next?' Nuclear Ambivalence and the Contradictions of Non-Proliferation Policy." *Economic and Political Weekly*, Vol. 45, No. 43, pp. 48–56.

Achen, Christopher. 2004. "A Methodological Education: Part I." *The Political Methodologist*, Vol. 12, No. 2, pp. 2–4.

Achen, Christopher and Duncan Snidal. 1989. "Rational Deterrence Theory and Comparative Case Studies." *World Politics*, Vol. 41, No. 2, pp. 143–169.

Albright, David, Paul Brannan, and Christina Walrond. 2010. "Did Stuxnet Take Out 1,000 Centrifuges at the Natanz Enrichment Plant?" *International Science and International Security Report*. Accessed via: http://isis-online.org/isis-reports/detail/did-stuxnet-take-out-1000-centrifuges-at-the-natanz-enrichment-plant/.

Albright, David and Corey Gay. 1998. "Taiwan: Nuclear Nightmare Averted," *Bulletin of the Atomic Scientists*, Vol. 54, No. 2, pp. 54–60.

Albright, David, and Andrea Stricker. 2010. "Iran's Nuclear Program." *Institute for Science and International Security (ISIS)*. Accessed via: http://iranprimer.usip.org/resource/irans-nuclear-program.

American Presidency Project. 1978. "Visit of Prime Minister Desai of India Joint Communique." Accessed via: http://www.presidency.ucsb.edu/ws/?pid=30952.

Arms Control Association. 2003. "Arms Control and Proliferation Profile: India." Accessed via: https://www.armscontrol.org/factsheets/indiaprofile.

Arms Control Association. 2019. "Chronology of U.S.-North Korean Nuclear and Missile Diplomacy." Accessed via: https://www.armscontrol.org/factsheets/dprkchron.

Art, Robert J., and Patrick M. Cronin, eds. 2003. *The United States and Coercive Diplomacy*. Washington, DC: United State Institute of Peace Press.

Asal, Victor, and Kyle Beardsley. 2007. "Proliferation and International Crisis Behavior." *Journal of Peace Research*, Vol. 44, No. 2, pp. 139–155.

Askari, Hossein G., John Forrer, Hildy Teegan, and Jiawen Yang. 2003. *Economic Sanctions: Examining Their Philosophy and Efficacy*. Westport, CT: Greenwood.

Associated Press. 2005. "Iran Would Rather be Hit by Sanctions than Back Down Over Nuclear Program." Accessed via: NTI 2011.

Associated Press. 2013. "North Korea Calls Nuclear Weapons Nation's Life." Accessed via: NTI 2011.

Bajpai, Kanti. 2009. "To War or Not to War: The India-Pakistan Crisis of 2001–2." In *Nuclear Proliferation in South Asia: Crisis Behaviour and the Bomb*, ed. Sumit Ganguly and S. Paul Kapur, New York, NY: Routledge Press, pp. 162–183.

Baker, Peter. 2015. "Obama Criticizes Huckabee, Trump, Cruz and Other Republicans." *The New York Times*. Accessed via: https://www.nytimes.com/2015/07/28/us/politics/obama-criticizes-huckabee-trump-cruz-and-other-republicans.html.

Baldwin, David A. 1971. "The Power of Positive Sanctions." *World Politics*, Vol. 24, No. 1, pp. 19–38.

Baldwin, David A. 1985. *Economic Statecraft*. Princeton, NJ: Princeton University Press.

Baldwin, David A. 2000. "The Sanctions Debate and the Logic of Choice." *International Security*, Vol. 24, No. 3, pp. 80–107.

Bapat, Navin, and T. Clifton Morgan. 2009. "Multilateral vs. Unilateral Sanctions Reconsidered: A Test Using New Data." *International Studies Quarterly*, Vol. 53, No. 4, pp. 1075–1094.

Bas, Muhammet, and Andrew Coe. 2016. "A Dynamic Theory of Nuclear Proliferation and Preventive War." *International Organization*, Vol. 70, No. 4, pp. 655–685.

BBC News. 2012. "North Korea 'Not Bound' by US Nuclear Deal." Accessed via: https://www.bbc.com/news/world-asia-17751864.

Beardsley, Kyle, and Victor Asal. "Winning with the Bomb." *Journal of Conflict Resolution*, Vol. 53, No. 2, pp. 278–301.

Beck, Nathaniel, Jonathan Katz, and Richard Tucker. 1998. "Taking Time Seriously: Time Series Cross-Section Analysis with a Binary Dependent Variable." *American Journal of Political Science*, Vol. 42, No. 4, pp. 1260–1288.

Beinart, Peter. 2015. "Why the Iran Deal Makes Obama's Critics So Angry." *The Atlantic*. Accessed via: https://www.theatlantic.com/international/archive/2015/07/iran-nuclear-deal-obama/398450/.

Bell, Mark, and Nicholas Miller. 2015. "Questioning the Effect of Nuclear Weapons on Conflict." *Journal of Conflict Resolution*, Vol. 59, No. 1, pp. 74–92.

Berkemeier, Molly, Paige Cone, Rupal Mehta, and Rachel Whitlark. 2019. "All Options on the (Latency) Table: Carrots and Sticks on Nuclear Reversal." *Working Paper*.

Beschloss, Michael R. 1991. *The Crisis Years: Kennedy and Khrushchev, 1960–1963*. New York: Edward Burlingame Books.

Betts, Richard K. 1977a. *Nuclear Blackmail and Nuclear Balance*. Cambridge, MA: Harvard University Press.

Betts, Richard K. 1977b. "Paranoids, Pygmies, Pariahs and Non-Proliferation." *Free Press*, No. 26, pp. 157–183.

Bhutto, Zulfikar Ali. 1974. "Prime Minister Secretariat Press Release." *Associated Press of Pakistan (APP) and Pakistan Television (PTV)*. Accessed via: NTI.

Blakely, Kenneth R. 2010. "The Libyan Conversion in Three Acts: Why Qadhafi Gave Up His Weapons of Mass Destruction Program." *Naval Postgraduate School*. Accessed via: https://calhoun.nps.edu/bitstream/handle/10945/5379/10Mar_Blakely.pdf?sequence=1&isAllowed=y.

Blanc, Alexis, and Brad Roberts. 2008. "Nuclear Proliferation: A Historical Overview." *Institute for Defense Analyses. IDA Document D-3447*.

Bleek, Philipp C. 2017. "When Did (and Didn't) States Proliferate? Chronicling the Spread of Nuclear Weapons." Discussion Paper. Cambridge, MA: Project on Managing the Atom, Belfer Center for Science and International Affairs, Harvard Kennedy School and the James Martin Center for Nonproliferation Studies, Middlebury Institute of International Studies.

Bleek, Philipp C., and Eric B. Lorber. 2014. "Security Guarantees and Allied Nuclear Proliferation." *Journal of Conflict Resolution*, Vol. 58, No. 3, pp. 429–454.

Boghani, Priyanka. 2018. "The U.S. and North Korea On the Brink: A Timeline." *PBS Frontline*. Accessed via: https://www.pbs.org/wgbh/frontline/article/the-u-s-and-north-korea-on-the-brink-a-timeline/.

Bowen, Wyn Q. 2006. "Libya and Nuclear Proliferation." *International Institute for Strategic Studies, Adelphi Paper 380*. London, UK: Routledge Press.

Bowen, Wyn Q., and Jonathan Brewer. 2011. "Iran's Nuclear Challenge: Nine Years and Counting." *International Affairs*, Vol. 84, No. 4, pp. 923–943.

Braun, Chaim, and Christopher F. Chyba. 2004. "Proliferation Rings: New Challenges to the Nuclear Nonproliferation Regime." *International Security*, Vol. 29, No. 2, pp. 5–49.

Braut-Hegghammer, Målfrid. 2006. "Rebel Without a Cause? Explaining Iraq's Response to Resolution 1441." *The Nonproliferation Review*, Vol. 13, No. 1, pp. 17–34.

Braut-Hegghammer, Målfrid. 2008. "Libya's Nuclear Turnaround: Perspectives from Tripoli." *The Middle East Journal*, Vol. 62, No. 1, pp. 55–72.

Braut-Hegghammer, Målfrid. 2016. *Unclear Physics: Why Iraq and Libya Failed to Build Nuclear Weapons*. Ithaca, NY: Cornell University Press.

Broad, William J. 2017. "U.S. Nuclear History Offers Clues to North Korea's Progress." *New York Times*. Accessed via: https://www.nytimes.com/2017/05/22/science/north-korea-nuclear-weapons.html.

Brodie, Bernard, ed. 1946. *The Absolute Weapon: Atomic Power and World Order*. New York: Harcourt, Brace & Co Press.

Brodie, Bernard. 1959. *Strategy in the Missile Age*. Princeton, NJ: Princeton University Press.

Brooks, Risa A. 2002. "Sanctions and Regime Type: What Works, and When?" *Security Studies*, Vol. 11, No. 4, pp. 1–50.

Brown, Robert L., and Jeffrey Kaplow. 2014. "Talking Peace, Making Weapons: IAEA Technical Cooperation and Nuclear Proliferation." *Journal of Conflict Resolution*, Vol. 58, No. 3, pp. 402–428.

Bueno de Mesquita, Bruce, and William H. Riker. 1982. "An Assessment of the Merits of Selective Nuclear Proliferation." *Journal of Conflict Resolution*, Vol. 26, No. 2, pp. 283–306.

Burr, William. 2011. "The Nixon Administration and the Indian Nuclear Program, 1972–1974." National Security Archive Electronic Briefing Book No. 367.

Burr, William. 2005. "Nixon/Kissinger Saw India as 'Soviet Stooge' in 1971 South Asia Crisis." Accessed via: http://nsarchive.gwu.edu/news/20050629/index.htm.

Burr, William, and Jeffrey T. Richelson. 2000. "Whether to 'Strangle the Baby in the Cradle': The United States and the Chinese Nuclear Program, 1960–64." *International Security*, Vol. 25, No. 3, pp. 54–99.

Campbell, Kurt M., Robert J. Einhorn, and Mitchell B. Reiss. 2004. *The Nuclear Tipping Point: Why States Reconsider Their Nuclear Choices*. Washington, DC: Brookings Institution Press.

Central Intelligence Agency. 1988. *Middle East-South Asia: Nuclear Handbook*. Accessed via: https://www.cia.gov/library/readingroom/docs/DOC_0000375197.pdf.

Cha, Victor D. 2002. "North Korea's Weapons of Mass Destruction: Badges, Shields, or Swords?" *Political Science Quarterly*, Vol. 117, No. 2, pp. 209–230.

Chang, Gordon H. 1990. *Friends and Enemies: The United States, China, and the Soviet Union, 1948–1972*. Stanford, CA: Stanford University Press.

Chellaney, Brahma. 1991. "South Asia's Passage to Nuclear Power." *International Security*, Vol. 16, No. 1, pp. 43–72.

Chiozza, Giacomo, and Hein E. Goemans. 2003. "Peace Through Insecurity: Tenure and International Conflict." *Journal of Conflict Resolution*, Vol. 4, No. 4, pp. 443–467.

Chiozza, Giacomo, and Hein E. Goemans. 2004. "International Conflict and the Tenure of Leaders: Is War Still *Ex Post* Inefficient?" *American Journal of Political Science*, Vol. 48, No. 3, pp. 604–619.

Clark, David H., and Timothy Nordstrom. 2005. "Democratic Variants and Democratic Variance: How Domestic Constraints Shape International Conflict." *Journal of Politics*, Vol. 6, No. 1, pp. 250–270.

Clary, Christopher. 2019. "Same as the Old Boss? Leaders and Nuclear Abandonment." *Working Paper*.

Coe, Andrew J., and Jane Vaynman. 2015. "Collusion and the Nuclear Nonproliferation Regime." *The Journal of Politics*, Vol. 77, No. 4, pp. 983–997.

Cohen, Avner. 1998. *Israel and the Bomb*. New York, NY: Columbia University Press.

Cone, Paige Price. 2019. "Pressing Pause on Proliferation: Conditions of Nuclear Reversal." *Under Review*.

Cone, Paige and Mehta, Rupal N. 2010. "Inducements in Interstate Relations." *Oxford Research Encyclopedia of Politics*. Oxford University Press.

Cooper, Helene. "Saudi Arabia Approves of Iran Nuclear Deal, U.S. Defense Chief Says." *New York Times*. Accessed via: https://www.nytimes.com/2015/07/23/world/middleeast/iran-nuclear-deal-saudi-arabia.html.

Corera, Gordon. 2006. *Shopping for Bombs: Nuclear Proliferation, Global Insecurity, and the Rise and Fall of the A.Q. Khan Network*. Oxford, UK: Oxford University Press.

Cortright, David, and George A. Lopez, eds. 1995. *Economic Sanctions: Panacea or Peacebuilding in a Post–Cold War World?* Boulder, Co: Westview Press.

Croco, Sarah E. 2011. "The Decider's Dilemma: Leader Culpability, War Outcomes, and Domestic Punishment." *American Political Science Review*, Vol. 105, No. 3, pp. 457–477.

Crumm, Eileen. 1995. "The Value of Economic Incentives in International Politics." *Journal of Peace Research*, Vol. 32, No. 3, pp. 313–330.

Daekwon, Son. 2017. "China's North Korea Solution." *The Diplomat*. Accessed via: https://thediplomat.com/2017/07/chinas-north-korea-solution/.

Davis, James. 2000. *Threats and Promises: The Pursuit of International Influence*. Baltimore, MD: Johns Hopkins University Press.

Debs, Alexander, and Nuno P. Monteiro. 2014. "Known Unknowns: Power Shifts, Uncertainty, and War." *International Organization*, Vol. 68, No. 1, pp. 1–31.

Debs, Alexander, and Nuno P. Monteiro. 2016. *Nuclear Politics: The Strategic Causes of Proliferation*. Cambridge, UK: Cambridge University Press.

Director of Central Intelligence (DCI). 1963. "Communist China's Advanced Weapons Program." Special National Intelligence Estimate (SNIE) 13-2-63. Accessed via: http://www.nsarchive.org.

Drezner, Daniel. 1999. *The Sanctions Paradox: Economic Statecraft and International Relations*. Cambridge, UK: Cambridge University Press.

Drury, A. Cooper. 1998. "Revisiting Economic Sanctions Reconsidered." *Journal of Peace Research*, Vol. 35, No. 4, pp. 497–509.

Early, Bryan R. 2015. *Busted Sanctions: Explaining Why Economic Sanctions Fail*. Stanford, CA: Stanford University Press.

Edelman, Eric, Dennis Ross, and Ray Takeyh. "Time to Take it to Iran." *Politico*. Accessed via: https://www.politico.com/magazine/story/2015/01/iran-yemen-coup-114532.

Erdbrink, Thomas. 2009. "Iran Signals Opening with U.S." *The Washington Post*.

Erdbrink, Thomas, and Rick Gladstone. 2015. "Iran's President Defends Nuclear Deal in Blunt Remarks." *New York Times*. Accessed via: https://www.nytimes.com/2015/07/24/world/middleeast/irans-president-defends-nuclear-deal-in-blunt-remarks.html.

Fassihi, Farnaz. 2016. "U.N.: Iran Keeping Commitments, but Flouting Spirit of Nuke Deal." *Wall Street Journal*. Accessed via: https://www.wsj.com/articles/u-n-iran-keeping-commitments-but-flouting-spirit-of-nuke-deal-1468933170.

Fearon, James D. 1994. "Signaling Versus the Balance of Power and Interests: An Empirical Test of the Crisis Bargaining Model." *Journal of Conflict Resolution*, Vol. 38, No. 2, pp. 236–269.

Fearon, James D. 1995. "Rationalist Explanations for War." *International Organization*, Vol. 4, No. 2, pp. 379–414.

Feaver, Peter Douglas. 1993. *Guarding the Guardians: Civilian Control of Nuclear Weapons in the United States*. Ithaca, NY: Cornell University Press.

Federation of American Scientists. 2013. "Prime Minister's announcement of India's three underground nuclear tests." Accessed via: www.fas.org/news/india/1998/05/vajpayee1198.htm.

Fey, Mark, and Kristopher W. Ramsay. 2006. "The Common Priors Assumption: A Comment on 'Bargaining and the Nature of War.'" *Journal of Conflict Resolution*, Vol. 50, No. 4, pp. 607–613.

Filson, Darren, and Suzanne Werner. 2002. "A Bargaining Model of War and Peace: Anticipating the Onset, Duration, and Outcome of War." *American Journal of Political Science*, Vol. 46, No. 4, pp. 819–838.

Fitzpatrick, Mark. 2006. "Assessing Iran's Nuclear Programme." *Survival*, Vol. 48, No. 3, pp. 5–26.

Foran, Virginia, and Lenoard Spector. 1997. "The Application of Incentives to Nuclear Proliferation." In *The Price of Peace: Incentives and International Conflict Prevention*, ed. David Cortright. Lanham, MD: Rowman & Littlefield, pp. 21–54.

Forland, Astrid.1997. "Norway's Nuclear Odyssey: From Optimistic Proponent to Nonproliferator." *The Nonproliferation Review*, Vol. 4, No. 2, pp. 1–16.

Forgey, Quint. 2018. "Trump Praises Kim Jong Un as 'Very Honorable.'" *Politico*. Accessed via: https://www.politico.com/story/2018/04/24/trump-praise-kim-jong-un-547610.

Frantz, Douglas, and Kathleen Collins. 2007. *The Nuclear Jihadist: The True Story of the Man Who Sold the World's Most Dangerous Secrets . . . and How We Could Have Stopped Him*. New York, NY: Twelve Publisher.

Fuhrmann, Matthew. 2009. "Spreading Temptation: Proliferation and Peaceful Nuclear Cooperation Agreements." *International Security*, Vol. 34, No. 1, pp. 7–41.

Fuhrmann, Matthew. 2012. *Atomic Assistance: How "Atoms for Peace" Programs Cause Nuclear Insecurity*. Ithaca, NY: Cornell University Press.

Fuhrmann, Matthew. 2019. "Influence without Bombs: The Logic of Latent Nuclear Deterrence." *Working Paper*.

Fuhrmann, Matthew, and Michael C. Horowitz. 2015. "When Leaders Matter: Rebel Experience and Nuclear Proliferation." *Journal of Politics*, Vol. 77, No. 1, pp. 72–87.

Fuhrmann, Matthew, and Sarah E. Kreps. 2010. "Targeting Nuclear Programs in War and Peace: A Quantitative Empirical Analysis, 1941–2000." *Journal of Conflict Resolution*, Vol. 54, No. 6, pp. 831–859.

Fuhrmann, Matthew, and Todd S. Sechser. 2014. "Signaling Alliance Commitments: Hand-Tying and Sunk Costs in Extended Nuclear Deterrence." *American Journal of Political Science*, Vol. 58, No. 4, pp. 919–935.

Fuhrmann, Matthew, and Benjamin Tkach. 2015. "Almost Nuclear: Introducing the Nuclear Latency Dataset." *Conflict Management and Peace Science*, Vol. 32, No. 4, pp. 443–461.

Galtung, Johan. 1967. "On the Effects of International Economic Sanctions: With Examples from the Case of Rhodesia." *World Politics*, Vol. 19, No. 3, pp. 378–416.

Gartzke, Erik, and Dong-Joon Jo. 2009. "Bargaining, Nuclear Proliferation, and Interstate Disputes." *Journal of Conflict Resolution*, Vol. 52, No. 2, pp. 9–33.

Gartzke, Erik, Jeffrey Kaplow, and Rupal N. Mehta. 2014. "The Determinants of Nuclear Force Structure." *Journal of Conflict Resolution*, Vol. 58, No. 3, pp. 481–508.

Gartzke, Erik, Jeffrey Kaplow, and Rupal N. Mehta. 2019. "Deterrence and the Structure of Nuclear Forces." *Working Paper*.

Gartzke, Erik, and Matthew Kroenig, eds. 2009. "A Strategic Approach to Nuclear Proliferation." *Journal of Conflict Resolution*, Vol. 53, No. 2, pp. 151–328.

Gaubatz, Kurt Taylor. 1991. "Election Cycles and War." *Journal of Conflict Resolution*, Vol. 3, No. 2, pp. 212–244.

Gavin, Francis J. 2004. "Blasts from the Past: Proliferation Lessons from the 1960s." *International Security*, Vol. 29, No. 3, pp. 100–135.

Gavin, Francis J. 2012. *Nuclear Statecraft: History and Strategy in America's Atomic Age*. Ithaca, NY: Cornell University Press.

Gavin, Francis J. 2015. "Strategies of Inhibition: U.S. Grand Strategy, the Nuclear Revolution, and Nonproliferation." *International Security*, Vol. 40, No. 1, pp. 9–46.

Gedda, George. 2002. "U.S. Says Iran Making Headway on Nuclear Weapons Program." *Associated Press*. Accessed via: https://www.mrt.com/news/article/U-S-Iran-Making-Headway-on-Nukes-7783688.php.

Geddes, Barbara. 1990. "How the Cases You Choose Affect the Answers You Get: Selection Bias in Comparative Politics." *Political Analysis*, Vol. 2, pp. 131–150.

Gelpi, Christopher, and Joseph M. Grieco. 2001. "Attracting Trouble: Democracy, Leadership Tenure, and the Targeting of Militarized Challenges, 1918–1992." *Journal of Conflict Resolution*, Vol. 45, No. 6 pp. 794–817.

Gearan, Anne, and John Hudson. 2018. "Trump Administration Insists Agreement Means North Korea Will Denuclearize." *The Washington Post.* Accessed via: https://www.washingtonpost.com/politics/trump-administration-insists-agreement-means-north-korea-will-denuclearize/2018/06/14/d97c59ac-6fea-11e8-bf86-a2351b5ece99_story.html?utm_term=.b0a2b17deefa.

George, Alexander. 1969. "The Operational Code: A Neglected Approach to the Study of Political Leaders and Decision-Making." *International Studies Quarterly,* Vol. 13, No. 2, pp. 190–222.

George, Alexander. 1971. "The Development of Doctrine and Strategy." In *The Limits of Coercive Diplomacy: Laos, Cuba, Vietnam,* ed. Alexander L. George, David Hal, and William Simons, 1–35. Boston, MA: Little, Brown.

George, Alexander. 1991. *Forceful Persuasion: Coercive Diplomacy as an Alternative to War.* Washington, DC: USIP Press.

George, Alexander. 1994. "Theory and Practice." In *The Limits of Coercive Diplomacy,* 2nd ed., ed. Alexander L. George and William E. Simons, 13–22. Boulder, CO: Westview Press.

George, Alexander L and Andrew Bennett. 2005. *Case Studies and Theory Development in the Social Sciences (A BCSIA book).* Cambridge, MA: Massachusetts Institute of Technology Press.

Gerzhoy, Gene. 2015. "Alliance Coercion and Nuclear Restraint: How the United States Thwarted West Germany's Nuclear Ambitions." *International Security,* Vol. 39, No. 4, pp. 91–129.

Gerzhoy, Gene, and Nicholas Miller. 2016. "Donald Trump Thinks More Countries Should Have Nuclear Weapons. Here's What the Research Says." *Washington Post's Monkey Cage.* Accessed via: https://www.washingtonpost.com/news/monkey-cage/wp/2016/04/06/should-more-countries-have-nuclear-weapons-donald-trump-thinks-so/?noredirect=on.

Gibbons, Rebecca Davis. 2019. "American Leadership and the Determinants of Commitment to the Nuclear Nonproliferation Regime." *Working Paper.*

Ghosn, Faten, Glenn Palmer, and Stuart Bremer. 2004. "The MID 3 Data Set, 1993–2001: Procedures, Coding Rules, and Description." *Conflict Management and Peace Science,* Vol. 21, No. 2, pp. 133–154.

Gochman, Charles, and Zeev Maoz. 1984. "Militarized Interstate Disputes, 1816–1976 Procedures, Patterns, and Insights." *Journal of Conflict Resolution,* Vol. 28, No. 4, pp. 585–616.

Goemans, H.E, Kristian Skrede Gleditsch, and Giacomo Chiozza. 2009. "Introducing Archigos: A Data Set of Political Leaders." *Journal of Peace Research,* Vol. 46, No. 2, pp. 269–283.

Goertz, Gary, Paul Diehl, and Alexandru Balas. 2016. *The Puzzle of Peace: Explaining the Rise of Peace in the International System.* Oxford, UK: Oxford University Press.

Goldgeier, James M. 1994. *Leadership Style and Soviet Foreign Policy: Stalin, Khrushchev, Brezhnev, Gorbachev.* Baltimore, MD: Johns Hopkins University Press.

Goldman, Russell. 2017. "How Trump's Predecessors Dealt with the North Korean Threat." *The New York Times.* Accessed via: https://www.nytimes.com/2017/08/17/world/asia/trump-north-korea-threat.html.

Goldschmidt, Bertrand. 1982. *The Atomic Complex.* La Grange Park, IL: American Nuclear Society.

Greenberg, Josh. 2015. "Netanyahu to Continue Campaign Against Iran Nuclear Deal." *The Wall Street Journal.* Accessed via: https://www.wsj.com/articles/netanyahu-to-continue-campaign-against-iran-nuclear-deal-1441281409.

Griffiths, James, and Serenitie Wang. 2017. "Is China Reinforcing Its Border with North Korea?" *CNN.* Accessed via: https://www.cnn.com/2017/07/25/asia/china-north-korea-border/index.html.

Guisinger, Alexandra, and Alastair Smith. 2002. "Honest Threats: The Interaction of Reputation and Political Institutions in International Crises." *Journal of Conflict Resolution,* Vol. 46. No. 2, pp. 175–200.

Haaas Richard, and Meghan O'Sullivan, eds. 2000. *Honey and Vinegar: Incentives, Sanctions, and Foreign Policy.* Washington, DC: Brookings Institution Press.

Haggard, Stephan, and Marcus Noland. 2012. "Economic Crime and Punishment in North Korea." *Political Science Quarterly,* Vol. 127, No. 4, pp. 659–683.

Halperin, Morton. 1974. *Bureaucratic Politics and Foreign Policy*. Washington, DC: Brookings Institution.

Harrell, Peter, and Juan Zarate. 2018. "How to Successfully Sanction North Korea: A Long-Term Strategy for Washington and Its Allies." *Foreign Affairs*. Accessed via: https://www.foreignaffairs.com/articles/north-korea/2018-01-30/how-successfully-sanction-north-korea.

Harvey, Frank P., and John Mitton. 2016. *Fighting for Credibility: U.S. Reputation and International Politics*. Toronto, CA: University of Toronto Press.

Hayes, Peter, and Chung-In Moon. 2011. "Park Chung Hee, the CIA, and the Bomb." *NAPSNet Special Reports*. Accessed via: http://nautilus.org/napsnet/napsnet-special-reports/park-chung-hee-the-cia-and-the-bomb/.

Hecker, Siegfried S. 2010. "Lessons Learned from the North Korean Nuclear Crises." *Daedalus*, Vol. 139, No. 1, pp. 44–56.

Heinonen, Olli. 2014. "Testimony Before the United States Senate Committee on Foreign Relations." *Belfer Center for Science and International Affairs*. Accessed via: https://www.foreign.senate.gov/imo/media/doc/Olli%20Heinonen%20Testimony%20140729.pdf.

Hersman, Rebecca K.C., and Robert Peters. 2006. "Nuclear U-Turns: Learning from South Korean and Taiwanese Rollback." *Nonproliferation Review*, Vol. 13, No. 3, pp. 539–553.

Hirschman, Albert. 1945. *National Power and the Structure of Foreign Trade*. Berkeley, CA: University of California Press.

Ho, Catherine. 2015. "Mega-Donors Opposing Iran Deal Have Upper Hand in Fierce Lobbying Battle." *Washington Post*. Accessed via: https://www.washingtonpost.com/news/powerpost/wp/2015/08/13/mega-donors-opposing-iran-deal-have-upper-hand-in-fierce-lobbying-battle/?noredirect=on&utm_term=.24404bada3ef.

Hoodbhoy, Pervez Amerali. 2011. "Pakistan's Nuclear Bayonet." *The Herald*. Accessed via: https://web.archive.org/web/20110218212415/http://www.dawn.com/2011/02/16/herald-exclusive-pakistans-nuclear-bayonet.html.

Horowitz, Michael, Rose McDermott, and Allan C. Stam. 2005. "Leader Age, Regime Type, and Violent International Relations." *Journal of Conflict Resolution*, Vol. 49, No. 5, pp. 661–685.

Horowitz, Michael C., and Allan C. Stam. 2015. "How Prior Military Service Influences the Future Militarized Behaviour of Leaders." *International Organization*, Vol. 68, No. 3, pp. 527–559.

Hufbauer, Gary C., Jeffrey J. Schott, Kimberly Ann Elliot, and Barbara Oegg. 2007. (HSE) *Economic Sanctions Reconsidered*. 3rd ed. Washington, DC: Peterson Institute for International Economics.

Huth, Paul K., and Bruce Russett. 1984. "What Makes Deterrence Work?: Cases from 1900 to 1980." *World Politics*, Vol. 36, No. 4, pp. 496–526.

Hymans, Jacques. 2001. "Of Gauchos and Gringos: Why Argentina Never Wanted the Bomb, and Why the United States Thought it Did." *Security Studies*, Vol. 10, No. 3, pp. 153–185.

Hymans, Jacques. 2006. *The Psychology of Nuclear Proliferation: Identity, Emotions, and Foreign Policy*. Cambridge, UK: Cambridge University Press.

Ignatius, David. 2016. "The Omani 'Back Channel' to Iran and the Secrecy Surrounding the Nuclear Deal." *Washington Post*. Accessed via: https://www.washingtonpost.com/opinions/the-omani-back-channel-to-iran-and-the-secrecy-surrounding-the-nuclear-deal/2016/06/07/0b9e27d4-2ce1-11e6-b5db-e9bc84a2c8e4_story.html.

India Today. 1978. "President Carter's visit turns out to be an eye-opener on state of Indo-US relations." *India Today Magazine*. Accessed via: https://www.indiatoday.in/magazine/indiascope/story/19780131-president-carters-visit-turns-out-to-be-an-eye-opener-on-state-of-indo-us-relations-822812-2014-10-29.

International Atomic Energy Agency. 2013. "IAEA, Iran Sign Joint Statement on Framework for Cooperation." *IAEA Press Release*.

Iran Press Service. 2002. "Iran Confirms Building New Nuclear Facilities." Accessed via: http://www.iran-pres-service.com/articles_2002/Dec_2002/iran_confirms_new_nucke_plants_141202.html.

Islam, Md. Thowhidul. 2013. "The Nuclearization Of Iran and The Policy Of Russia." *Asian and African Studies*, Vol. 22, No. 2, pp. 248–278.

Jaipal, Rikhi. 1977. "The Indian Nuclear Explosion." *International Security*, Vol. 1, No. 4, pp. 44–51.

Jervis, Robert. 1976. *Perception and Misperception in International Politics*. Princeton, NJ: Princeton University Press.

Jervis, Robert. 1983. "Deterrence and Perception." *International Security*, Vol. 7, No. 3, pp. 3–30.

Jervis, Robert. 1989. *The Meaning of the Nuclear Revolution*. Ithaca, NY: Cornell University Press.

Jo, Dong-Joon, and Erik Gartzke. 2007. "Determinants of Nuclear Weapons Proliferation: A Quantitative Model." *Journal of Conflict Resolution*, Vol. 51, No. 1, pp. 167–194.

Jones, Daniel, Stuart Bremer, and J. David Singer. 1996. "Militarized Interstate Disputes, 1816–1992: Rationale, Coding Rules, and Empirical Patterns." *Conflict Management and Peace Science*, Vol. 15, No. 2, pp. 163–213.

Kahl, Colin H. 2012. "Not Time to Attack Iran: Why War Should Be a Last Resort." *Foreign Affairs*. Accessed via: https://www.foreignaffairs.com/articles/iran/2012-01-17/not-time-attack-iran.

Kapur, S. Paul. 2007. *Dangerous Deterrent: Nuclear Weapons Proliferation and Conflict in South Asia*. Stanford, CA: Stanford University Press.

Keohane, Robert O., and Joseph S. Nye. 1997. *Power and Interdependence: World Politics in Transition*. Boston, MA: Little, Brown.

Kerr, Paul K. 2019. "Iran's Nuclear Program: Status." *Congressional Research Service*.

Kertzer, Joshua D. 2016. *Resolve in International Politics*. Princeton, NJ: Princeton University Press.

Khan, Munir Ahmad. 1974. "India's nuclear explosion: Challenge and Response," *International Atomic Energy Agency and Pakistan Atomic Energy Commission*. Accessed via: https://www.iaea.org/sites/default/files/then_and_now.pdf.

Kim, Dongsoo. 2015. "The Obama Administration's Policy Toward North Korea: The Causes and Consequences of Strategic Patience." *Journal of Asian Public Policy*, Vol. 9, No. 1, pp. 32–44.

King, Gary, Robert Keohane, and Sidney Verba. 1994. *Designing Social Inquiry*. Princeton, NJ: Princeton University Press.

Kissinger, Henry. 1957. *Nuclear Weapons and Foreign Policy*. New York, NY: Harper Press.

Korte, Gregory. 2017. "Trump Orders Chinese Trade Investigation despite Cooperation on North Korea." *USA Today*. Accessed via: https://www.usatoday.com/story/news/politics/2017/08/14/trump-orders-chinese-trade-investigation-despite-cooperation-north-korea/565899001/.

Kroenig, Matthew. 2009a. "Exporting the Bomb: Why States Provide Sensitive Nuclear Assistance." *American Political Science Review*, Vol. 103, No. 1, pp. 113–133.

Kroenig, Matthew. 2009b. "Importing the Bomb: Sensitive Nuclear Assistance and Nuclear Proliferation." *Journal of Conflict Resolution*, Vol. 53, No. 2, pp. 161–180.

Kroenig, Matthew. 2010. *Exporting the Bomb: Technology Transfer and the Spread of Nuclear Weapons*. Ithaca, NY, Cornell University Press.

Kroenig, Matthew. 2012. "Time to Attack Iran: Why a Strike Is the Least Bad Option." *Foreign Affairs*. pp. 76–86.

Kroenig, Matthew. 2014. "Force or Friendship? Explaining Great Power Nonproliferation Policy." *Security Studies*, Vol. 2, No. 1, pp. 1–32.

Kugler, Jacek. 1984. "Terror Without Deterrence: Reassessing the Role of Nuclear Weapons." *Journal of Conflict Resolution*, Vol. 28, No. 3, pp. 470–506.

Lake, David A., and Robert Powell, eds. 1999. *Strategic Choice and International Relations*. Princeton, NJ: Princeton University Press.

Landler, Mark. 2018. "Trump Abandons Iran Nuclear Deal He Long Scorned." *The New York Times*. Accessed via: https://www.nytimes.com/2018/05/08/world/middleeast/trump-iran-nuclear-deal.html.

Lanoszka, Alexander. 2018. *Atomic Assurance: The Alliance Politics of Nuclear Proliferation*. Ithaca, NY: Cornell University Press.

Lacy, Dean, and Emerson M.S. Niou. 2004. "A Theory of Economic Sanctions and Issue Linkage: The Roles of Preferences, Information, and Threats." *Journal of Politics*, Vol. 66, No. 1, pp. 25–42.

Leeds, Brett Ashley. 1999. Domestic Political Institutions, Credible Commitments, and International Cooperation. *American Journal of Political Science*, Vol. 43, No. 4, pp. 979–1002.

Leeds, Brett Ashley, Jeffrey M. Ritter, Sara McLaughlin Mitchell, and Andrew G. Long. 2002. "Alliance Treaty Obligations and Provisions, 1815 –1944." *International Interactions*, Vol. 28, No. 3, pp. 237–260.

Levite, Ariel. 2002/2003. "Never Say Never Again: Nuclear Reversal Revisited." *International Security*, Vol. 26, No. 3, pp. 59–88.

Liberman, Peter. 2001. "The Rise and Fall of the South African Bomb." *International Security*. Vol. 26, No. 2, pp. 45–86

Lindsay, Jon R. 2013. "Stuxnet and the Limits of Cyber Warfare." *Security Studies*, Vol. 22, No. 3, pp. 365–404.

Liptak, Kevin and Nicole Gaouette. 2018. "Trump Withdraws from Iran Nuclear Deal, Isolating Him Further from World." *CNN*. Accessed via: https://www.cnn.com/2018/05/08/politics/donald-trump-iran-deal-announcement-decision/index.html.

Litwak, Robert. 2007. *Regime Change: U.S. Strategy through the Prism of 9/11*. Washington, DC: Woodrow Wilson Center Press and The Johns Hopkins University Press.

Long, Austin. 2015. "If You Really Want to Bomb Iran, Take the Deal." *Washington Post's Monkey Cage*. Accessed via: https://www.washingtonpost.com/news/monkey-cage/wp/2015/04/03/if-you-really-want-to-bomb-iran-take-the-deal/.

Lyndon B Johnson Library (LBJL). "The Bases for Direct Action Against Chinese Communist Nuclear Facilities," April 22, 1964, Document #111, "China Memos Vol. 1, 12/63-9/64 [2 of 2]," National Security File, Country File, Asian and the Pacific, Cambodia, China, Box 237, Papers of Lyndon Baines Johnson President, 1963–1969.

MacLeod, Scott. 2006. "Behind Gaddafi's Diplomatic Turnaround." *TIME Magazine*. Accessed via: http://content.time.com/time/world/article/0,8599,1195852,00.html.

Malici, Akan and Stephen G. Walker. 2016. Role Theory and Role Conflict in U.S.-Iran Relations: Enemies of Our Own Making. New York, NY: Routledge Press.

Malinowski, Tom. 2017. "How to Take Down Kim Jong Un." *Politico*. Accessed via: https://www.politico.com/magazine/story/2017/07/24/how-to-take-down-kim-jong-un-215411.

Marshall, Monty G., Ted Robert Gurr, and Keith Jaggers. 2010. "Polity IV Project: Political Regime Characteristics and Transitions, 1800–2009. Dataset Users' Manual." Center for Systemic Peace. Accessed via: http://www.systemicpeace.org/polity/polity4.htm .

Mattiacci, Eleonora, and Benjamin T. Jones. 2016. "(Nuclear) Change of Plans: What Explains Nuclear Reversals?" *International Interactions*, Vol. 42, No. 3, pp. 530–558.

McGillivray, Fiona, and Alastair Smith. 2006. "Credibility in Compliance and Punishment: Leader Specific Punishments and Credibility." *Journal of Politics*, Vol. 68, No. 2, pp. 248–256.

Mearsheimer, John J. 1990. "Back to the Future: Instability in Europe After the Cold War." *International Security*, Vol. 15, No. 1, pp. 5–56.

Mearsheimer, John J. 1993. "The Case for a Ukrainian Nuclear Deterrent." *Foreign Affairs*, Vol. 72, No. 3, pp. 50–66.

Mehta, Rupal N. 2016. "Is a Nuclear-Armed Japan Inconceivable?" *War on the Rocks*. Accessed via: https://warontherocks.com/2016/06/is-a-nuclear-armed-japan-inconceivable/.

Mehta, Rupal N. 2017. "Roundtable Review: Frank P. Harvey and John Mitton's New Book, *Fighting for Credibility: U.S. Reputation and International Politics*." H-Diplo. Accessed via: https://networks.h-net.org/node/28443/discussions/950042/issf-roundtable-10-3-fighting-credibility-us-reputation-and.

Mehta, Rupal N., and William Spaniel. 2019. "The Patience Gap: Temporal Preferences and Nuclear Negotiations." *Working Paper*.

Mehta, Rupal N., and Rachel E. Whitlark. 2017. "The Benefits and Burdens of Nuclear Latency." *International Studies Quarterly*, Vol. 61, No. 3, pp. 517–528.

Mehta, Rupal N., and Rachel E. Whitlark. 2016. "Unpacking the Iranian Nuclear Deal: Nuclear Latency and U.S. Foreign Policy." *The Washington Quarterly*, Vol. 39, No. 4, pp. 45–61.

Melham, Hisham. 2015. "President Obama's Perilous Road to Iran." *Al-Arabiyya*. Accessed via: http://english.alarabiya.net/en/views/news/middle-east/2015/04/04/President-Obama-s-perilous-road-to-Iran.html.

Meyer, Stephen M. 1984. *The Dynamics of Nuclear Proliferation*. Chicago, IL: University of Chicago Press.

Miller, Nicholas L. 2014. "The Secret Success of Nonproliferation Sanctions." *International Organization*, Vol. 68, No. 4, pp. 913–944.

Miller, Nicholas L. 2018. *Stopping the Bomb: The Sources and Effectiveness of U.S. Nonproliferation Policy*. Ithaca, NY: Cornell University Press.

Miller, Nicholas L., and Vipin Narang. 2018. "North Korea Defied the Theoretical Odds: What Can We Learn from its Successful Nuclearization?" *Texas National Security Review*, Vol. 1, No. 2, pp. 58–75.

Miller, Zeke. 2018. "Trump Tempers Iran Rhetoric, Says He's Ready for New Deal." *AP News*. Accessed via: https://www.apnews.com/eb9376eb3b264b5f9fbe48d774a9ad99.

Monteiro, Nuno P., and Alexandre Debs. 2014. "The Strategic Logic of Nuclear Proliferation." *International Security*, Vol. 39, No. 2, pp. 7–51.

Montgomery, Alexander H., and Scott D. Sagan. 2009. "The Perils of Predicting Proliferation." *Journal of Conflict Resolution*, Vol. 53, No. 2, pp. 302–328.

Morgan, T. Clifton, Navin Bapat, and Yoshi Kobayashi. 2014. "The Threat and Imposition of Sanctions: Updating the TIES dataset." *Conflict Management and Peace Science*, Vol. 3, No. 5, pp. 541–558.

Morgan, T. Clifton, and Valerie Schwebach. 2002. "Fools Suffer Gladly: The Use of Economic Sanctions in International Crises." *International Studies Quarterly*, Vol. 41, No. 1, pp. 27–50.

Morrow, Daniel, and Michael Carriere. 1999. "The Economic Impact of the 1998 Sanctions on India and Pakistan." *The Nonproliferation Review*, Vol. 6, No. 4, pp. 1–16.

Morrow, James D. 1989. "Capabilities, Uncertainty, and Resolve: A Limited Information Model of Crisis Bargaining." *American Journal of Political Science*, Vol. 33 No. 4, pp. 941–972.

Mufson, Steven and Robin Wright. 2007. "Iran Adapts to Economic Pressure." *The Washington Post*.

Müller, Harald, and Andreas Schmidt. 2008. "The Little Known Story of Deproliferation: Why States Give Up Nuclear Weapon Activities." *ISA Convention Paper*.

Nanto, Dick K., and Mark E. Manyin. 2010. "China-North Korea Relations." *Congressional Research Service*.

Narang, Neil, and Rupal N. Mehta. 2019. "The Unforeseen Consequences of Extended Deterrence: Moral Hazard in a Nuclear Protégé." *Journal of Conflict Resolution*, Vol. 63, No. 1, pp. 218–250.

Narang, Vipin. 2013. "What Does It Take to Deter? Regional Power Nuclear Postures and International Conflict." *Journal of Conflict Resolution*, Vol. 57, No. 3, pp. 478–508.

Narang, Vipin. 2014. *Nuclear Strategy in the Modern Era: Regional Powers and International Conflict: Regional Powers and International Conflict*. Princeton, NJ: Princeton University Press.

Narang, Vipin. 2015. "Nuclear Strategies of Emerging Nuclear Powers: North Korea and Iran." *The Washington Quarterly*, Vol. 38, No. 1, pp. 73–91.

Narang, Vipin. 2009. "Pride and Prejudice and Prithvis: Strategic Weapons Behavior in South Asia." In *Inside Nuclear South Asia*, ed. Scott D. Sagan, Stanford, CA: Stanford University Press, pp. 137–183.

Nasr, Vali. 2017. "How Hassan Rouhani Won in Iran: The Nuclear Deal Was Not Enough." *The Atlantic*. Accessed via: https://www.theatlantic.com/international/archive/2017/05/iran-election-rouhani-shia/527577/.

Nephew, Richard. 2017. *The Art of Sanctions: A View from the Field*. New York, NY: Columbia University Press.

Neuman, Scott. 2018. "North Korea Reportedly Expanding Ballistic Missile Production Facility." *NPR*. Accessed via: https://www.npr.org/2018/07/02/625267839/north-korea-reportedly-expanding-ballistic-missile-production-facility.

Niksch, Larry A. 2009. "North Korea's Nuclear Weapons Development and Diplomacy." *Congressional Research Service*.

Nincic, Miroslav. 2010. "Getting What You Want Positive Inducements in International Relations." *International Security*, Vol. 35, No. 1, pp. 138–183.

Nitikin, Mary Beth. 2013. "North Korea's Nuclear Weapons: Technical Issues." *Congressional Research Service*.

Noorani, A.G. 2001. "The Nuclear Guarantee Episode." *Frontline*, Vol. 18, No. 12. Accessed: https://frontline.thehindu.com/static/html/fl1812/18120940.htm.

Nuclear Threat Initiative. 2006. Brazil's Nuclear Ambitions. Accessed via: http://www.nti.org/analysis/articles/brazils-nuclear-ambitions/.

Nuclear Threat Initiative. 2010. "Pakistan." Accessed via: http://www.nti.org/learn/countries/pakistan/.

Nuclear Threat Initiative. 2011. "Iran's Nuclear Chronology." Accessed via: http://www.nti.org/media/pdfs/iran_nuclear.pdf?_=1316542527/.

Nuclear Weapons Archive. 2001. "India's Nuclear Weapons Program: The Long Pause: 1974–1989." Accessed via: http://nuclearweaponarchive.org/India/IndiaPause.html.

O'Neill, Barry. 2006. "Nuclear Weapons and National Prestige." *Cowles Foundation Discussion Paper No. 1560*.

Office of the Secretary of Defense. 1996. *Proliferation: Threat and Response*. Washington, DC: Office of the Secretary of Defense, pp. 1–83.

Organski, A.F.K., and Jacek Kugler. 1980. *The War Ledger*. Chicago, IL: University of Chicago Press.

Panda, Ankit, and Vipin Narang. 2017. "North Korea's ICBM: A New Missile and A New Era." *War on the Rocks*. Accessed via: https://warontherocks.com/2017/07/north-koreas-icbm-a-new-missile-and-a-new-era/.

Pape, Robert A. 1996. *Bombing to Win: Air Power and Coercion in War*. Ithaca, NY: Cornell University Press.

Pape, Robert A. 1997. "Why Economic Sanctions Do Not Work." *International Security*, Vol. 22, No. 2, pp. 9–136.

Paul, T. V. 2000. *Power vs. Prudence: Why Nations Forgo Nuclear Weapons*. Montreal, CN: McGill-Queen's University Press.

Perkovich, George. 2002. *India's Nuclear Bomb: The Impact on Global Proliferation, Updated Edition with a New Afterword*. Berkeley, CA: University of California Press.

Petrovics, Ariel. 2019. "Nuclear Proliferation and Foreign Policy Effectiveness: Examining the conditions for effectively inducing deproliferation. *Working Paper*.

Pevehouse, Jon. 2002. "With a Little Help from My Friends? Regional Organizations and the Consolidation of Democracy." *American Journal of Political Science*, Vol. 46, No. 3, pp. 611–626.

Pew. 2017. "U.S. Image Suffers as Publics Around World Question Trump's Leadership." Accessed via: http://www.pewglobal.org/2017/06/26/u-s-image-suffers-as-publics-around-world-question-trumps-leadership/.

Pifer, Steven. 2018. "The Future of the INF Treaty." *Brookings Institute*. Accessed via: https://www.brookings.edu/testimonies/the-future-of-the-inf-treaty/.

Politico. 2012. "Text of Obama's AIPAC Speech." *Politico*. Accessed via: https://www.politico.com/story/2012/03/text-of-obamas-aipac-speech-073588.

Porter, Gareth. 2012. Understanding Iran's Diplomatic Strategy." *Al-Jazeera–US and Canada*. Accessed: https://www.aljazeera.com/indepth/opinion/2012/04/2012422833676280.html.

Potter, William, and Gaukhar Mukhatzhanova. 2010. *Forecasting Nuclear Proliferation in the 21st Century*. Stanford, CA: Stanford University Press.

Powell, Robert. 1999. *In the Shadow of Power: States and Strategies in International Politics.* Princeton, NJ: Princeton University Press.

Powell, Robert. 2003. "Nuclear Deterrence Theory, Nuclear Proliferation, and National Missile Defense." *International Security*, Vol. 27, No. 4, pp. 86–118.

Press, Daryl G. 2005. *Calculating Credibility: How Leaders Assess Military Threats.* Ithaca, NY: Cornell University Press.

Quester, George H. 1973. *The Politics of Nuclear Proliferation.* Baltimore, MD: Johns Hopkins University Press.

Quillen, Chris. 2002. "Iranian Nuclear Weapons Policy: Past, Present, and Possible Future." *Middle East Review of International Affairs*, Vol. 6, No. 2, pp. 17–24.

Rapp-Hooper, Mira. 2018. "The Singapore Summit's Three Big Takeaways." *Washington Post's Monkey Cage.* Accessed via: https://www.washingtonpost.com/news/monkey-cage/wp/2018/06/12/the-singapore-summits-three-big-takeaways/?utm_term=.041991f7dcb9.

Rauchhaus, Robert. 2009. "Evaluating the Nuclear Peace Hypothesis: A Quantitative Approach." *Journal of Conflict Resolution*, Vol. 53, No. 2, pp. 258–277.

Reardon, Robert. 2010. *Nuclear Bargaining: Using Carrots and Sticks in Nuclear Counter-Proliferation.* MIT Dissertation.

Reiss, Mitchell. 1995. *Bridled Ambition: Why Countries Constrain their Nuclear Capabilities.* Washington, DC: Woodrow Wilson Center Press.

Renshon, Jonathan. 2006. *Why Leaders Choose War: The Psychology of Prevention.* Westport, CT: Praeger Security International.

Renshon, Jonathan, Allan Dafoe, and Paul Huth. 2018. "Leader Influence and Reputation Formation in World Politics." *American Journal of Political Science*, Vol. 62, No. 2, pp. 325–339.

Reuters. 2007. "Iran Won't Negotiate over Atomic Rights: President." Accessed via: https://www.reuters.com/article/us-iran-nuclear-ahmadinejad/iran-wont-negotiate-over-atomic-rights-president-idUSBLA33947120071023.

Reuters. 2015. "Israel Not Bound by Deal with Iran: Netanyahu." Accessed via: https://www.reuters.com/article/us-iran-nuclear-netanyahu-bound-idUSKCN0PO1VI20150714.

Reuters. 2017. "France Says Rouhani Re-Election Strengthens Hope of Iran Nuclear Deal Application." Accessed via: https://af.reuters.com/article/idAFKCN18G0XI.

Rezaian, Jason, and Joby Warrick. 2013. "Moderate Cleric Hassan Rouhani Wins Iran's Presidential Vote." *The Washington Post.* Accessed via: https://www.washingtonpost.com/world/iranians-await-presidential-election-results-following-extension-of-polling-hours/2013/06/15/3800c276-d593-11e2-a73e-826d299ff459_story.html?noredirect=on.

Riedel, Bruce. 2016 "What the Iran Deal Has Meant for Saudi Arabia and Regional Tensions." *Brookings Institute Blog.* Accessed via: https://www.brookings.edu/blog/markaz/2016/07/13/what-the-iran-deal-has-meant-for-saudi-arabia-and-regional-tensions/.

RT. 2013. "Echoing Obama: Iran Says 'All Options on the Table' If Nuclear Program Is Attacked." Accessed via: https://www.rt.com/news/iran-nuclear-obama-israel-369/.

Rublee, Maria Rost. 2009. *Nonproliferation Norms: Why States Choose Nuclear Restraint.* Athens, GA: University of Georgia Press.

Russett, Bruce. 1989. "The Real Decline in Nuclear Hegemony." In *Global Changes and Territorial Challenges: Approaches to World Politics for the 1990s*, ed. Ernst-Otto Czempiel and James N. Rosenau, 177–193. Lexington, MA: Lexington Books.

Sabet, Farzan. 2016. "Iran's 2016 Elections: Change or Continuity?" *Carnegie Endowment for International Peace.* Accessed via: http://carnegieendowment.org/2016/06/09/iran-s-2016-elections-change-or-continuity-pub-63782.

Sagan, Scott D. 1993. *The Limits of Safety: Organizations, Accidents, and Nuclear Weapons.* Princeton: NJ, Princeton University Press.

Sagan, Scott D. 1996/1997. "Why Do States Build Nuclear Weapons?: Three Models in Search of a Bomb." *International Security*, Vol. 2, No. 3, pp. 54–86.

Sagan, Scott D. 2010. "Nuclear Latency and Nuclear Proliferation." In *Forecasting Nuclear Proliferation in the 21st Century*, ed. William Potter and Gaukhar Mukhatzhanova, Stanford, CA: Stanford University Press, pp. 80–101.

Sagan, Scott D. 2017. "The Korean Missile Crisis: Why Deterrence Is Still the Best Option." *Foreign Affairs*. Accessed via: https://www.foreignaffairs.com/articles/north-korea/2017-09-10/korean-missile-crisis.

Sagan, Scott D., and Kenneth N. Waltz. 1995. *The Spread of Nuclear Weapons: A Debate*. New York, NY: Norton Press.

Sagan, Scott D., and Kenneth N. Waltz. 2003. *The Spread of Nuclear Weapons: A Debate Renewed*. New York, NY: Norton Press.

Sagan, Scott. D., ed. 2009. *Inside Nuclear South Asia*. Stanford, CA Stanford University Press.

Sang-Hun, Choe. 2012. "North Korea Says It Will Abandon Deal with U.S." *New York Times*. Accessed via: https://www.nytimes.com/2012/04/18/world/asia/north-korea-says-it-will-abandon-deal-with-united-states.html.

Sanger, David. "Iranian Overture Might Complicate Relations with Israel." *The New York Times*. Accessed via: https://www.nytimes.com/2009/02/10/world/americas/10iht11websanger.20084025.html.

Sanger, David, Edward Wong, Steven Erlanger, and Eric Schmitt. 2019. "U.S. Issues New Sanctions as Iran Warns It Will Step Back From Nuclear Deal." *The New York Times*. Accessed via: https://www.nytimes.com/2019/05/08/us/politics/iran-nuclear-deal.html.

Samore, Gary, ed. 2015. "The Iran Nuclear Deal: A Definitive Guide." *Belfer Center Report*. Accessed via: https://www.belfercenter.org/publication/iran-nuclear-deal-definitive-guide.

Sartori, Anne. 2005. *Deterrence by Diplomacy*. Princeton, NJ: Princeton University Press.

Saunders, Elizabeth N. 2011. *Leaders at War: How Presidents Shape Military Interventions*. Ithaca, NY: Cornell University Press.

Schaffer, Brenda. 2003. "Iran at the Nuclear Threshold." *Arms Control Today*.

Schelling, Thomas C. 1960. *The Strategy of Conflict*. Cambridge, MA: Harvard University Press.

Schelling, Thomas C. 1966. *Arms and Influence*. New Haven, CT: Yale University Press.

Schultz, Kenneth A. 2005. "The Politics of Risking Peace: Do Hawks or Doves Deliver the Olive Branch?" *International Organization*, Vol. 59, No. 1, pp. 1–38.

Sechser, Todd S. 2011. "Militarized Compellent Threats, 1918-2001." *Conflict Management and Peace Science*, Vol. 28, No. 4, pp. 377–401.

Sechser, Todd, and Matthew Fuhrmann. 2017. *Nuclear Weapons and Coercive Diplomacy*. Cambridge, UK: Cambridge University Press.

Serjoie, Kay Armin. 2018. "Iran's Wave of Protests Show a Split at the Heart of the Country." *TIME Magazine*. Accessed via: http://time.com/5084426/iran-protests-populist-islamic-republic/.

Shen, Zhihua and Yafeng Xia. 2012. "Between Aid and Restriction: The Soviet Union's Changing Policies on China's Nuclear Weapons Program, 1954–1960." *Asian Perspective*, Vol. 36, No. 1, pp. 95–122.

Shinkman, Paul D. 2017. "If Trump Doesn't Want a World Leadership Role, China Will Take It." *U.S. News and World Report*. Accessed via: https://www.usnews.com/news/world/articles/2017-06-02/following-trumps-paris-agreement-decision-china-poised-to-overtake-us-global-leadership.

Shultz, George. 1984. "Preventing the Proliferation of Nuclear Weapons." *Department of State Bulletin*, Vol. 84, No. 2093, p. 18.

Signorino, Curtis S., and Jeffrey M. Ritter. 2001. "Tau-b or Not Tau-b: Measuring the Similarity of Foreign Policy Positions." *International Studies Quarterly*, Vol. 43, No. 1, pp. 115–144.

Sinai, Joshua. 1997. "Libya's Pursuit of Weapons of Mass Destruction." *The Nonproliferation Review*, Vol. 4, No. 3, pp. 92–100.

Singh, Sonali, Christopher Way. 2004. "The Correlates of Nuclear Proliferation." *Journal of Conflict Resolution*, Vol. 48, No. 6, pp. 859–885.

Slantchev, Branislav. 2003. "The Power to Hurt: Costly Conflict with Completely Informed States." *American Political Science Review*, Vol. 47, No. 1, pp. 123–135.

Smith, Alastair, and Allan C. Stam. 2004. "Bargaining and the Nature of War." *Journal of Conflict Resolution*, Vol. 48, No. 6, pp. 783–813.

Solingen, Etel. 1994. The Political Economy of Nuclear Restraint. *International Security*, Vol. 19, No. 2, pp. 126–169.

Solingen, Etel. 2007. *Nuclear Logics: Contrasting Paths in East Asia and the Middle East*. Princeton, NJ: Princeton University Press.

Solingen, Etel, ed. 2012. *Sanctions, Statecraft, and Nuclear Proliferation*. Cambridge, UK: Cambridge University Press.

Sorkin, Jerry. 2005. "Missing the Target on Nonproliferation?" *Middle East Quarterly*, Vol. 12, No. 1, pp. 45–50.

Spaniel, William 2019. *Bargaining over the Bomb: The Successes and Failures of Nuclear Negotiations*. Cambridge, UK: Cambridge University Press.

Spector, Leonard, Mark G. McDonough, and Evan S. Medeiros. 1995. *Tracking Nuclear Proliferation: A Guide in Maps and Charts, 1995*. Washington, DC: Carnegie Endowment for International Peace.

Squassoni, Sharon A., and Andrew Feickert. 2004. "Disarming Libya: Weapons of Mass Destruction." *Congressional Research Service: The Library of Congress*.

Staw, Barry M. 1997. "The Escalation of Commitment: An Update and Appraisal." In *Organizational Decision Making*, ed. Zur Shapira. New York, NY: Cambridge University Press, pp. 191–215.

Stein, Janice Gross. 2013. "Threat Perception in International Relations." *The Oxford Handbook of Political Psychology*, 2nd ed., ed. Leonie Huddy, David O. Sears, and Jack S. Levy. Oxford, UK: Oxford University Press, pp. 364–394.

Steinhauer, Jennifer. 2015. "Democrats Hand Victory to Obama on Iran Nuclear Deal." *New York Times*. Accessed via: https://www.nytimes.com/2015/09/11/us/politics/iran-nuclear-deal-senate.html.

Sublette, Carey. 2011. "Pakistan's Nuclear Weapons Program: 1998: The Year of Testing." Accessed via: http://nuclearweaponarchive.org/.

Taleblu, Behnam Ben and Richard Goldberg. 2018. "Here's How the U.S. and EU Can Thwart Iranian Missile Programs." *Foreign Policy*. Accessed via: https://foreignpolicy.com/2018/01/30/heres-how-the-u-s-and-eu-can-thwart-iranian-missile-programs/.

Tellis, Ashley J., C. Christine Fair, and Jamison Jo Medby. 2001. *Limited Conflicts Under the Nuclear Umbrella: Indian and Pakistani Lessons from the Kargil Crisis*. Santa Monica, CA: RAND Corporation. https://www.rand.org/pubs/monograph_reports/MR1450.html.

Terry, Sue Mi. 2019. "Assessment of the Trump-Kim Hanoi Summit." *CSIS Critical Questions Report*. Accessed via: https://www.csis.org/analysis/assessment-trump-kim-hanoi-summit.

Thatcher, Jonathan. 2003. "US: No Plans for Military Action in Iran." *Reuters*.

Thayer, Bradley. 1994. "The Risk of Nuclear Inadvertence: A Review Essay." *Security Studies*, Vol. 3, No. 3, pp. 428–493.

The Guardian. 2013. "Iran Ready to Talk If US Shows 'Goodwill,' Says New President." Accessed via: https://www.theguardian.com/world/2013/aug/06/iran-ready-to-talk-us-goodwill-hassan-rouhani.

United Nations Security Council. 1998. "Resolution 1172." Accessed via: http://www.mofa.go.jp/mofaj/gaiko/naruhodo/data/pdf/data6-1.pdf.

USAID. 2007. "U.S. Overseas Loans and Grants Greenbook." Accessed via: https://www.usaid.gov/data/dataset/49c01560-6cd7-4bbc-bfef-7a1991867633.

U.S. Department of State. 1975. "Memorandum for the Assistant to the President for National Security Affairs: Department of State Response to NSSM 219 [Nuclear Cooperation with Iran]. Washington National Records Center, OSD Files: FRC 330–78–0058, Box 66, Iran 300–900, 1975."

U.S. Department of State. 2009a. "Preventative Diplomacy—Indian Nuclear Test Preparations." Case No. M-2009-00895. Doc No. C17601493.

U.S. Department of State. 2009b. "Implications of an Indian Nuclear Weapon Test." U.S. Department of State. Case No. M-2009-00895. Doc No. C17601520.

U.S. Government Printing Office. 1975. "Nonproliferation Issues: Hearings before the Subcommittee on Arms Control, International Organizations and Security Agreements of the Committee on Foreign Relations." United States Senate. Accessed via: http://www.archive.org/stream/nonproliferation00unit/nonproliferation00unit_djvu.txt.

United Nations Office of Disarmament Affairs. 1970. "Treaty on the Non-Proliferation of Nuclear Weapons (NPT)." Accessed via: https://www.un.org/disarmament/wmd/nuclear/npt/.

Verdier, Daniel. 2008. "Multilateralism, Bilateralism, and Exclusion in the Nuclear Proliferation Regime." *International Organization*, Vol. 62, No. 1, pp. 439–476.

Volpe, Tristan. 2017. "Atomic Leverage: Compellence with Nuclear Latency." *Security Studies*, Vol. 26, No. 3, pp. 517–544.

Walsh, James. 2000. *Bombs Unbuilt: Power, Ideas, and Institutions in International Politics.* Cambridge, MA: MIT Doctoral Dissertation.

Ward, Alex. 2019. "North Korea Tested a Missile over the Weekend. The Trump Admin Flubbed the Response." *Vox*. Accessed via: https://www.vox.com/world/2019/5/6/18531121/north-korea-missile-test-trump-pompeo.

Waltz, Kenneth N. 1979. *Theory of International Politics*. New York, NY: McGraw Hill.

Waltz, Kenneth N. 1990. "Nuclear Myths and Political Realities." *American Political Science Review*, Vol. 84, No. 3, pp. 731–745.

Way, Christopher. 2019. "Nuclear Proliferation Dates." *Working Paper*. Accessed via: http://falcon.arts.cornell.edu/crw12/documents/Nuclear%20Proliferation%20Dates.pdf.

Way, Christopher, and Jessica L. P. Weeks. 2014. "Making It Personal: Regime Type and Nuclear Proliferation." *American Journal of Political Science*, Vol. 58, No. 3, pp. 705–719.

White House. 2017. "Presidential Executive Order on Imposing Additional Sanctions with Respect to North Korea." Accessed via: https://www.whitehouse.gov/presidential-actions/presidential-executive-order-imposing-additional-sanctions-respect-north-korea/.

Whitlark, Rachel Elizabeth. 2017. "Nuclear Beliefs: A Leader-Focused Theory of Counter-Proliferation." *Security Studies*, Vol. 26, No. 4, pp. 545–574.

Whitlark, Rachel Elizabeth, and Rupal N. Mehta. 2019. "Hedging Our Bets: Why Does Nuclear Latency Matter." *The Washington Quarterly*, Vol. 42, No. 1, pp. 41–52.

Wilson, Scott, and Colum Lynch. 2013. "Obama, Iranian President Speak by Phone." *Washington Post*. Accessed via: https://www.washingtonpost.com/politics/2013/09/27/228f6ece-27af-11e3-b75d-5b7f66349852_story.html?noredirect=on.

Wolford, Scott. 2007. "The Turnover Trap: New Leaders, Reputation, and International Conflict." *American Journal of Political Science*, Vol. 51, No. 4, pp. 772–788.

Woods, Kevin M., David D. Palkki, and Mark E. Stout, eds. 2010. *A Survey of Saddam's Audio Files, 1978–2001: Toward an Understanding of Authoritarian Regimes*. Alexandria, VA: Institute for Defense Analyses.

INDEX

For the benefit of digital users, indexed terms that span two pages (e.g., 52–53) may, on occasion, appear on only one of those pages.

Tables are indicated by *t* following the page number